EQUIP

Your Personal Journey to the Kingdom

Peter Tsukahira

EQUIP - Your Personal Journey to the Kingdom

First Edition, December 2020

Published by Peter Tsukahira
P. O. Box 7231
Haifa, 31073 Israel
www.petertsukahira.com

ISBN 978-965-599-292-2

Inspiration for front cover image by Steve Carpenter
Cover design by Jordan Silver
Layout by Lee Uzziah

Acknowledgments

I am grateful to God for my family members and so many dear friends who contributed to this book and helped me develop these teachings over the years. May the Lord be gracious to you and may His face shine upon each of you. My prayer is that this book will be useful to others on their discipleship journey and that we will all share in God's reward.

Peter Tsukahira
Mt. Carmel
December 2020

Table of Contents

Part 4 – Law and Grace

My Personal Journey

After coming to the Lord in 1973 out of a rebellious countercultural background, it was clear that I needed to be completely "re-educated" in the understanding of my new faith. Less than a year later, I began the study of foundational biblical truths at a school in Dallas and then enrolled in a seminary affiliated with a large charismatic church in California.

Back in my first months as a believer, I had heard the Lord's call to serve Him first in Japan and then in Israel, without any idea how this could happen. During the time at seminary, I had worked in the fledgling computer industry. In 1982, having completed my Master of Divinity degree, my wife and I left for Japan where I was employed by a major Japanese high-tech company in Tokyo.

This was a time of unprecedented economic growth as well as the beginning of a spiritual renewal in Japan. I had the opportunity to pastor alongside a man who had spent many years there and to help establish a congregation for both the international and Japanese communities.

In 1987, the Lord opened a door for us to emigrate to Israel with our two-year-old daughter and to settle on Mt. Carmel in the northern city of Haifa. We saw there was a need for a Spirit-led expression for Messianic believers in our city and after the Gulf War ended in early 1991, we connected with David and Karen Davis, who had come from New York to pioneer the first biblically based drug rehabilitation center in Israel.

Together, we founded the Carmel Congregation, which has been reaching out to both Jews and Arabs, as well as providing humanitarian aid and shelter to many needy and desperate persons. The network of ministries continues to grow and now a younger generation of leaders we trained as disciples is moving the community forward with their own gifts and callings, and we are witnessing the beginnings of a great harvest among Israelis.

Almost half of my life has been lived in Israel. When we came as new immigrants, the nation was less than forty years old and still fighting for its survival among many hostile neighbors. These were the years before Israel became known for its tremendous accomplishments in innovation and technology, and for most people, it was just another tiny country in the Middle East. The international world, including the evangelical churches, were not really aware of what was taking place in the nation.

In the early nineties, I began traveling to teach about the biblical and prophetic significance of Israel's restoration as a modern nation and the re-emergence of Israeli Messianic communities. The excitement of seeing God's prophetic words coming to life was more than emotion. I knew we were part of a historic event and a heavenly revelation that needed to be shared. Participating in worship services where Jesus (or *Yeshua*, His Hebrew name) is being honored as Messiah and King in His own land, by His own people, and in His own language of Hebrew for the first time in two thousand years was and still is one of the great events of our time. I wanted all Christians to see this truth as the fulfillment of God's promises in Scripture as well as a present-day reality. When I traveled and taught, I felt it was vital for Christians in every nation to realize that God had never forsaken His covenant with Abraham and the people of Israel despite their unfaithfulness. God had not "replaced" Israel with the church as had been taught for many centuries by Christian leaders. The survival of the Jews after so much wandering and persecution and their return to the very land God had promised their fathers was a powerful statement of God's faithfulness throughout all generations. I saw it as important evidence that God would also uphold His promises to Christians through the covenantal sacrifice of His own Son, Jesus. Eventually, I began to suspect that there was more to Israel's existence than meets the eye—even to my eyes of faith. By the end of the nineties, the impact of the "resurrection" of Israel as a modern nation and the re-emergence of Israeli Messianic communities was already moving through the worldwide church, changing many hearts and minds.

Eventually, I began to suspect that there was more to Israel's existence than meets the eye—even to my eyes of faith.

But sadly, it seemed that most of the church was not ready to move ahead with what God had intended by bringing this huge historical event to pass. I was reminded of a tragic event that happened during the American Civil War. In the spring and summer of 1864, when the war between North and South was in its final stages, the opposing armies were deadlocked around a strategic town called Petersburg in Virginia. If the North could break through the South's battle lines at Petersburg, then the southern capital, Richmond, would fall and the war would end.

Eventually, a plan was made by the North to dig a tunnel under their enemy's lines, detonate a massive explosive charge, blast a breakthrough, take the city, and end the war. When the day of the attack came, the underground explosion worked as planned but the attacking troops were not trained or even adequately instructed to charge through the resulting gap and conquer their objective. In confusion, they milled around the impressive crater long enough for the southern forces to recover from their surprise, regroup, and throw them back with many losses. The war dragged on for nearly a year longer and many more lives were needlessly lost. It is clear to me now that a prophetic "explosion" of biblical proportions took place in our time but like the northern armies who were so impressed by the huge crater that they didn't advance in battle towards the real goal, we, the church, are looking at the "miracle" of Israel's rebirth but not understanding what we need to do next. The significance of Israel's restoration and the emergence of an indigenous believing body is an unprecedented prophetic breakthrough. Even the disciples of Jesus asked Him about this restoration in their last moments with Him on earth (Acts 1:6).

However, it is a breakthrough that must not be seen as an end in itself but rather as a means toward an even greater goal. God's goal is not the restoration of Israel for its own sake. His goal is the restoration of the kingdom of God as He intended it to be. Jesus never said that the regathering of Israel or even the salvation of all Israel was God's ultimate objective, but He said to pray in this way, "Your kingdom come. Your will be done, on earth as it is in heaven" (Matthew 6:10).

He emphasized God's kingdom as His disciples' highest earthly priority with these words, "But seek first His kingdom and His righteousness, and all these things will be added to you" (Matthew 6:33). Jesus predicted that His message of God's kingdom would impact the world before His return. He said, "This gospel of the kingdom shall be preached in the whole world as a testimony to all the nations, and then the end will come" (Matthew 24:14). I began to realize that Israel's unique contribution is to bring the good news of God's messianic kingdom to all other nations. Israel was chosen by God as His instrument to be a "blessing to all the families of the earth" (Genesis 12:3) and a "light to the nations" as described in Isaiah 60:1-3. But an inwardly focused light that only shines upon itself is darkness, a "black hole."

Israel's destiny is to be God's servant nation, His human, national instrument that is a model of God's kingdom to the world. As I grew in this understanding, my own messages began to pivot from teachings *about* Israel to teaching that comes *from* Israel. Going beyond just explaining Israel's significance to Christians, I began teaching about the kingdom of God and the call to make disciples of the kingdom in every nation. This is the great command of our Lord (the "Great Commission" found in Matthew 28:18-20), which He personally gave to His Israeli disciples and it is again today coming "out of Zion."

God's intention for this end time shift in focus back to Israel is signaled in these words given to us from both the prophets Isaiah and Micah: Now it will come about that in the last days the mountain of the house of the Lord will be established as the chief of the mountains and will be raised above the hills and all the nations will stream to it. And many peoples will come and say, "Come, let us go up to the mountain of the Lord, to the house of the God of Jacob that He may teach us concerning His ways and that we may walk in His paths." For the law will go forth from Zion and the word of the Lord from Jerusalem. (Isaiah 2:2-3 and Micah 4:1-2)

These next fifty-two chapters represent the unfolding of the teachings I have received during my journey. A deeper understanding of God's purposes for His people Israel through the ancient Hebrew Scriptures illuminates our path to the kingdom of God and reveals the necessity of bearing fruit as disciples. I want to share with you what the Lord has shown me about the call to make disciples of His kingdom and give you what He has freely invested in my life over the years.

Introduction

> Thus says the Lord, "Stand by the ways and see and ask for the ancient paths, where the good way is, and walk in it and you will find rest for your souls." (Jeremiah 6:16)

This book is a manual for taking the next step in discipleship beyond the basic spiritual instruction provided by many good churches and ministries. The modern restoration of Israel as a nation has triggered a parallel restoration of Christianity's Hebraic roots. This book is a modern approach to discipleship based on these "ancient paths." It is arranged into five parts, each addressing essential elements for equipping Jesus' disciples to be spiritually fruitful in the end times. All other books and materials cited in the following chapters are identified at the end of the book in the References section.

As a manual, it can be used in several ways. The Table of Contents can be scanned to find topics of particular interest and the chapters can be used as individual short teachings. Alternatively, since the topics are progressively related, the chapters may be read one after another over a period of time. It has fifty-two chapters with some short questions for discussion and a point for prayer at the end of each chapter. The chapters are designed to be used as a weekly study for training that will last one year.

The material is meant to be inspirational and biblical rather than academic and is for Christians called to the marketplace and other professions as well as pastors and ministry leaders. As time goes on, teaching materials to support each topic, including video teachings and other online resources, will also be available.

* * *

God chose the people of Israel and entrusted them with the task of receiving, writing, and preserving the special revelation known to the world as the Bible. Most of the Bible was written about people from Israel and events that took place in the land of Israel. God's story, by His design, is entwined with the story of Israel. Even today, thousands of years after the Bible was written, you cannot interact with what it says about the people of Israel and this land in an honest way and remain unchanged. The chapters that follow in this book are the result of many years of teaching in Israel and the nations. Some of these truths were first written about in my earlier books, but they are now converging into a single body of teaching. I see this process as a restoration of the "gospel of the kingdom" that was lost to the church centuries ago.

Today, a single clear truth emerges from the preaching of God's kingdom: The most important factor limiting the coming of His kingdom to earth is the lack of disciples. Although we should always pray and more prayer is needed, prayer by itself will not bring the kingdom of God. The coming of God's kingdom is also not hindered by our lack of vision for winning the world or the resources necessary for massive evangelistic campaigns. The limiting factor is the relative scarcity of real disciples of God's kingdom who know God and know what to do with their own gifts and callings.

The most important factor limiting the coming of His kingdom to earth is the lack of disciples.

So far, we have failed to effectively equip the majority of people in the church and mobilize them for the work of the kingdom. We need more mature, gifted, and anointed leaders who can fulfill the callings Paul wrote about in Ephesians chapter 4: "And He gave some as apostles, and some as prophets, and some as evangelists, and some as pastors and teachers, for the equipping of the saints for the work of service, to the building up of the body of Christ; until we all attain to the unity of the faith, and of the knowledge of the Son of God, to a mature man, to the measure of the stature which belongs to the fullness of Christ" (Ephesians 4:11-13). The key words in the inspired passage above are *equipping* and *all*. When the greatest leaders among us are servants in the manner of Jesus, who sacrificed Himself to equip the rest, then the great body of Christ will surge forward again to win and disciple the nations.

This book is my small contribution to this great task. My prayer is that you will be encouraged and equipped in your calling as you read these pages and apply the truths they contain to your life.

Part 1

Disciples of the Kingdom

Go therefore and make disciples of all the nations, baptizing them in the name of the Father and the Son and the Holy Spirit, teaching them to observe all that I commanded you; and lo, I am with you always, even to the end of the age. (Matthew 28:19-20)

Chapter 1

Organic Growth

Almost fifteen years after praying to make Jesus the Lord of my life and beginning to follow Him, I moved to Israel and became one of the founders and a pastor in a new Messianic congregation reaching out simultaneously to Jews, Arabs, and other Gentiles. By that time, I had completed two years of Bible school in the United States and several more years of seminary, where I earned an advanced degree. In addition, I had completed five years of pastoring in a growing church in Japan. Naively, I thought I had enough experience to prepare me for effective ministry!

In our new Israeli congregation, we pastors wanted to bring another man, Reuven Ross, to minister alongside of us. However, he had one condition: He would first take us through a ten-session course he called "The Vision of Discipleship." In the beginning I thought, *Come on now, we are disciples already. We are ministry leaders by now!* In spite of my hesitancy, he was insistent and so we agreed. By the third session, my mind was completely changed and I was thinking, *Personal and intentional discipleship is so important to the Lord. How could I have missed this?*

Over the years, Reuven and his wife Yanit's books on discipleship, *Go and Make Disciples!* and *The Call to Radical Discipleship* became standard texts in our new believer and leadership programs. They are translated into several languages and we continue to use them regularly. Reuven and Yanit wrote, "Every living species must somehow reproduce in order to survive. Any successful army must produce trained soldiers. A manufacturer must create finished products in order to stay in business. In the same way, the Church must produce disciplined and sanctified lives for it to grow and reproduce in a healthy way."

Once we catch the vision and understand the meaning of discipleship, it is easy to see that the making of disciples is essential for God's kingdom to grow. The organization of people into churches and denominations does not by itself produce new growth. Church building projects, evangelistic rallies, worship services, prayer meetings, and effective administration all may contribute to growth, but these activities *facilitate* rather than *produce* growth. Large public meetings, anointed worship, and dynamic prayer are some of the outward signs of growth, but making disciples is God's way to build His kingdom. The cost in time and resources required by any church activity or project should be measured against its effectiveness in ultimately producing discipled lives. Unless a church is making new disciples, even if its numbers are growing, it is actually dying.

Robert E. Coleman in his powerful book *The Master Plan of Evangelism* (which is actually about discipleship but includes a foreword by evangelist Billy Graham) wrote, "It all started by Jesus calling a few men to follow him. This revealed immediately the direction his evangelistic strategy would take. His concern was not with programs to reach the multitudes, but with men whom the multitudes would follow. Remarkable as it may seem, Jesus started to gather these men before he ever organized an evangelistic campaign or even preached a sermon in public. Men were to be his method of winning the world to God."

Unless a church is making new disciples, even if its numbers are growing, it is actually dying.

If you are like me and not a biologist, you may think that plants grow by putting out more leaves, becoming bushier, taller, or producing flowers and seeds. Someone aware of what goes on inside plants knows that their growth is an organic process that includes photosynthesis, which is the ability of the leaves to turn sunlight into chemical energy. The roots absorb moisture along with vital nutrients and the cellular structure converts the energy and nutrients into producing more cells. Plant DNA guides the growth by directing production of new cells to the appropriate places. Ultimately a healthy plant produces fruit with seeds that contain the DNA and other material to start new plants according to their kind.

The growth of plants and other living organisms is always an inner process that remains focused on the production of new cells. The same basic design is found in animals and humans as well. Cells are the basic building blocks of all living organisms. Each cell contains the DNA (identity) of the body and each grows by dividing itself to produce new cells. Organic growth is always at the cellular level and this is also where deadly diseases like cancer and viruses attack.

Think of disciples as the living "cells" of God's kingdom. That is why replicating what God, by grace has accomplished in individuals through discipleship is a central truth of the Bible. Great leaders and prophets had disciples. Moses' disciple was Joshua, who led Israel into the Promised Land. Elijah's disciple was Elisha, who received from God a double portion of his mentor's anointing. Jesus had the twelve apostles, who changed the world after He ascended into heaven.

New growth in God's kingdom is also organic in the sense that God's people are described as a body and not as an organization. An organization grows by developing new plans, programs, projects, and fitting people into that framework. Certainly, we do need organizations and planning when projects need to be accomplished. But achieving goals and finishing projects is not how the body of the Lord grows. As a body, the church always grows through the process of producing new and healthy disciples. Disciples are the "cells" that, guided by the "DNA" of God's purposes, result in the overall maturity of the body as a whole.

"But speaking the truth in love, we are to grow up in all aspects into Him who is the head, even Christ, from whom the whole body, being fitted and held together by what every joint supplies, according to the proper working of each individual part, causes the growth of the body for the building up of itself in love" (Ephesians 4:15-16).

Powerful industrial corporations understand that, while pursuing good organizational planning, growth through finding the right people is more important in the long run. The most successful companies have ways to recruit and develop the type of people who bring with them real and long-term growth. In a best-selling book about businesses in America, *Good to Great*, author Jim Collins wrote,

> First Who…Then What. We expected that good-to-great leaders would begin by setting a new vision and strategy. We found instead that they *first* got the right people on the bus, the wrong people off the bus, and the right people in the right seats—and *then* they figured out where to drive it. The old adage "People are your most important asset" turns out to be wrong. People are not your most important asset. The *right* people are.

God's process of developing ordinary people into "right" people and guiding them into the right place in His kingdom is called discipleship.

Discussion Questions

1. How are disciples in God's kingdom like the cells of a plant?
2. Why don't church programs and other projects by themselves cause God's kingdom to grow?
3. Why does the Bible describe God's kingdom as a "body"?

Prayer Point

Lord, show me what it means to be a disciple and help me to become spiritually mature so that I can fulfill my role in Your body.

Chapter 2

What is a Disciple?

A disciple is someone who is trained by the Lord to be teachable and able to teach others. A disciple is someone disciplined in obedience and who is developing a lifestyle of following the Lord. Here's what the great prophet Isaiah wrote: "The Lord God has given me the tongue of disciples, that I may know how to sustain the weary one with a word. He awakens me morning by morning, He awakens My ear to listen as a disciple. The Lord God has opened My ear and I was not disobedient nor did I turn back" (Isaiah 50:4-5).

The word used by Isaiah twice in these verses is *limudim,* which means the ones who are learning and hearing God's voice. Some years ago, I heard that a certain minister from another country was visiting Israel. I had heard about this man's reputation as a leader who had made many disciples, planted churches, and influenced his region.

To meet him, I drove about an hour to the Sea of Galilee just to have dinner at his hotel. After the meal, I asked him to tell me the secret of his fruitfulness in ministry. His answer was something like this, "If I can get the majority of my people to simply hear the voice of God on a daily basis, all the rest is easy!"

A disciple is someone who is developing a lifestyle of following the Lord.

I don't think I will ever forget his words. If a disciple begins to hear directly from the Lord, then God can do the important work in his or her life.

Of course, there will always be obstacles and opposition. A disciple is someone under spiritual authority and identified fully with the Lord, who is learning from God. Jesus said, "A disciple is not above his teacher, nor a slave above his master. It is enough for the disciple that he become like his teacher, and the slave like his master. If they have called the head of the house Beelzebub, how much more will they malign the members of his household!" (Matthew 10:24-25).

Disciples will be misunderstood and face trials and tests in life, but true disciples of Jesus end up with powerful spiritual authority. Here's a conversation between Jesus and seventy people He was training as disciples. "'The one who listens to you listens to Me, and the one who rejects you rejects Me; and he who rejects Me rejects the One who sent Me.' The seventy returned with joy, saying, 'Lord, even the demons are subject to us in Your name'" (Luke 10:16-17).

Disciples are called to create other disciples. Here are the verses that have become known as Jesus' "Great Commission."

"And Jesus came up and spoke to them, saying, 'All authority has been given to Me in heaven and on earth. Go therefore and make disciples of all the nations, baptizing them in the name of the Father and the Son and the Holy Spirit, teaching them to observe all that I commanded you; and lo, I am with you always, even to the end of the age'" (Matthew 28:18-20).

The seventeenth chapter of John's gospel has been called Jesus' "High Priestly Prayer." I prefer to call it Jesus' "final performance report" to His Father in heaven. In this prayer, Jesus is telling God that His essential work on earth is finished because His disciples are ready to carry on. The prayer is almost entirely focused on His disciples. Jesus prayed, "I glorified You on the earth, having accomplished the work which You have given Me to do. Now, Father, glorify Me together with Yourself, with the glory which I had with You before the world was" (John 17:4-5).

What was the work that Jesus had accomplished when He prayed this prayer? The work of salvation and atonement for the sins of the world was accomplished on the cross and by His resurrection from the dead. All this would come later. When Jesus prayed this prayer in John 17, He was referring to His work of training the disciples that God had given Him. He said,

> I have manifested Your name to the men whom You gave Me out of the world; they were Yours and You gave them to Me, and they have kept Your word. Now they have come to know that everything You have given Me is from You; for the words which You gave Me I have given to them and they received them and truly understood that I came forth from You, and they believed that You sent Me. I ask on their behalf; I do not ask on behalf of the world, but of those whom You have given Me; for they are Yours; and all things that are Mine are Yours, and Yours are Mine and I have been glorified in them. (John 17:6-10)

Then Jesus prayed for all of us from every nation and ethnic group who over the centuries would follow the example of His disciples. "I do not ask on behalf of these alone, but for those also who believe in Me through their word; that they may all be one; even as You, Father, are in Me and I in You, that they also may be in Us, so that the world may believe that You sent Me" (John 17:20-21).

Discussion Questions

1. How would I describe a disciple of Jesus?
2. Let's read through John chapter 17. Is it focused on Jesus' disciples?
3. Would I describe myself as one of Jesus' disciples now? Why or why not?

Prayer Point

Lord, please open the eyes of my heart to see why disciples are so important to You. Help me to be one of those who hears Your voice on a regular basis.

Chapter 3

Coming Out of the Crowd

Here's a biblical event recorded by Matthew that illustrates the gap between disciples of Jesus and the many who are content to only watch from the crowd. This story takes place in the town of Capernaum, a place that Jesus made His headquarters during the years of His Galilean ministry. He often came and went from this town, a prosperous fishing and trading center on the northern shore of the Sea of Galilee, which was also near the main Roman road.

Jesus met five of His disciples in Capernaum and almost all the rest came from nearby towns in the northern Galilee. We know that Peter's mother-in-law lived in Capernaum and it is thought that Jesus often stayed in that same home where

He once healed her of an illness (Matthew 8:14-15).

Over the years, I have visited the site of ancient Capernaum many times. It has been archeologically restored and when you walk among its old stones, it is easy to imagine the scene described by Matthew. The shore is less than two minutes' walk from the edge of the town, which may not have been much more than two thousand people in total population at the time of Jesus. Directly behind some of the small homes built of stones there is a little pebbly beach, where, according to the Bible, Jesus went on that day.

> That day Jesus went out of the house and was sitting by the sea. And large crowds gathered to Him, so He got into a boat and sat down, and the whole crowd was standing on the beach. And He spoke many things to them in parables, saying, "Behold, the sower went out to sow and as he sowed, some seeds fell beside the road, and the birds came and ate them up. Others fell on the rocky places, where they did not have much soil and immediately they sprang up, because they had no depth of soil. But when the sun had risen, they were scorched; and because they had no root, they withered away. Others fell among the thorns, and the thorns came up and choked them out. And others fell on the good soil and yielded a crop, some a hundredfold, some sixty, and some thirty. He who has ears, let him hear." (Matthew 13:1-9)

So many people had gathered to hear the Lord that they

had to put Him into one of their small fishing boats and push Him off from the shore so that all could see Him. It could not have been more than ten or fifteen meters because they needed to hear Him as well. There must have been someone in the boat with Him to hold it steady, and judging from the size of the beach, there were at least three or four hundred people gathered there.

Jesus spoke to them in parables and the one that is recorded by Matthew is called the parable of the sower. Afterward, Jesus must have signaled to the man in the boat with Him to bring it to the shore. The crowd began to drift away and Jesus, with His disciples, began to walk off in another direction. At that point, when they were alone with their Master, the disciples had a question for Him. They said, "Why do You speak to them in parables?" (Matthew 13:10).

I'm sure the disciples asked this simple question politely and respectfully. However, if I am not mistaken, there was confusion, frustration, and even irritation in their hearts. I think they were asking, "Lord, why did You speak to them *like that*?" Because it is obvious the people did not respond enthusiastically to what Jesus said. The crowd walked away unimpressed and unconvinced.

And who was in that crowd? All the friends, family members, former employers, and other people that some of Jesus' disciples had known all their lives! Also, why were so many local people waiting on the beach when Jesus arrived? Someone must have told them that He would speak to them that day. Someone must have invited them—probably those same disciples. The disciples very likely went out the day before and convinced everyone they knew to come and listen to the Lord. If that was the case, they certainly must have wanted His most convincing sermon. A miracle or two would also have been welcome! Instead, Jesus told the crowd of fishermen and tradesmen what amounted to an agricultural story. The disciples were disappointed and confused.

Understanding their perplexity and knowing the thoughts in their minds, Jesus gave them a deep and astounding answer when they were alone with Him. In verse 11 it is written, "Jesus answered them, 'To you it has been granted to know the mysteries of the kingdom of heaven, but to them it has not been granted.'" If the disciples were confused before, now they must have been shocked. They were thinking, *You mean that You spoke to them that way on purpose? You knew that they would be unconvinced and unmoved no matter what You said?*

But Jesus had more to say to them. "For whoever has, to him more shall be given, and he will have an abundance; but whoever does not have, even what he has shall be taken away from him. Therefore I speak to them in parables because while seeing they do not see, and while hearing they do not hear, nor do they understand" (Matthew 13:12-13).

Jesus was saying there is a big gap between the people who merely sit in the crowd and the people who sit at the Master's feet. Disciples have made their decisions to always be with the Lord. When the crowd goes home, true disciples will still be waiting to hear the Lord's words and trying to follow His instructions.

Jesus knew that the people of Capernaum, on the whole, thought they had more important things to do than listen to Him and obey. They had businesses to run, families to raise, meals to cook, gossip to share, and shopping errands waiting for them. They had come to see Jesus because of curiosity or to please a friend or family member who invited them, but not out of a desire to find a new life with God.

Then, when everyone else was gone, Jesus turned to the twelve men who were becoming His disciples and said, "But blessed are your eyes, because they see; and your ears, because they hear. For truly I say to you that many prophets and righteous men desired to see what you see, and did not see it and to hear what you hear, and did not hear it. Hear then the parable of the sower" (Matthew 13:16-17).

Jesus was saying there is a big gap between the people who merely sit in the crowd and the people who sit at the Master's feet.

Jesus' parable from His sermon earlier that day was explained only to His disciples and not to the crowd. He told them that the sower is God and that the seeds are the words of God's kingdom. The soil is the condition of people's hearts. Some people hear the Word of God and do not understand it. Their hearts are like the soil found beside the road where the seed never begins to grow. Within minutes, the birds come and snatch it away. It is a picture of the devil stealing God's Word from some hearts. Other people's hearts are like stony ground where the Word of God is received with joy but never becomes rooted so that when hardship or persecution arises, it withers way. Yet others are like good soil overgrown with thorns so that although the seed of God's Word grows there, it is choked out by daily pressures, worries, the false promises of wealth and fame, and so their lives remain spiritually barren.

But some of the precious words of God's kingdom fall on hearts that are like good soil. These are hearts that are soft and open and ready for something new and beautiful to grow. In these people, God's Word begins to flourish and in time produces fruit that ultimately more than makes up for all the seed that is lost on others along the way.

I think at this point in the explanation the disciples must have realized that Jesus was speaking about them. They had been chosen to be good soil and they were called to produce an abundance of spiritual fruit!

However, one of them might have asked, "Lord, if we, your disciples, are the 'good soil' and are expected to produce fruit for God's kingdom, why didn't You tell us this yesterday, before we went out and invited everyone we knew to come and hear You speak? Why didn't You just say, 'Guys, tomorrow is a discipleship retreat day. Just Me and the twelve of you. Clear your schedules!'"

But if the disciples wanted to know why Jesus even bothered to speak to the crowd, isn't the answer obvious? He taught the crowd as an illustration for the disciples' sake!

They had just seen God's sower go out and sow the seed of His Word. They knew the people in the crowd so well. They knew which ones would hardly be able to remember what was said a few minutes after the meeting was over. They knew which ones might be enthusiastic for a while and then go back to the way they had been. They knew many who were simply too busy with other things to care about changing their lives. They saw the big gap between being in the crowd and just hearing God's Word and becoming a disciple. They also began to realize the special nature and destiny of their own calling.

Discussion Questions:

1. Why did Jesus always focus His attention on the disciples?
2. Do I feel like I am one of the people in the crowd or already among Jesus' disciples?
3. Are Christian ministries today concentrating on producing disciples?

Prayer Point:

Lord, cause me to come out of the crowds who gather just to hear about You. I want to hear your voice and follow You wherever You go. Please help me to be a disciple.

Chapter 4

Destiny of a Disciple

Discipleship is a process of molding a person's character into an eternal identity. Today there is much emphasis around the world on personal identity. Is it what you wear? How good you look? What gender, what race, what religion you have in your background? I believe every person is born with a God-given destiny that God, out of love, determines before we were born. Then, in faith, He releases us into a broken and dangerous world that is dominated by human free will.

The Bible speaks of all people as a tri-unity: spirit, soul, and body. Our spirits are the seats of our inner intentions and motives. Our spirits are where the Holy Spirit resides and begins to rule when we become believers. The human spirit is the most private, secret, intimate place of the inner man or woman. Our spirit can be dead or alive, full of darkness or light. Proverbs 20:27 says, “The spirit of a man is the lamp of the Lord, searching all the inner depths of his heart.” It could be said that each person is a spirit, has a soul and lives in a body.

The human soul is different from our spirit. It is our minds, that is, our thoughts, our will, and emotions. The New Testament Greek word for soul is *psuche* from which the English word psychology (literally “science of the soul”) is formed. The soul is very powerful and many people live their lives guided and controlled by their souls. They strive for informed and right thoughts, a self-disciplined will, and positive, loving feelings. These are all beneficial for living a better life but, of course, there are problems. The problems have to do with conflict, pain and fear. When we are hurt, betrayed, falsely accused, physically injured, or ill, our righteous thoughts, our disciplined wills, and our good emotions often desert us. We all struggle to deal sometimes with dark thoughts and violent emotions. Tragically, sometimes the soul can even become a doorway to the demonic and be used to guide some people to dysfunction, crime or even suicide.

The body has to do with our physical being along with its basic needs, instincts, and appetites. Our behavior, words, and actions come from our bodies. In popular culture, so much emphasis is placed on our bodies that some people may think that having a “good” or sexually attractive body is the most important part of a person’s identity!

Our physical appearance, how we are shaped, how we dress, what we eat, whether we are physically fit—all these are the subject of countless books and videos. Young celebrities often define a certain minimum physical standard of acceptance. "Body shaming" can be the result of not meeting those culturally determined physical requirements.

While it is interesting and even instructive to try analyzing the different components of someone's personality and character, the truth is that people are meant to be whole. We all have different parts of our lives, but God's plan is for all the complex elements to be aligned to His good purpose and original design. The best word for this alignment is *integrity*. Integrity is more than honesty. In English, the word is based on the word *integer*, which means a whole number.

Civil engineers think of well-designed buildings as having structural integrity. All the parts are aligned into a single whole and the result is stability and strength. God's plan is for a disciple's body, soul, and spirit to become integrated and aligned to God's design. The result is peace in our lives. The Hebrew word for peace is *shalom* and it means more than the absence of conflict. In Hebrew, the word *shalom* is closely related to words like *whole* (*shalem*) and *perfect* (*mushlam*).

The apostle Paul, who made many disciples among the early believers, wrote, "Now may the God of peace Himself sanctify you completely; and may your whole spirit, soul, and body be preserved blameless at the coming of our Lord Jesus Christ" (1 Thessalonians 5:23).

How do disciples develop integrity and wholeness? The journey begins with the power of God's Word speaking into our spirits. Jesus said, "It is the Spirit who gives life; the flesh profits nothing. The words that I speak to you are spirit, and they are life" (John 6:63).

> The journey begins with the power of God's Word speaking into our spirits.

First, we must remove confusion between Jesus' words that feed our spirits and other messages we might receive that only touch our thoughts and emotions. God's words are not just Bible verses. God's voice is His Spirit of truth that penetrates to our innermost being and produces convictions. The Bible sometimes uses the word flesh to refer to both body and soul. The voice of God is like a sword that pierces our fleshly outer life and lays bare who we are inside. "For the word of God is living and active and sharper than any two-edged sword, and piercing as far as the division of soul and spirit, of both joints and marrow, and able to judge the thoughts and intentions of the heart" (Hebrews 4:12).

Truths that are rooted in our spirits become convictions that determine inner thoughts and motives. These, in turn, begin to control our emotions and our wills. The result is that different behavior aligned with God's will emerges from our lives. New ways of speaking, new actions can be seen by others around us. Discipleship is a change that starts from the inside and moves out! It is a personal transformation that all starts with a call from God.

Let's follow this process in the life of one of Jesus' disciples, a man called Simon who was also named Peter. His discipleship journey began with the Lord's command, "Follow me!" "Now as Jesus was walking by the Sea of Galilee, He saw two brothers, Simon who was called Peter, and Andrew his brother, casting a net into the sea; for they were fishermen. And He said to them, 'Follow Me, and I will make you fishers of men.' Immediately they left their nets and followed Him" (Matthew 4:18-20).

After Simon had been following Jesus for more than one year, the voice of God was beginning to penetrate deep into his spirit. He and the other disciples were realizing that Jesus was more than just another man; more than a great teacher and miracle worker. At this crucial turning point, Jesus took the twelve out of the lower Galilee, where most of their ministry work was centered, several days walk to the north where He could spend time with them away from the crowds. They visited a town called Caesarea Philippi and had an important private talk there.

"Now when Jesus came into the district of Caesarea Philippi, He was asking His disciples, 'Who do people say that the Son of Man is?' And they said, 'Some say John the Baptist; and others, Elijah; but still others, Jeremiah, or one of the prophets.' He said to them, 'But who do you say that I am?' Simon Peter answered, 'You are the Christ, the Son of the living God'" (Matthew 16:13-16).

Simon was a natural leader and he loved Jesus, but he had another side to him that was unreliable, impulsive, boastful, and cowardly. On that day in Caesarea Philippi, I'm sure Simon was the first to speak out after Jesus asked such an important question. He probably wanted to make sure he was first, ahead of James, his brother Andrew, and all the others. In his answer, Simon blurted out what he was thinking in his heart regarding the hidden but true identity of Jesus. He said that Jesus was more than a man; He was Israel's chosen and long-awaited Messiah, the only begotten eternal Son of God!

Perhaps there was a moment of silence after Simon's

response. Everyone was waiting to see if he had given the right answer! But then, Jesus confirmed with a blessing the truth that God had revealed and placed deep in Simon's spirit. However, in the very next moment, Jesus took the opportunity to speak words of God's Spirit directly into Simon's inner man. These were words about Simon's identity and God's plan for him.

Jesus prophesied this disciple's destiny. God's Word went into his heart. However, it still had to be worked out in his life. "And Jesus said to him, 'Blessed are you, Simon Barjona, because flesh and blood did not reveal this to you, but My Father who is in heaven. I also say to you that you are Peter, and upon this rock I will build My church; and the gates of Hades will not overpower it. I will give you the keys of the kingdom of heaven; and whatever you bind on earth shall have been bound in heaven, and whatever you loose on earth shall have been loosed in heaven'" (Matthew 16:17-19).

Discussion Questions:

1. What is the difference between spirit, soul, and body?
2. Have I ever heard God speak inside my spirit? How did I know it was God and what did He say?
3. Why does integrity mean wholeness and not just honesty?

Prayer Point:

Lord, You are the living Word of God. Please speak life and truth into my innermost being. Call me by name and show me what You have planned for me.

Chapter 5

Identity of a Disciple

Identity is a vitally important part of being a disciple. The awakening of God's identity in us happens when God speaks His Word into our spirits. Jesus said in effect to Simon, "By revelation from God you have correctly identified Me. Now, allow Me to correctly identify you!" Jesus told this impulsive, unreliable man that he was called to be a rock of stability who would not only be a leader in the community of believers but also would wield astonishing spiritual authority. These were Spirit words, liberating words of truth, but we know Simon, now called Peter, still struggled to develop into the integrity of his calling.

Even after that inspired conversation with the Lord at Caesarea Philippi, Simon Peter continued with his pattern of contradicting the Lord and trying to correct Him. This was especially evident when the Lord spoke of His impending death. What is revealed is that Simon Peter inwardly believed Jesus was mistaken about the future and weak to the point of needing protection. Simon Peter's pride was connected to proving he knew more about earthly realities than the Lord Himself and that as a true disciple he would be the one to protect the Master from harm. Eventually, Jesus had to rebuke him for holding these well-meaning but mistaken thoughts and feelings that arose from this disciple's soul rather than from his spirit.

"From that time Jesus began to show His disciples that He must go to Jerusalem, and suffer many things from the elders and chief priests and scribes, and be killed, and be raised up on the third day. Peter took Him aside and began to rebuke Him, saying, 'God forbid it, Lord! This shall never happen to You.' But He turned and said to Peter, 'Get behind Me, Satan! You are a stumbling block to Me; for you are not setting your mind on God's interests, but man's'" (Matthew 16:21-23).

Months later, with the end of His earthly life fast approaching, Jesus and the disciples went up to Jerusalem for the Passover. At their last supper together, Jesus took the unleavened Passover bread and the cup of wine from their celebration and initiated with them a new covenant sealed by the sacrifice of His own body and blood. Afterward, on their way to Gethsemane on the Mount of Olives, He told them about God's difficult but perfect plan that was unfolding that night. We need to see this as part of the discipleship process for Peter and the others.

Then Jesus said to them, "You will all fall away

> because of Me this night, for it is written, 'I will strike down the shepherd, and the sheep of the flock shall be scattered.' But after I have been raised, I will go ahead of you to Galilee." But Peter said to Him, "Even though all may fall away because of You, I will never fall away." Jesus said to him, "Truly I say to you that this very night, before a rooster crows, you will deny Me three times." Peter said to Him, "Even if I have to die with You, I will not deny You." All the disciples said the same thing too. (Matthew 26:31-35)

As we know, Jesus' words were prophetic and all the disciples lost their courage and ran for their lives. When the crisis came, and he was confronted, Peter denied even with cursing that he knew the Lord. Then, when the rooster crowed, he knew that he had failed at his point of pride. Jesus had *always* been right and that meant Peter had always been wrong. He did not understand human situations better than the Lord nor was he able to defend Him. Peter went out and wept bitterly, not just for his friend's sake but for his own now shattered self-image.

In the aftermath of Jesus' crucifixion and his shameful failure to stand with Him, Peter's whole world was broken. For him, the dream that had begun with Jesus' words, "Follow Me!" three years earlier was over. Not only was Jesus dead, but Peter knew he was not the same self-confident young man he had been when they started. What else was left for him to do but return in humiliation to his hometown and try to get his old job back?

John records in his gospel that after His resurrection,

true to His words, Jesus met His disciples again on a little beach on the shores of the Sea of Galilee not far from where they first met.

> So when they had finished breakfast, Jesus said to Simon Peter, "Simon, son of John, do you love Me more than these?" He said to Him, "Yes, Lord; You know that I love You." He said to him, "Tend My lambs." He said to him again a second time, "Simon, son of John, do you love Me?" He said to Him, "Yes, Lord; You know that I love You." He said to him, "Shepherd My sheep." He said to him the third time, "Simon, son of John, do you love Me?" Peter was grieved because He said to him the third time, "Do you love Me?" And he said to Him, "Lord, You know all things; You know that I love You." Jesus said to him, "Tend My sheep. "Truly, truly, I say to you, when you were younger, you used to gird yourself and walk wherever you wished; but when you grow old, you will stretch out your hands and someone else will gird you, and bring you where you do not wish to go." Now this He said, signifying by what kind of death he would glorify God. And when He had spoken this, He said to him, "Follow Me!" (John 21:15-19)

Three times Jesus asked His disciple, "Do you love Me?" Three times Peter answered Him in the affirmative, but it is as if he is struggling to say, "Of course, I love you. I always did. But I'm not the same man I was before. I thought with

You we would change the world. I was going to be with You, bringing God's kingdom back to Israel. Now I know I could never achieve that. It was just my foolish dream."

By the time the Lord asked the same question a third time, however, I think Peter realized Jesus was not asking him to change the world but only to take care of the little flock of other disciples who remained. Peter is different now. He is ready to believe in the Lord's perfect knowledge and simply trust and obey Him by faith. Jesus said a few very deep words about the future sacrifice of Peter's life and then said to him, "Follow Me!"

Between those two commands of "Follow Me!" spoken to the same man in nearly the same location but three years apart, is God's work of molding a person into a disciple. Libraries of books have been written about this process of spiritual growth to maturity. The outer man of body and soul must yield so that the inner man of the spirit can live. The old lessons of life must be unlearned so that new truth can find its place in the heart of a true disciple. The Gospels themselves offer a series of glimpses into this transformation like the individual frames of a motion picture.

Taken together, a moving image emerges of what God wants from each of us and what the world needs today. Scottish theologian Reverend A. B. Bruce, in his nineteenth-century classic on discipleship, *The Training of the Twelve,* wrote, "The careful, painstaking education of the disciples secured that the Teacher's influence on the world should be permanent; that His kingdom should be founded on the rock of deep and indestructible convictions in the minds of the few, not on the shifting sands of the superficial evanescent impressions on the minds of the many."

Each of us has a name and an identity as a disciple that God already knows.

In the book of Acts, Peter emerges as a rock-like figure of faith. He preaches with boldness and power in the face of the gospel's enemies. His shadow falling on the paving stones had the power to heal the sick. He raised a godly woman from the dead and opened the door of God's kingdom to Jews on Pentecost. He did the same with Gentiles in the home of Cornelius, the Roman centurion. It is sometimes hard to recognize that this apostle is the same brash young fisherman that Jesus originally called to follow Him in the Galilee. The transformation is so complete. Yet this is the picture of what God intends for us all. Each of us has a name and an identity as a disciple that God already knows. Each of us has a destiny reserved from before our birth. Like Peter, we need to answer the Master's "Follow Me!" and submit to the process of transformation into a disciple.

Discussion Questions:

1. Why did Simon Peter have to change?
2. Is discipleship a process in my life or a single decision I made?
3. Have I ever felt like I failed God? What did I learn from that experience?

Prayer Point:

Lord, please help me through my weaknesses and failings to find the identity that is mine forever. I am trusting in You alone because no one else understands me like You do!

Chapter 6

Socks and Shoes of Discipleship

Discipleship may be roughly divided into two categories — socks and shoes. Everybody needs socks and this describes the entry-level discipleship that every believer needs. Basic discipleship addresses and answers questions like, "Who is God? What are the Scriptures? How to worship and pray? How to begin living a holy life?"

A great many churches and ministers do adequate to excellent work in these areas. However, you don't send your children out to school wearing just their socks. They need shoes. People of all ages need different kinds of shoes, depending on the type of work, play, or other activities they are going to be doing. A young person studying to become a dancer needs different shoes from someone working on a construction site. Effective discipleship must provide both socks and shoes to people of the kingdom. The shoes kind of discipleship is vocation-oriented and intended to help each believer find his or her personal calling and become effective and fruitful as a follower of Jesus in it. Mature Christians must be equipped to do their professional work effectively as disciples.

The great majority of God's people are not called to be professional ministers. Using biblical Israel as a model, only one of the twelve tribes was assigned a priestly role by God. This meant less than 10 percent of the people in God's kingdom worked full time in religion. Based on my experience as a minister, in general, this ratio is still evident in the church today. Most Bible schools and seminaries are designed to produce professional ministers of some kind. What about discipleship training for the rest of God's people? Everyone in the kingdom should be given the opportunity to find their God-given calling and trained to be spiritually effective as God's witnesses in society. Non-ministers should not be expected to be simply spectators or financial supporters while only a few trained ministers do the work of extending God's kingdom!

New growth for God's kingdom is not going to be found in the existing churches. People attending churches should already be on the path of spiritual development and discipleship. New growth will always come from the surrounding society, which is full of unbelievers who are not yet part of any church fellowship!

If the 90 percent of God's people who work professionally every day among unbelievers are not discipled to

Disciples are empowered to be people whose lives bear witness of God's kingdom wherever they go.

become genuine examples, agents, or ambassadors of God's kingdom, the goal of reaching the world will never be accomplished. We must find a way to fulfill Jesus' words in Matthew 24:14 (NKJV) "And this gospel of the kingdom will be preached in all the world as a witness to all the nations, and then the end will come."

A key word in that passage is *witness* although some translations say *testimony*. The New Testament Greek word in the text is *marturion* from which we derive the English word *martyr*. It means more than simply preaching an evangelistic message. The meaning is more about becoming, by sacrifice, a living example. The same word in its plural form is found in Acts 1:8 when Jesus foretells the outpouring of God's Spirit on Pentecost and its purpose: "But you will receive power when the Holy Spirit has come upon you and you shall be My *witnesses* both in Jerusalem, and in all Judea and Samaria, and even to the remotest part of the earth."

Jesus was speaking to and about His disciples. Disciples are empowered to be people whose lives bear witness of God's kingdom wherever they go.

Throughout the world, there are a great many organizations and associations that exist to encourage, teach, and reach out to non-ministers who work in various professions and different walks of life. Health care and legal professionals have established some very effective Christian support and training groups. Christian businesspeople have formed numerous and powerful networks and a multitude of other para-church associations are active in various countries and internationally. However, along with the recent growth of what is being called the "marketplace movement," most of these groups are functioning outside the core activities of the existing church.

It is easy for Christians in ministry to lapse into a focus on the practice of our faith as an end in itself. Especially in ministry, the way we worship carries the risk of becoming separated from God's purposes as described in the Bible. The first question of the *Westminster Shorter Catechism*, one of the formative documents of the Protestant Reformation, asks, "What is the chief end of man?" The answer given is, "Man's chief end is to glorify God, and to enjoy him forever."

While beautiful and godly, these words fall short of the example and command of Jesus to focus on making disciples. It was His expectation that this work would take place in the whole world before His return. Disciples of Jesus have an almost infinite variety of gifts and callings. However, what God gives to each person has an eternal purpose. None of our human activities whether religious or non-religious should be considered worthy simply for their own sake.

This was the error of the Pharisees in the days of the Lord's earthly ministry. They were so focused on the *form* of their religion they had lost sight of its *goal*. They, like us, believed their faith had been given to them by God and had Scriptures to back them up. God is holy and He deserves our best church services, prayers, and songs, but He is also intensely functional. God has purposes for the surrounding world that He will fulfill come what may. God passionately loves the people of the societies in which we live and commanded us to make them into disciples.

God's contention with Israel at the time of Jesus' ministry was not that they did not believe in God, the patriarchs, or the inspired Scriptures. The problem was that they were not producing the results God expected from their beliefs. By refusing to be a light to the other nations Israel was denying the function for which it had been chosen and gifted. From a divine perspective, Israel had become dysfunctional and God was saying through His Son, Jesus, "Change your ways or I will set you aside while I accomplish my plan through others."

Now, 2000 years later, the church that Jesus established has reached a turning point that is similar to the one reached by Israel. Will we go on prioritizing our familiar forms of ministry or focus on producing what the Lord explicitly said was our task? This means a big turn for many, a pivot toward restoring God's kingdom on the earth.

Dr. George Eldon Ladd, who taught for many years at Fuller Theological Seminary, in his small but helpful book, *The Gospel of the Kingdom,* wrote, "Therefore, the Church is not the Kingdom of God; God's Kingdom creates the Church and works in the world through the Church." The churches that do not prioritize God's kingdom purposes, specifically the production of effective disciples, risk being set aside by God as He moves powerfully to complete His work in this age.

In Jesus' day, the Pharisees were the dominant religious group in Israel. They prided themselves on honoring the Scriptures and keeping the lamp of Jewish life burning under the Roman occupation. Jesus did not hate the Pharisees, although He was often saddened or angered by their response to the gospel of the kingdom. He saw a future and hope for all Pharisees, even among the scribes, who were their teachers and theologians. In Matthew 13:52 we see, "And Jesus said to them, 'Therefore every scribe who has become a disciple of the kingdom of heaven is like a head of a household, who brings out of his treasure things new and old.'"

There is an old spiritual song, written by an unknown author, that was sung generations ago among African American slaves and subsequently recorded by many well-known singers and musicians. It is called "All God's Children Got Shoes." Slaves in America were often forced to live and work without shoes but they hoped God would give them shoes in heaven. The words are, "I got shoes, you got shoes, all God's children got shoes. When I get to heaven, I'm gonna put on my shoes, I'm gonna walk all over God's heaven!"

Today, we are not slaves and we don't need to wait until heaven to put on our shoes. But truly, all God's children need shoes. It is time to stop sending the people of Jesus' flock out to do their work for God with only socks on their feet. Wearing shoes means ensuring that every disciple knows how to act, pray, worship, believe, grow spiritually, share encouragement, and faith, while at the same time effectively functioning professionally in the surrounding society.

There are so many different kinds of shoes needed, so this task requires the involvement of everyone in the kingdom. Extending this metaphor, there some ministries today that may only be equipping believers to wear plastic flip-flops. These believers are only spiritually equipped to visit the closest mall or go to the beach! On the other hand, if they go to the mall or the beach as disciplined servants of God who are living for the benefit of others, won't there be some value for God's kingdom? The point is that it is time for all Christians to put on their shoes and go to work, school, or to whatever duty we are assigned. "For God has not given us a spirit of timidity, but of power and love and discipline" (2 Timothy 1:7). One of the terms used in making sure all disciples have on both socks and shoes is "holistic mission." Dr. Kim Tan, chairman of SpringHill Management, a private fund management company specializing in biotech and social venture capital investments and co-founder of the Transformational Business Network wrote, "In recent years a movement has grown called 'Business as Mission' though it has its antecedents in the original goals of many earlier companies – Boots (the pharmacy chain) and Guinness (the brewery) to name but two. I contend however that for those called and gifted, business *is* mission. For those called to politics, politics *is* mission. Arts *is* mission, hairdressing *is* mission, banking *is* mission. . . . Holistic mission is about living out our discipleship in every area of life that we have been called to."

Discussion Questions:

1. What is the difference between socks and shoes when it comes to discipleship?
2. Are there many Christians who go to work wearing only socks as disciples?
3. How can we help everyone in God's kingdom to be equipped with both socks *and* shoes?

Prayer Point:

Lord, please teach me and develop my ability to live as a disciple in every area of my life. At home, at work, at church, at play, with my family, and with my friends, let my entire life be a graceful expression of Your Lordship.

Chapter 7

Giving Up to Gain More

Although the inner motives of our hearts are vital in following the Lord, there are three important behaviors that define the lifestyle of every disciple. Each of these activities has to do with giving up something in pursuit of receiving the blessing and approval of God. They are found in Jesus' teaching in "The Sermon on the Mount" and give us practical wisdom about what God considers normal behavior in His kingdom. In Matthew chapter 6, the topics of giving to the poor, prayer, and fasting were introduced by Jesus with the words *when* and *whenever*.

This means He expected His disciples to already be doing these things as a part of their daily lives. Jesus said,

"So when you give to the poor, do not sound a trumpet before you, as the hypocrites do in the synagogues and in the streets, so that they may be honored by men. Truly I say to you, they have their reward in full. But when you give to the poor, do not let your left hand know what your right hand is doing, so that your giving will be in secret; and your Father who sees what is done in secret will reward you" (Matthew 6:2-4).

Giving to other people who have financial need or debts beyond their means is a godly activity because God cares for every single person and has special compassion for the poor. In Proverbs 19:17 we read, "One who is gracious to a poor man lends to the LORD and He will repay him for his good deed." This means that you are doing God's work when you help poor people and He promises to repay you! Great men of God in past generations who discovered this truth include John Wesley, who is known to have taught, "Earn all you can, save all you can, give all you can!" Disciples who give freely discover that it is impossible to outdo God when it comes to generosity. When we are generous in our giving to poor people, without fail we find that God is generous to us.

However, this is not a transactional matter like paying for an insurance policy, nor is it random like putting money into a slot machine. Giving to the poor is a behavior that over time develops godly generosity of heart that is pleasing to God and consistently rewarded by Him. In His sermon, Jesus goes on to say that we shouldn't be giving with the motive to receive payment or praise from other people. As disciples, we will be happy and blessed when we learn and apply the truth. Paul the apostle said this to the disciples he made in Ephesus: "In everything I showed you that by working hard in this manner you must help the weak and remember the words of the Lord Jesus, that He Himself said, 'It is more blessed to give than to receive'" (Acts 20:35).

The second behavior in the normal life of disciples is prayer. Jesus said, "But you, when you pray, go into your inner room, close your door and pray to your Father who is in secret, and your Father who sees what is done in secret will reward you" (Matthew 6:6). While in ministry it is often required to pray publicly and corporate prayer is certainly important, Jesus made it clear that it is the *habit* of private prayer that gets the best results from God (John 15:7). He also said that God prefers conversation with us more than the use of memorized or recited written prayers.

The practice of prayer means giving up time and our sense of self-importance to humbly enter the presence of our sovereign Lord and have a meaningful conversation with Him. The reward is spiritual growth and maturity.

The secret of effective prayer lies in developing ongoing dialog with God, who is your loving Father in heaven. Once you begin to genuinely trust Him, you will also start learning to tell Him the truth. Jesus said God is looking for people who will worship Him in Spirit and in truth (John 4:23).

Some people have no one in their life to whom they can deeply and honestly confide. Others resist or are emotionally blocked from telling the truth to anyone, and still others do not even admit to themselves what is really going on inside of them. Because the world around us is so often deceitful and cruel, we learn to hide our hearts at an early age. That is why it takes everyone some effort to begin an honest conversation with God. However, once the conversation starts, you will never want it to end! For many disciples it is the discovery of God as our all-knowing and patiently loving

Father that opens the door to secret and powerful prayer.

Andrew Murray, one of the great writers on the subject of prayer from an earlier generation, wrote, "Beloved fellow-disciple! We begin to see what the reason is that we know so little of daily answers to prayer, and what the chief lesson is which the Lord has for us in His school. It is all in the name of Father. We thought of new and deeper insight into some of the mysteries of the prayer-world as what we should get in Christ's school; He tells us the first is the highest lesson, we must learn to say, 'Abba, Father!'"

Talking things over with our heavenly Father on a regular basis solves all kinds of human problems. Paul wrote to the Thessalonians that we should "pray without ceasing" (1 Thessalonians 5:17). This means praying through the busyness of our daily schedules. It might be the spiritual equivalent of a soldier on the battlefield who is staying in contact with headquarters by radio in real time! The ability to pray whenever and wherever necessary is an essential part of the spiritual equipment every disciple needs to accomplish the work of God's kingdom.

The third expected behavior for disciples is fasting. Jesus said, "Whenever you fast, do not put on a gloomy face as the hypocrites do, for they neglect their appearance so that they will be noticed by men when they are fasting. Truly I say to you, they have their reward in full. But you, when you fast, anoint your head and wash your face so that your fasting will not be noticed by men, but by your Father who is in secret and your Father who sees what is done in secret will reward you" (Matthew 6:16-18).

Fasting is the deliberate giving up of food for brief or prolonged periods of time. Fasting, even for just a meal or two, can be challenging because eating is so important to all of us. Aside from the nutrition our bodies need for health and survival, sharing meals together has a central place in our families and cultures. We all are accustomed to eating at regular times during the day and our bodies start to demand food whether we need the caloric input or not. Many of us also have special "comfort foods" that often bring us a personal sense of reward or well-being. Fasting disrupts all of that.

So why fast? Fasting is the discipline of purposefully weakening ourselves physically and emotionally in order to allow the inner person, our spirit man or woman, to grow in strength. At a certain point in the life of every disciple, the inner person must assert his or her authority over the fleshly desires of the physical. Paul prayed for his disciples in this way: "For this reason I bow my knees before the Father from whom every family in heaven and on earth derives its name, that He would grant you, according to the riches of His glory, to be strengthened with power through His Spirit in the inner man" (Ephesians 3:14-16).

By faith, we interact with the unseen realm of spiritual reality. God is invisible and His voice is rarely heard by human ears. But we perceive what cannot be seen and we hear the voice of God in our spirits. Fasting loosens our grip on the physical while upgrading our ability to grasp the hand of God and "see" the truth of God's Word by revelation. Paul went on to pray, "so that Christ may dwell in your hearts through faith; and that you, being rooted and grounded in love, may be able to comprehend with all the saints what is the breadth and length and height and depth, and to know the love of Christ which surpasses knowledge, that you may be filled up to all the fullness of God" (Ephesians 3:17-19).

In his helpful book, *Celebration of Discipline*, Richard Foster explains how spiritual disciplines offer a door to liberation to believers who practice them. His writing is enlightening as well as practical and this book is known and recommended around the world. In the chapter on fasting he wrote, "Fasting reminds us that we are sustained: 'by every word that proceeds from the mouth of God' (Matt. 4:4). Food does not sustain us; God sustains us. In Christ, 'All things hold together' (Col. 1:17). Therefore, in experiences of fasting, we are not so much abstaining from food as we are feasting on the word of God. Fasting is feasting!"

> Deliberate giving up of what we rightfully have is a path to spiritual freedom.

I am personally very glad to have the discipline of fasting in my spiritual equipment as a disciple of the Lord. I know that when I am facing a severe crisis or have a problem I cannot solve by my own abilities, I can turn to prayer with fasting to improve my "grip" on the Lord. God's grace flows more easily and powerfully upon me when I deliberately deny myself food and focus on Him. Spiritual breakthroughs have often come to me as the result of personal and corporate prayer with fasting. The Bible contains many stories of people who fasted and received blessing and deliverance from God: Moses, David, Elijah, Esther, Daniel, Anna, Paul, and Jesus all fasted with powerful results. Books like Foster's give useful guidance on the type and length of fast to choose when the time comes.

All three of these disciplines—giving to the poor, prayer, and fasting—show us that deliberate giving up of what we rightfully have is a path to spiritual freedom. When we sow sacrificial seeds of time, money, and effort into improving our walk with God, the result is a harvest of abundant fruitfulness. God wants all of His children to be free from want and full of every good thing. Spiritual disciplines like these are vital in the process of equipping God's people for their fruitful work of service in His kingdom!

Discussion Questions:

1. What are the three behaviors Jesus taught for disciples in Matthew chapter 6?
2. Is spiritual discipline necessary for me to grow as a disciple with God?
3. Would fasting with prayer improve my spiritual life? What results am I seeking?

Prayer Point:

Lord, please help me learn spiritual discipline so that I can always be at my best for You. Show me how to invest my life to increase Your blessings and give me a hunger for more of You!

Chapter 8

Hearts of Gold

Since ancient times, gold has been used as a measure and symbol of wealth. Gold is mentioned more than four hundred times in the Bible. Genesis 13:2 says, "Now Abram was very rich in livestock, in silver and in gold." According to the book of Revelation, the streets of the New Jerusalem, which comes down out of heaven, are made of "pure gold" (Revelation 21:21). The purity of gold determines its worth. Typically, jewelry is a mixture of gold with other metals like copper or silver in an alloy. Today, gold comes in a wide variety of jewelry items, coins, and investment-grade bars that are valued by the purity of the gold. Karats are the most common measurement of purity.

Now I believe that God does not have fire—He is the fire.

One-karat gold means one twenty-fourth pure gold, so 24-karat gold means 100 percent pure gold.

There are many ways to mine and process gold ore, but the principle of removing impurities from gold by refining in fire at high temperature hasn't changed much over the centuries. A furnace that is hot enough to liquify metal causes impurities to separate from the gold so they can be removed by the refiner. This process, called smelting, becomes a picture in the Bible of how God works in human lives to produce a pure and undivided heart. Read the following verses from the prophet Malachi, who wrote more than four hundred years before Jesus' day.

> "Behold, I am going to send My messenger, and he will clear the way before Me. And the Lord, whom you seek, will suddenly come to His temple; and the messenger of the covenant, in whom you delight, behold, He is coming," says the LORD of hosts. "But who can endure the day of His coming? And who can stand when He appears? For He is like a refiner's fire and like fullers' soap. He will sit as a smelter and purifier of silver and He will purify the sons of Levi and refine them like gold and silver, so that they may present to the LORD offerings in righteousness." (Malachi 3:1-3)

I used to think that God had many kinds of fire to suit His purposes: fire for revival, fire for judgment, fire of trials and adversity, fire of godly passion, fire of the Holy Spirit, and more. Now I believe that God does not have fire—He *is* the fire. In the words of the Bible, "For our God is a consuming fire" (Hebrews 12:29). As we seek to draw closer to Him, we approach a holy, invisible flame that begins to refine our hearts the way a refiner watches the intense heat of the furnace start to separate the pure gold from what is impure. The worthless dross is skimmed off and discarded, but what is precious remains.

The main area where our hearts need the spiritual fire of God is in finding freedom from rebellion. Rebellion against God is evil and inspired by the devil. Satan fell from his high position of serving God because of rebellion, and according to the Bible, he tempted Adam and Eve to do the same. Since the fall of the first man and woman, all of humankind is rebellious by nature. In every heart, the spirit of rebellion has set up "strongholds" against God that must be identified, dismantled, and cleared out of the life of a disciple. A stronghold is an area of stubborn resistance to God's will that develops where our rebellious nature and areas of personal weakness are exploited by spiritual evil. In these areas, sins and wrong habits become entrenched and rooted in our personalities. Various obsessive behaviors and addictions are among the evidences of evil strongholds in our lives.

Miners and treasure hunters know that you hardly ever find valuable gold lying exposed on the ground. You have to dig for gold. You hunt for treasure. It takes time and effort and costs you something. Because of the difficulty, not everyone is successful. There are people who give up or run out of resources and have to stop. This is also true in developing a heart of gold for the Lord. It is a spiritual struggle to remain in the heat and light of God's presence long enough for the impurities deep in our lives to be exposed and removed. Drawing compromised or contaminated areas of our lives out of their dark hiding places into the light where they are visible is not pleasant or easy. It can be very hard work. However, when we fully entrust ourselves to God's hands, His presence confronts spiritual strongholds and has the power to destroy and remove them.

Everyone has inner problems that arise from hurts, bitterness, guilt, and unforgiveness in our past. Healing these wounded areas starts by admitting we have these inner issues and talking about them while surrounded by the love and grace of God. This too is part of God's refining process. He is looking for hearts that are pure gold all the way through, not just gold plated on the outside. Honesty about our real motives exposes inner thoughts to the flames in God's purifying furnace.

Getting to the place where we are truthful about our real intentions requires divine help. The words that God speaks to us are more effective than the hands of a skilled surgeon in reaching to our inner core. "For the word of God is living and active and sharper than any two-edged sword, and piercing as far as the division of soul and spirit, of both joints and marrow, and able to judge the thoughts and intentions of the heart" (Hebrews 4:12).

Anyone who truly desires purity can begin developing a life that has eternally beautiful qualities now. Acquiring a heart that is like gold in the eyes of God is a quest and an adventure that takes effort and commitment. Under the loving guidance of our heavenly Father, we take responsibility for our own thoughts and actions. Our efforts are an investment in eternal life and its rewards. Like all good investments, over a period of time, it will grow many times over in value. To the "lukewarm" church at Laodicea in Revelation chapter 3, the Spirit of the Lord said,

> I advise you to buy from Me gold refined by fire so that you may become rich, and white garments so that you may clothe yourself, and that the shame of your nakedness will not be revealed; and eye salve to anoint your eyes so that you may see. Those whom I love, I reprove and discipline; therefore be zealous and repent, Behold, I stand at the door and knock; if anyone hears My voice and opens the door, I will come in to him and will dine with him, and he with Me. He who overcomes, I will grant to him to sit down with Me on My throne, as I also overcame and sat down with My Father on His throne. (Revelation 3:18-21)

A strategic battleground in the fight for a spiritually valuable life is finding and holding onto sexual purity. Sex is a powerful, God-given drive in almost everyone and it is part of God's good design for humans. The drive for sexual intimacy has been compared to a river that cannot be stopped but must be directed and kept within its banks or else its life-giving flow will become destructive and dangerous. Paul's words to the Ephesians captures the standard for disciples of God's kingdom: "But immorality or any impurity or greed

We need to endure the uncomfortable heat of God's presence until our hearts start to shine with His light and look more like pure gold.

must not even be named among you, as is proper among saints" (Ephesians 5:3). There are two sides to developing a lifestyle of sexual purity: God's side and yours. Jesus is the only completely pure person, so His spiritual presence in your heart will always be necessary. Worship and praise to the Lord is one way to enter His presence. We experience purity in the presence of the Lord when He surrounds us like a shield. The more we learn to cultivate a consistent lifestyle that has Jesus at the core, the more we are progressively transformed by God's Spirit into His likeness. Jesus is the only perfect human and His Spirit working in us is the true mark of eternal perfection in our lives.

The other side of being pure is the human side and it means never giving up our struggle with the flesh. We cannot be holy without God's presence, but we must never cease resisting temptation and our own sinful desires. In their challenging book, *Every Man's Battle*, Christian authors Stephen Arterburn and Fred Stoeker wrote, "Holiness is not some nebulous thing. It's a series of right choices. You needn't wait for some holy cloud to form around you. You'll be holy when you choose not to sin. You're already free from the *power* of sexual immorality; you are not yet free from the *habit* of sexual immorality, until you choose to be—until you say, "That's enough! I'm choosing to live purely!"

Walking a path of purity requires managing to live in the tension between God's responsibility and yours. Successfully handling the tension between God's Spirit and your flesh takes effort and concentration, but when we have faith in God, our weakness pulls His strength toward us. Paul discovered this secret access to God's power. He wrote, "God has chosen the weak things of the world to shame the things which are strong" and "for when I am weak, then I am strong" (1 Corinthians 1:27 and 12:10). We need to endure the uncomfortable heat of God's presence until our hearts start to shine with His light and look more like pure gold.

Stay on this path! Don't be quick to jump out of God's fiery presence when things get hot! Disciples of the kingdom learn to not allow disappointments and setbacks to turn them away from their calling and eternal destiny. We want to offer to the Lord hearts of pure gold.

Discussion Questions:

1. What does it mean to have a pure heart?
2. Does God desire and encourage purity in every area of my life?
3. Will God answer my prayers for purity? Is there something I must also do?

Prayer Point:

Lord, I know You have called me with a holy calling. Please help me to develop a pure heart and a godly lifestyle that honors You every day.

Part 2

Restoring Foundations

He was looking for the city which has foundations, whose architect and builder is God. (Hebrews 11:10)

Chapter 9

Restoration of All Things

The word *restoration* in a biblical sense points to God's original and perfect plan for everything. The Bible is specific about God's intentions for Israel, the nation He created and chose for eternal purposes in the service of all humanity. Israel was intended to be a great nation that would bless all the other peoples of the world (Genesis 12:1-3). Israel would inherit a land promised by God, disobey and be scattered throughout the world only to be regathered according to God's plan (Ezekiel 36:22-24).

Modern history points to the fact that we are in an age of profound restoration for Christianity. The creation of the modern state of Israel demonstrates that the people of Israel are being restored to their promised land after nearly two millennia of wandering. At the same time, with the re-emergence of Messianic Jewish communities, we see the good news of God's kingdom, as preached by Jesus, being restored to the people who were the first to bring this message to the world. These are prophetic milestones that point to the "restoration of all things" prophesied by the apostle Peter.

Restoration means a recovery of the original or a return to our beginnings.

A short time after the death and resurrection of Jesus, Peter and John encountered a lame man at one of the main entrances to the great temple in Jerusalem. After healing the man in the name of Jesus, Peter began to preach to the Jews who gathered around him in the temple compound. He said, "Therefore repent and return, so that your sins may be wiped away, in order that times of refreshing may come from the presence of the Lord; and that He may send Jesus, the Christ appointed for you, whom heaven must receive until the period of restoration of all things about which God spoke by the mouth of His holy prophets from ancient time" (Acts 3:19-21).

Restoration means a recovery of the original or a return to our beginnings. God's prophets spoke many times about restoration. Here are two out of the many significant examples from the Bible that are being fulfilled in our time. The first is a promise from God saying to the people of Israel that He will restore them to the land that was promised to their fathers. The second example is of an end time restoration of the spirit and power of Elijah.

> "For behold, days are coming," declares the LORD, "when I will restore the fortunes of My people Israel and Judah." The LORD says, "I will also bring them back to the land that I gave to their forefathers and they shall possess it" (Jeremiah 30:3-4).

> "Behold, I am going to send you Elijah the prophet before the coming of the great and terrible day of the Lord. He will restore the hearts of the fathers to their children and the hearts of the children to their fathers so that I will not come and smite the land with a curse" (Malachi 4:5-6).

The prophet Malachi said that Elijah would bring a restoration of God's planned alignment between God's children and their fathers. In the Bible, particularly in the writing of the apostle Paul, the phrase "the fathers" refers specifically to the patriarchs of Israel. One way to understand these verses is to recognize Christians of all nations today as the children of Abraham by faith (Galatians 3:7-9). The spirit and power of Elijah are now working to restore Christian hearts to the worldview and faith of their biblical fathers: Abraham, Isaac, and Jacob. This is not a return to ancient Christian traditions but something far more radical.

The original meaning of the English word *radical* comes from the phrase *forming the root*. Restoration of the Hebraic origins of Christian faith can only be termed "radical" because it is a reconnection with our Jewish "roots," Paul wrote in his letter to the Romans. "But if some of the branches were broken off, and you [Gentiles], being a wild olive, were grafted in among them [the Jews] and became partaker with them of the rich root of the olive tree, do not be arrogant toward the branches; but if you are arrogant, remember that it is not you who supports the root, but the root supports you" (Romans11:17-18).

How is this related to the days of Elijah's ministry? In 1 Kings 18:30, it is recorded: "Then Elijah said to all the people, 'Come near to me.' So all the people came near to him. And he repaired the altar of the Lord which had been torn down." "All the people" of Israel were a younger generation who no longer worshipped the God of their fathers or followed His commands. When Elijah first confronted his people and asked, "How long will you hesitate between two opinions . . .?" (1 Kings 18:21), none of the younger leaders would answer him or respect his authority. This may be seen as a picture of the Christian world developing over the centuries to the point of rejecting its biblical and Hebraic origins.

When Elijah restored (Hebrew root word: rapha meaning healed) the altar of the Lord that had been torn down, he was calling the new generation back to the faith of their fathers. There had been altars to the Lord in Israel previously, but they had been destroyed or neglected. When Elijah prayed at the altar he had restored, the fire of the Lord fell and the young leaders worshipped God. The heart of the next generation was restored to their fathers who had provided them an example of faith. They turned back to Abraham who believed God, Moses, who had led them through the wilderness and to the faith of Joshua and the judges. They were restored to faith in the living God of Israel.

Elijah's ministry provides a picture of end time restoration for Israel and the church. This prophetic restoration is not only a biblical truth but meant to be a personal experience for all believers who are the Lord's disciples. Everyone who is chosen by the Lord is called to return, turn back to God's original plan. Jesus said, "Elijah is coming and will restore all things" (John 17:10-13) and then He said Elijah already came in the person of John the Baptist. These words remind us of the way we view the kingdom of God as something that is both already here but also coming in the future. Malachi's prophecy states Elijah will be sent before the "great and terrible day of the Lord," that is, before Jesus' return.

This final restoration of God's kingdom was the subject of the last question the disciples asked Jesus before He ascended into heaven, "Lord, is it at this time You are restoring the kingdom to Israel?" (Acts 1:6). Today, God has begun the restoration of His kingdom to Israel and is working powerfully to extend His lawful reign through personal discipleship and fatherly mentoring in every nation of the world.

Discussion Questions:

1. Why is the modern restoration of Israel important to Christians as part of God's end time plan?
2. In what way and why does the church need to be restored?
3. What would a personal restoration in my life be like?

Prayer Point:

Lord, please restore my faith to its biblical roots and let me be a part of restoring Your kingdom on earth in my time.

Chapter 10

Contextualization "Time Warp"

Contextualization refers to finding ways of presenting the biblical message that are culturally relevant to different times and peoples. For example, if you were called to bring the Bible's message to a tribal group in a distant jungle that had never seen a sheep before, then contextualization would be a challenge. Would you first organize a pre-Bible class explaining about sheep, lambs, and shepherds so that later you could tell them about Jesus, the Lamb of God and the Good Shepherd? An alternative would be to use a substitute animal that is familiar to them. What about the "pig of God" or the "snake of God"? Would those animals work? Of course not!

The truth about God in the Scriptures is timeless, spiritual, and transcultural, but it has been handed down to us in the context of a particular people and culture. That is the nation of Israel. From this one people, we have received essentially everything we know for certain about God. The people of Israel received inspiration from God and wrote the Bible, both the Old and New Testaments. From them come almost all the original heroes of our faith: Abraham, Isaac, Jacob, Joseph, Moses, Joshua, David, Elijah, Isaiah, Jeremiah, Ezekiel, Daniel, Jesus, Peter, and Paul. The entire Bible comes to us in the context of Israel's unique culture. The challenge of Christianity as it spread throughout the world for the last two thousand years has been to make the Bible's eternal message culturally relevant to people who do not share Israel's background.

The truth about God in the Scriptures is timeless, spiritual, and transcultural, but it has been handed down to us in the context of a particular people and culture.

Now, after nearly two thousand years of wandering, the people of Israel have returned to their land and become a nation again. When we begin to bring the message of the entire Bible, both Old and New Testaments, back to the people of Israel today and try to contextualize its meaning for them, we fall through a strange "time warp." Our feet begin landing in a place that at first seems strange to us, that is, the context of the Bible as it was originally written. This return can only be called a great restoration. As we progress further and more understanding and revelation emerges, a powerful authentic gospel appears. The words of the biblical text are being restored to their original meaning; their ancient light flaring up again to light our path to God's house.

We realize that for nearly two thousand years Gentile believers in the Bible from lands outside of Israel have abstracted the Bible's message, that is, pulled it away from its original meaning to fit it into other cultural and historic contexts. For example, Jerusalem became whatever principal city where Christians happened to be at the time or a purely heavenly, almost mythic reality. Passover became Easter and the coming of God's kingdom was a far-off eternal event.

This "spiritualization" of the divine message over time hardened into church traditions and accepted doctrines. Now, many of those abstractions, cultural distortions, and religious traditions are being chipped away by the powerful events of our time. Israel is a nation again! Messianic Jews in Israel are worshipping Jesus as their Jewish Messiah and using the language of Hebrew once more. The emphasis in Israel is on building Messianic communities and reaching out to every area of society so that "all Israel will be saved" (Romans 11:26). Around the world, the church also is beginning a major course adjustment, a great realignment to biblical truth and a return to its ancient Hebraic beginnings.

When I was a young pastor, I believed that the kingdom of God was my church fellowship. My job as a minister was to serve God by convincing as many people as possible to join my church. They joined by believing several doctrines I taught and praying certain prayers, but most of all by attending the weekly worship service. If the number of people attending that weekly service was growing, I knew that I was doing my part in extending God's kingdom on earth.

Along with others on the pastoral leadership team, I spent hours, sometimes days preparing for the weekly service. When the service was over, I could relax and then begin preparing for the next week's service. What the people in the congregation did with their lives during the week was significantly less important to me than what they did in the service. If they worshipped, listened, and prayed in that service, then I felt what I was doing and saying must be right.

Now after many years, I realize that the emphasis of Jesus' ministry was the reverse of mine. When we see Jesus in the actual context of the Bible's words, it is clear that when He ministered to people in public meetings it was so that their daily lives after the meeting would be different. What their lives were like after they went home was more important than the meeting itself!

How many of our church services are focused on producing a religious experience that may make people feel better about themselves but fails to significantly change their lives? Faith comes by hearing the words of God. The Bible contains those words, but we have to listen for the way they were spoken and not as we have decided to hear them. The inspiration of the Bible is in what God meant when He spoke to the writers, not whatever we may think those words mean today. An accurate understanding of the original context of God's words will always help us to understand what His words really mean and what He is saying to us today.

Discussion Questions:

1. How has the Bible's message been contextualized for my culture?
2. What are some of the differences between the way Jesus and His disciples ministered and how Christian ministries function today?
3. Am I interested in visiting Israel? Why or why not?

Prayer Point:

Lord, help me to understand more of the original meaning of your words and contextualize your timeless message to my own culture more effectively.

Chapter 11

"De-Greecing" God's House

Bible teacher David Pawson invented the term "de-Greecing" and has taught for years about how the early influence of Greek thinking on Christianity gave rise to unbiblical thinking and behavior that persists to this day. He said, "Those who think the foundation of Western civilization is Judeo-Christian are mistaken. It is far more Greco-Roman." Pawson goes on to cite four examples of where ancient Greek influence dominates Western culture in obvious ways: architecture (public buildings look like Greek temples), politics (democracy), sport (Olympic games), and entertainment (exaltation of leisure and human beauty).

Pawson's focus, however, is on the influence of Greek

thinking in the church and how to remove it. He said, "The root of Christianity is in quite a different world from Greece. Your Bible tells you where our roots are. Our roots are in the Hebrew world—the Jewish world. That world was almost the opposite in every respect of ancient Greece. The Old Testament is totally Hebrew and was actually completed before the Greeks appeared on the scene."

In order to restore the original meaning of the Bible, we have to see how much the Bible's message was changed as Christianity developed in the West.

In order to restore the original meaning of the Bible, we have to see how much the Bible's message was changed as Christianity developed in the West. The writers of the entire Bible and virtually all of its main characters are Jews. But Paul and other apostles of the New Testament age took the Hebrew Bible's good news west, into the Greek-speaking world. Jesus and His disciples spoke and prayed in Hebrew but the entire New Testament and particularly Paul's epistles were written in Greek. This was more than a language change. It represented a change in worldview.

The early history of Christianity is well researched and documented, as are the writings of Augustine, Bishop of Hippo (354-430), who had a profound and lasting influence on Christian theology both Catholic and Protestant. Augustine was a student of Greek philosophy and did much to create a synthesis between the Hebraic understanding found in the Bible and the thinking of Greek- and Latin-speaking Gentile Christians.

Thomas Aquinas (1225-1274) was an Italian philosopher and theologian who likewise mixed Greek philosophy with the Bible, deeply influencing the church for centuries. Gradually, Greek ideas dominated Christian thinking and theology.

When the Protestant reformers came on the scene in the sixteenth century, they did much to turn the church back toward the Bible as the sole authority for faith and doctrine. However, the reformers failed to restore respect for Israel, the Jews, and the Hebraic understanding behind the Scriptures. Greek thinking remained entrenched in Protestantism.

The Greek mind is dualistic; that is, it sees a sharp contrast between what is earthly and what is heavenly, between the physical and the spiritual. The Hebrew mind is more holistic. God is one and Lord of both heaven and the earth. Humans are made in His image, so all of human life, including the earthly as well as its eternal aspects are meant to be lived out in God's creation. The Greek mind is logical and takes things apart to see how they work. This, of course, had a powerful influence on the development of modern scientific thinking. The Hebrew mind is more concerned with values that derive from the character of God and the meaning they give to life and community.

Rabbi Lord Jonathan Sacks, who served as chief rabbi of the United Hebrew Congregations of the Commonwealth, wrote, "Western civilization was born in the synthesis between Athens and Jerusalem brought about by Pauline Christianity and the conversion of Emperor Constantine in 312, turning a small and often persecuted sect into the official religion of the Roman Empire. It was an astonishing, improbable event and it eventually transformed the world.

Christendom drew its philosophy, science, and art from Greece, its religion from Israel."

Over the centuries, Greek thinking molded the Christian worldview in the synthesis that Rabbi Sacks mentions. European Christians believed God created the universe and this gave them the faith to investigate through science, which they learned from the Greeks.

At first, this seemed like a huge success. It resulted in the spectacular rise in the influence of science on our lives today, even to the sad extent of forcing biblical faith to the sidelines of society. The success of modern science made the West powerful and wealthy, but cold, lonely, and confused at the same time. Rabbi Sacks wrote, "Science takes things apart to see how they work, [biblical] religion puts things together to see what they mean."

Now Israel has been restored to her land and Messianic Jewish disciples of Jesus are working to restore His truth to its original Hebraic context. Today a great restoration has begun. Christianity is turning back from Athens and Rome toward Jerusalem!

This restoration is beginning to impact not only the way Christians today read the Old Testament but also how we understand the words of the New Testament. The earliest church "fathers," who wrote before the fourth century AD, state that Matthew wrote his gospel in the Hebrew language, and others used it as a source. Since the discovery of the Dead Sea Scrolls in 1947, modern scholars see an increasing amount of evidence that the earliest gospel was written in Hebrew and then translated into the Greek text that we use as the basis for our English translations today.

Christian scholars David Bivin and Roy Blizzard's book,

Understanding the Difficult Words of Jesus, sheds important light on the Hebraic background of the New Testament. They wrote, "The assumption that the entire New Testament was originally communicated in Greek has led to a considerable amount of misunderstanding on the part of scholars and lay-persons alike. Today, as a result of recent research, we know that the key to our understanding of this material is Hebrew."

Bivin and Blizzard cite compelling evidence that Hebrew and not Aramaic, and certainly not Greek, was the daily language of the Jews in the days of Jesus. They show fascinating examples of Hebrew language and Hebraic understanding underlying the New Testament Greek text. For example, in His Sermon on the Mount, Jesus is quoted as saying, "Do not store up for yourselves treasures on earth, where moth and rust destroy, and where thieves break in and steal. But store up for yourselves treasures in heaven, where neither moth nor rust destroys, and where thieves do not break in or steal; for where your treasure is, there your heart will be also" (Matthew 6:19-21).

The next two verses say, "The eye is the lamp of the body; so then if your eye is clear, your whole body will be full of light. But if your eye is bad [Greek: *poneros* meaning evil], your whole body will be full of darkness. If then the light that is in you is darkness, how great is the darkness!" (Matthew 6:22–23). And then Jesus concludes with: "No one can serve two masters; for either he will hate the one and love the other, or he will be devoted to one and despise the other. You cannot serve God and wealth" (Matthew 6:24).

For centuries many Christians have wondered why Jesus inserted a statement about eyesight in the middle of His teaching about having the right attitude toward money. But this is evidence of the Hebrew language and culture "peeking" through the Greek New Testament text! Having a "bad eye" or an "evil eye" (Hebrew: *ayin raa*) is a Hebrew idiom that means to be stingy. It can be found in Deuteronomy 15:9 and Proverbs 28:22.

The opposite is having a "good eye" (Hebrew: *ayin tov*), which means to be generous, and is found in Proverbs 22:9. Jesus used Hebrew idiom in His parable of the laborers in the vineyard found in Matthew chapter 20. In this parable, the master of the vineyard asks the complaining original workers why they are resentful because he generously rewarded the others who came to work late in the day. "Take what is yours and go your way. I wish to give to this last man the same as to you. Is it not lawful for me to do what I wish with my own things? Or is your eye evil [*poneros*] because I am good?" (Matthew 20:14-15 NKJV).

To Hebrew-speaking Jews, the whole teaching in the Sermon on the Mount would have made perfect sense: Since God is your Father and provides everything you need for your life, your real treasure is truly in heaven. Then, if you demonstrate your faith through generosity, you will find your everyday life permeated with God's presence! Modern readers of the English Bible might think having a "clear eye" or a "good eye" means having good eyesight or being single-minded in our pursuit of God. Two thousand years ago, the Greek translators copied an inspired Hebrew story correctly word for word and then the English translators did the same. We got the right words and lost the "Jewish" meaning.

We should not be surprised at the scale of this change in the Christian mind today. It is like a tsunami that originates from a giant subterranean earthquake. The modern restoration of Israel is a prophetic earthquake. We can use this word *prophetic* not just because the return of the Jewish people to their land is predicted in the Bible but in the same sense that the gospels in the New Testament are considered prophetic.

The gospels document historic events that took place less than one hundred years before they were written. They were written while the eyewitnesses were still alive to explain the significance of the things they had seen and heard. At this writing, it is still less than a century since the founding of Israel as a modern nation. The significance of this historically unique and prophetic event is still sending shock waves through the Christian world. The process of "de-Greecing" God's house has already begun.

Discussion Questions:

1. Does it matter to me that Jesus, His disciples, and the writers of the Bible were Hebrew-speaking Jews?
2. What words in Hebrew do I know and use that are from the Bible?
3. Do I think of Christianity as a "Western" religion?

Prayer Point:

Lord, help me to use the Bible's ancient truth to live out Your will "on earth as it is in heaven" with faith and courage. I don't want to separate spiritual or heavenly truth from the way I live my daily life.

Chapter 12

New Architecture for the Church

According to the Bible, what we call the "church" (New Testament Greek: *ekklesia*) is the people from every nation, tribe, and tongue who have been called and chosen by God to be followers of His Son, Jesus. This group of people is intended to be the evidence of God's kingdom on earth and God's instrument for extending His reign everywhere. *Christianity* is the term that historically applies to the religious expression of faith in Jesus among "the nations." The Hebrew term for "the nations" is *goyim,* which is also translated "Gentiles" in the Bible. In general, that word has come to mean non-Jewish people. Christianity carries the message of God's kingdom and His salvation for the world and is a movement that has been growing and developing among Gentiles for nearly two thousand years.

> Christianity has repeatedly met the challenge of reform.

Like a ship on a long journey, however, changes in course must be made from time to time. Now we have reached an important turning point. In times past, Christianity has repeatedly met the challenge of reform. Although church history seems to change with glacial slowness, today such a time has come again. Christianity as we know it needs a redesign; that is, new architecture.

Paul the apostle called himself a wise "master builder." The Greek text uses the word *architekton* from which we derive the English word *architect*. God's kingdom is portrayed as a building. God is the owner of the building and Paul was apostolically commissioned by Him to lay a foundation for others to build upon. He wrote, "According to the grace of God which was given to me, like a wise master builder [*architekton*] I laid a foundation, and another is building on it. But each man must be careful how he builds on it" (1 Corinthians 3:10-11).

Paul wrote to Jesus' Gentile disciples in Ephesus regarding the foundation he had laid. He told them that God had chosen him to bring non-Jews to faith in Jesus in order to work on building the house of God. But they should be clear about the nature of the foundation upon which they built. "So then you are no longer strangers and aliens, but you are fellow citizens with the saints, and are of God's household, having been built on the foundation of the apostles and prophets, Christ Jesus Himself being the cornerstone, in whom the whole building, being fitted together, is growing into a holy temple in the Lord" (Ephesians 2:19-21).

We know that it was God's choice for His Son, Jesus, to come to us from Israel, the nation chosen to be God's example for all peoples (Genesis 12:3). Jesus is the cornerstone and there is no other. However, the rest of the foundation, according to Paul, is "the apostles and prophets." Paul is not referring to whomever we now consider apostolic or prophetic. There is a difference between "apostles and prophets" and "*the* apostles and prophets."

All of today's apostolic and prophetic ministry is based on and draws its legitimacy from the biblical prophets and the original apostles of Jesus. Jesus is the cornerstone, and the biblical prophets and apostles are the other foundation stones of God's household. All of these anointed leaders, including Jesus Himself, are, by God's design, from one people group, the people of Israel. This means biblical Israel is the "cement" that binds the foundation stones of God's house together.

God's choice of Israel is not accidental, nor is the fact that after two thousand years of wandering, the people of Israel, though scattered and few in number, have returned to their land. These facts are of deep significance for all of Christianity. Biblically, Israel is God's example of His kingdom for both Jews and Gentiles. We will examine this truth more closely in the rest of this book.

According to the New Testament, the distinction between Jews (Israel) and Gentiles (the nations) and God's plan to bring both together in "one new man" (Ephesians 2:15) are strategic issues in God's overall plan for the world. Because we are Christians and students of the Bible, it is also very important for us to notice the different manner in which the New Testament writers addressed Jews and Gentiles, respectively, in Scripture.

When Jesus appeared in Israel and later, when the New Testament was written, the Hebrew Bible had been known to the Jews for over a thousand years. Almost every child grew up hearing the stories written in God's Word. Religious leaders were national figures and they were expected to be experts in biblical interpretation. Two thousand years ago, the Gentiles, on the other hand, knew virtually nothing about God. Paul wrote to the Gentile Ephesians that before he brought them the gospel, they had been spiritually dead in trespasses and sins (Ephesians 2:1).

Paul wrote: "Remember that you were at that time separate from Christ, excluded from the commonwealth of Israel, and strangers to the covenants of promise, having no hope and without God in the world" (Ephesians 2:12). To these same Gentiles, Paul explained that they were not required to first become Jews to find salvation and enter the kingdom of God. It was not by their efforts or religious striving but rather by God's freely given grace, which was received by faith in Jesus, His Messiah. These inspired words were certainly good news to those who were not Jewish and just coming out of spiritual darkness. Since the days of Paul until now, the message that Jesus Christ died for us sinners, was buried, and rose on the third day so that we who believe in Him might be forgiven and have eternal life has been the core of the gospel preached to the nations.

However, this is not the complete message of the New Testament. Especially when we reexamine the Scriptures specifically written for Jewish disciples of Jesus. As we shall see later, these verses are strong in their emphasis on the authority of God's laws as opposed to proclaiming only His grace and mercy that are offered through faith in Jesus (Matthew 5:17-19). Scriptures written for the Jews in the New Testament are equally emphatic in stating that without good works it is impossible to have a living or saving faith (James 2:14, 17).

This is a definite change from the emphasis on faith without good works and grace without God's law found in some parts of the Protestant world today. Bible teaching that is not aligned with Scripture produces weak and unstable disciples. A Christian population that is not feeding on the whole Bible will lack depth and credibility in their faith. Biblically weak Christians may also become prey for religious manipulators who divert kingdom resources to build ministry reputations or for personal financial gain.

Now, after nearly two thousand years of Christian history, we Gentile Christians have libraries of spiritual books literally at our fingertips. At the click of a mouse, we have the benefit of centuries of debate, biblical criticism, and scholarly discourse that have enabled us to refine our understanding of the Bible. The truth is that today, we are more like the Jews of Jesus' day than the biblically ignorant Gentiles of ancient Ephesus and Corinth. But still, we continue to emphasize those verses meant for the Gentiles whom Paul encountered on his earliest missionary journeys and ignore the others.

Our generation needs a fresh revelation of biblical truth that restores the church to its original foundations and renews it as a powerful expression of God's kingdom. The foundation of the church is Jesus, the Living Word, along with the inspired words of the biblical prophets and apostles. The nation of Israel is what connects the foundation stones and holds them together.

Standing on that foundation are two massive columns that support the entire structure according to God's "blueprint." The first of these columns is law and grace, two great truths held together in tension as one. The relationship between law and grace and their essential unity gives this biblical truth internal strength like the steel rods placed under great pressure in modern, pre-stressed concrete building columns. The second great column consists of faith and works, two truths similarly held together in tension.

Over the centuries, the whole structure has been groaning in misalignment and is deeply in need of maintenance and renovation. Today's church needs new architecture.

Discussion Questions:

1. Why should my faith be Bible-based?
2. Can I identify some areas where the church needs to become more biblical?
3. How can truths like law and grace held "in tension" produce strong faith?

Prayer Point:

Lord, thank You for laying eternal foundations for my life through what the words of Scripture contained in the books of the Bible reveal. Please help me to align my personal faith and my responsibility in the church with your inspired words.

Chapter 13

Restoring the Unity of the Bible

Over the centuries, scientists and scholars, like archeologists, historians, and Bible translators, have done excellent work discovering, researching, and preserving the ancient texts of the Scriptures, as well as uncovering the cultural context of the original authors. Because of modern biblical scholarship, our current translations of the Bible are more accurate and more faithful to the original texts than many other earlier attempts. The Bible contains the greatest story that has ever been told and this amazing, ancient document actually becomes more accurate as time goes on!

Everything we know to be true about God ultimately comes from one book, the Bible. To become a medical doctor today, a person must study a small library of books. After that, there are years of examinations, internships, and more study before anyone is considered qualified to practice medicine. The process of becoming a lawyer or a judge follows a similar pattern but uses a different library of books that must be read and mastered. However, to become a disciple of the Lord and lead others to eternal life, there is only one book that must be studied, understood, and followed. That book is the Bible.

The Bible is comprised of sixty-six books that are really like chapters written by forty different authors over several thousand years. It is less than eight hundred thousand words in English. The average person reads about two hundred words per minute, so that means it takes only a little more than ten minutes of reading a day to read through the entire Bible in one year. There is no reason why every believer who wants to be a disciple of the Lord cannot have a general knowledge of what the entire Bible says from start to finish, that is, from Genesis to Revelation.

Today, most Christians habitually de-emphasize the portion of the Bible we call the Old Testament. It is in the Old Testament that God's kingdom is most clearly described as a nation in which social responsibility and legal accountability before God were required. Just calling the first portion of the Bible the "Old" Testament reveals a dimension of our disdain for it. To Jewish people, this part of the Bible is known as the *Tanach*, which is an acronym for three Hebrew words that are translated as law, prophets, and writings.

In most of our Christian Bible schools and seminaries, young ministers are taught that the really important part of the Bible is the New Testament. Most Bible translation societies translate only the New Testament into new languages for as yet unreached people groups. Christians are taught that the New Testament has all the essentials we need to know about salvation and the practice of our faith. But we are told, if there is anything unclear in it, we have a wonderful and also inspired reference work called the Old Testament to help us.

This is exactly backward! How much of the New Testament was in the Bible that Jesus knew? Jesus continually quoted and referred to the Scriptures in His teachings. He affirmed the inspiration and unbreakable nature of the words of God that had been preserved in the Hebrew Bible. He was raised in the synagogue where the Scriptures were revered and the entire five books of Moses and many of the prophets were read through publicly each year. The Hebrew Scriptures were not only considered religion; they formed the core of Israel's everyday culture.

What Bible did the apostle Paul leave with his new Gentile converts in Asia Minor and Europe? Of course, Paul's Bible did not contain any of the New Testament. When Paul wrote to his spiritual son, Timothy, "All Scripture is inspired by God and profitable for teaching, for reproof, for correction, for training in righteousness so that the man of God may be adequate, equipped for every good work" (2 Timothy 3:16-17), the Gospels as we know them had not been written and Paul was certainly not referring to his own letters as Scripture! When Paul wrote, "All Scripture . . .," he was obviously and only referring to the Old Testament.

Near the end of his life, Paul, while imprisoned in Rome, spoke to the leaders of the Jewish community. He was, "explaining to them by solemnly testifying about the kingdom of God and trying to persuade them concerning Jesus, from both the

Law of Moses and from the Prophets . . ." (Acts 28:23).

All of the apostles who were authorized by God to write the New Testament were Jews. The lone possible exception is Luke, the writer of the Gospel of Luke and Acts, who might have been a Gentile. All of these writers had a deep understanding of the Hebrew Scriptures and they quote often from them. So much of the Hebrew Bible is found in Paul's writings that his letter to the Romans has been called a Messianic Jewish commentary on the *Tenach*.

The term *Old Testament* was introduced in Europe during the early centuries of Christianity. At that time, the New Testament writings were being canonized, that is, collected, copied, and regarded as God's inspired Word. Even though many centuries have now passed we should never forget that the writers of the New Testament were Jews who were chosen by God. They understood the revelation of Jesus in relation to what God had already revealed in the Hebrew Scriptures.

The Old and New Testaments are integrally woven together by unbreakable fibers of truth. All the New Testament writers knew and respected the Hebrew Scriptures as the inspired and inerrant Word of God. They were called and gifted by God to write His words by the same Holy Spirit who inspired the Hebrew prophets. The Old and New Testaments, therefore, are one continuous revelation from one God with one plan and purpose for all of mankind.

In his book, *Recovering the Unity of the Bible: One Continuous Story, Plan, and Purpose*, Dr. Walter Kaiser Jr. (former President of Gordon-Conwell Theological Seminary) wrote: "Accounting for all of this unity in the midst of obvious diversity spread over these centuries with some sixty-six contributions of some forty different writers in three languages on three continents is mind-boggling. There can be no real answer unless we also receive the claim of the writers that there was a supernatural aspect and a guiding mind at work in their writings as well. If God was behind the production of all these contributions, then the unity is the result of a driving plan and the harmony reflects what he has willed and purposed."

Because we divide the Bible into Old and New Testaments and de-emphasize the first part, most Christians are not aware of the biblical connection between Israel as God's chosen nation and the kingdom of God as presented in the New Testament. One of the results has been to "spiritualize" God's kingdom and over-emphasize the other-worldliness of our Christian faith. For example, the "promised land" becomes heaven and God's rule is understood as a religious experience. One verse that is used to spiritualize God's kingdom is Jesus' statement to Pilate, "My kingdom is not of this world" (John 18:36). When this verse is spiritualized, it implies that Jesus' kingdom is not meant to be an earthly reality.

This is a misinterpretation of what He said. The discussion with Pilate was about the responsibility to judge. Both men knew that Pilate's authority originated in Rome, but Jesus claimed His authority came from heaven. Pilate reasoned that Roman authority did not include the kingdom of heaven and said, "I find no guilt in him." Jesus was *not* saying that His kingdom was intended to be devoid of earthly influence or consequences.

The result of spiritualizing God's kingdom is that Christians tend to see the transformation of society and molding cultural values as an unplanned by-product of religious activity rather than the purposeful outcome of God working through His disciples. Unless churches have a powerful vision of God's kingdom impacting all of society, they will become and remain sub-cultures. Christians should not be trying to dominate or control non-believing society by political means. Nor should Christians impose or force a system of religious observance on anyone.

However, the biblical model of Israel as the example of God's kingdom reveals an entire nation and culture ruled by God. God's kingdom is a healthy functioning society filled with justice and mercy with a vital religious "heart" that serves to renew and equip the other parts. God's kingdom grows through godly influence and example, not by dominating the cultural discussion but by uplifting those who are being crushed under powerful people and events beyond their control.

Biblical Israel shows us that worship of God is interwoven with our family life and our daily work. God's commands and His holidays throughout the year were focused on how the people of Israel made their living and treated others around them. Today, most of our important church activities are organized around meetings: prayer meetings, home cell meetings, church services, conferences, evangelistic rallies, etc. We tend to identify these meetings with

Biblical Israel shows us that worship of God is interwoven with our family life and our daily work.

advancing the kingdom of God, and the number of people who gather usually determines the level of perceived success. The overall result of our focus on meetings is a Christianity that knows how to gather people together but not how to equip and send them to serve in the surrounding culture. It produces and encourages a "spectator" attitude.

When we restore the unity of the entire Bible, we see that the gospel of the kingdom produces freedom, justice, creativity, and a better society for everyone. When this truth is translated into action by people of faith in a wide spectrum of different vocations, an entire culture can be influenced to love and follow God.

Discussion Questions:

1. Have I read every book of the Bible in the last year or two?
2. Do I have questions about how the Old Testament fits together with the New Testament?
3. Why should the Bible be regarded as one single book with many chapters and authors?

Prayer Point:

Lord, please help me to see the entire Bible as one continuous revelation directly from You. Open my eyes to the inspiration behind *all* the words of the Bible.

Additional Note:

I strongly recommend reading through the entire Bible on an annual basis. There are numerous good resources available to help us read through both the Old and New Testaments in a single year by giving us selected short daily readings. There are also a wide variety of excellent resources available for purchase or free online with Bible-based daily devotional readings.

Chapter 14

Interpreting the Bible

Almost all of the Bible was written by people without special academic qualifications to write sacred literature. The writers were, for the most part, ordinary people who were inspired by God to write what they knew by faith and what they had experienced to be true. We have access to the same Spirit who inspired the writers of the Bible, so the first step in interpreting what they wrote is to pray! Ask the Holy Spirit to awaken your mind and speak to your heart through the words of Scripture. After that, read carefully what they wrote, paying attention to each word.

Not having been written by experts, the Bible is designed to be understood by ordinary people. There are a handful of guidelines that can help us all in learning to understand the Scriptures. If we stick to these principles and develop our interpretive skills through practice, almost all of the Bible will become easily understandable and its secrets will begin to be revealed. Here are five of the most important rules to follow:

1. When the words of the Bible make good sense, don't keep looking for some other hidden meaning. Make sure you understand the meaning of the words you are reading and check, if necessary, by using the internet or other easy-to-acquire study tools available to you.
2. Context is "king." This means that each verse was not written on its own but is part of a thought, prayer, teaching, historic event, or prophecy that the writer received or experienced. Sometimes a verse on its own can be given a special meaning by the Holy Spirit, but when studying the Bible, the original meaning of that verse will be found in the context of the other verses around it. Learn to read the Bible in paragraphs as well as sentences and try to understand the entire thought that is being communicated.
3. Let the Bible interpret the Bible. All Christians must simply be familiar with the whole book! Many times, when we have questions about the meaning of a particular word, verse, or thought in the Bible, if we just go on reading something else in the Bible will help us understand what that word, verse, or thought means. It is important to try to use the "whole counsel" of the Bible because important themes are often repeated and written about in different ways or from a different perspective.

4. Use your "forensic" mind. The Bible is a window into God's eternal kingdom. It does not show us everything there is to know but provides enough to guide our lives of faith. Jesus gave a great many teachings and performed many miracles, but only some of them are recorded in the New Testament. He ministered to people countless times, but we have the record of only some of those occasions. Like the work of editing separate scenes in a movie, we need to think about assembling the pieces and putting the storyline together.
5. Talk to other people about your ideas regarding the meaning of the Scriptures. Take the opportunity to teach a Bible study when it is offered to you. You will have to study what others have written about the Bible and this is often the best way to learn and develop your own interpretive skills.

When you come to the epistles that make up about half of the New Testament, try thinking of Paul's letters as "intercepted" communications. We don't know all the people he was writing to and we don't know exactly what their lives were like or the challenges they faced. However, using the knowledge we have, a realistic picture can be pieced together. This reconstruction is vital to getting to the meaning of the verses themselves.

Using the Scripture verses from Paul's letters to develop doctrinal rules for the believing community is important. However, correct doctrine is not the final goal. Doctrine helps us know how to live our lives of faith, but our values and the reasons why we live for God are equally important.

These motivations of the heart are seen in the lives of the people who wrote the words for us.

To improve your understanding of the Bible, learn to use a few important tools. First of all, if you are an English speaker, start with a good word-for-word modern translation of the Bible. There are many versions of the Bible available on the market. Almost all are useful to some degree, but they are not all the same! Some are newer editions of translations that are centuries old; some are paraphrases; some are a particular minister's or a church's ideas about what the Bible says.

> Doctrine helps us know how to live our lives of faith, but our values and the reasons why we live for God are equally important.

An accurate, full translation of the Bible is a disciple's most useful tool! Although it may be easy for us to buy a copy, a good translation of the Bible is very valuable and takes years to produce. Each new translation requires committees of qualified linguists and scholars to collaborate using the most recent research while going directly to the ancient languages of the biblical texts. The goal is to produce a modern text that is as faithful as possible to the original.

Some modern translations, like the New International Version (NIV), are thought-for-thought translations in which the translators read a passage in the original language and devised the best passage in English to represent it. This makes the Bible more readable but inevitably the translators' thoughts and interpretations become mixed into the translation. Word-for-word translations try to capture the original meaning of each word and then assemble those words into coherent sentences. In my opinion, the best modern word-for-word English translations are the New American Standard Bible (NASB) and the New King James Version (NKJV).

No translation is perfect, however, and we should all be aware that the original writers and characters in the Bible did not speak in English! Although the oldest texts of the New Testament we have are all in Greek, we know that Jesus and His disciples did not speak to each other in that language. Over the centuries, many scholars have taught they spoke a Semitic language called Aramaic but prayed and studied the Scriptures in Hebrew. However, more recently, there is growing evidence that Hebrew was also Jesus' and the disciples' daily language. Despite these language barriers, some of the Bible translations we have today are amazingly accurate. Having said that, it is still important for every disciple to know how to use a concordance.

A concordance is a book with all the English words in the Bible linked to the original word in the biblical text. Each original word (in Hebrew, Aramaic, or Greek) is accessible with its dictionary definition. These days, this information is also easily available online or as part of a good Bible app for your smartphone, computer, or tablet.

With a concordance, if you have a question about the meaning of any word in the Bible, you can immediately go to the same text the translators use and do some quick research yourself! In some Bible apps you merely have to touch the screen over a single word and your built-in concordance will instantly give you the dictionary definition of the original word written in English.

If you learn to use these basic tools and rules of interpretation, after a while, your ability to read the Bible and understand it will increase. You will begin feeding yourself spiritually and will become less dependent on the teaching of others. This confidence in knowing what the words of the Bible say will contribute to your faith and maturity in the Lord. "As a result, we are no longer to be children, tossed here and there by waves and carried about by every wind of doctrine, by the trickery of men, by craftiness in deceitful scheming; but speaking the truth in love, we are to grow up in all aspects into Him who is the head, even Christ" (Ephesians 4:14-15).

As a final step rather than a first one, read as much as you can from the commentaries, teaching books, and articles of others. Once you have formed your opinion of what a passage in the Bible means, read the work of others and compare your findings with theirs. Be ready to take correction and learn. Others have been studying the Bible for many years and have uncovered historical facts, put together timelines of events, and worked on apparent contradictions. Watch the videos of recommended Bible teachers and preachers on the internet. You will not agree with everyone, but some teachers have amazing insights that will help you go further. Gradually, you will develop confidence in the conclusions you are forming. These conclusions in turn solidify into convictions and that is how your faith grows.

Discussion Questions:

1. Why is it important for every Christian to interpret the Bible correctly?
2. Why should I pray before trying to understand God's Word?
3. Is it easy for me to learn the original meaning of a verse and use a concordance?

Prayer Point:

Lord, thank You for putting tools of Bible interpretation into my hands. Please give me confidence that as I read the Bible, my faith will grow and I will understand what Your words mean.

Additional Note:

Digital Bible study tools are increasing each year in number and usefulness. Many of them are available for free online or can be purchased and downloaded at reasonable prices. Some of the study tools I have found most useful are listed in the reference material for this chapter at the end of the book.

Chapter 15

Israel and God's Kingdom

Most biblical scholars agree the kingdom of God was the central topic of Jesus' teaching ministry. According to Matthew, He began His ministry with the proclamation, "Repent, for the kingdom of heaven is at hand" (Matthew 4:17). Matthew recorded that "Jesus was going throughout all Galilee, teaching in their synagogues and proclaiming the gospel of the kingdom, and healing every kind of disease and every kind of sickness among the people" (Matthew 4:23). Matthew's intended audience was mostly Jews, so he often used the term *kingdom of heaven* in place of *kingdom of God*, although they mean the same thing. This is because religious Jews, even to this day, seek to honor God by sanctifying

If we believe that the kingdom of God begins with Jesus, it is like coming into a long movie in the middle or diving into a television series after the first few episodes.

and protecting His name from common usage.

Jesus followed up the proclamation of God's kingdom by teaching His disciples to pray for the coming of the kingdom. In His great Sermon on the Mount, He said, "Pray, then, in this way: 'Our Father who is in heaven, hallowed be Your name. Your kingdom come. Your will be done, on earth as it is in heaven" (Matthew 6:9-10). At one point He emphasized the priority of God's kingdom to His disciples by teaching that the kingdom is worth more than any other earthy reward. He said, "But seek first His kingdom and His righteousness, and all these things will be added to you" (Matthew 6:33).

Jesus' method of teaching included the frequent use of parables. The parables are stories taken from life experiences familiar to Jesus' hearers and are meant to illustrate truth about God's kingdom. Many of His parables began with the same words, "The kingdom of heaven is like . . ." followed by His illustration. In Matthew chapter thirteen, there are six such parables, all beginning with those words. All together the phrase *kingdom of heaven* is found thirty-two times in the New Testament and kingdom of *God* sixty-six times.

As a result of this amount of Scriptural evidence pointing to the centrality of God's kingdom in Jesus' teaching, many Christians believe the Bible's teaching of this theme begins in the New Testament. After all, Jesus is the King of the kingdom and He proclaimed that it was "at hand." Why shouldn't we believe that it begins with Him?

If we believe that the kingdom of God begins with the ministry of Jesus, it is like coming into a long movie in the middle or diving into a television series after the first few episodes. If you come into the story halfway through, eventually you will find out how it ends. If you pay attention, you can usually figure out who are the main characters. But you will not understand why it ends the way it does. Nor will you have insight into the character and motivation of the people you encounter in the second half of the story. All that is established in the beginning. So it is with the kingdom of God. It does not begin with Jesus in the New Testament but much earlier in the Bible and with a people called Israel.

When God wanted a people who would become the example of His kingdom, He did not recycle an existing nation but rather, He created a new nation starting with one man. God found in Abraham a man of loyalty, integrity, obedience, and faith. Abraham had the character qualities that allowed him to become a friend of God. God called him to be separated, set apart from his own ethnic roots, and then made promises to him. The promises included a pledge that he would become the father of a "great nation" (Genesis 12:2).

Later, God made a covenant with Abraham and promised his "seed," this new ethnic group, a specific land with specific borders (Genesis 15:18-21). But God also told Abraham that He had a larger purpose in choosing him. God's eternal intention, revealed at the very beginning for the people of Israel, was always that this new nation would be His means of blessing all the people of the world.

Before the centuries of captivity in Egypt, the people of Israel were a close-knit family group led by a lineage of patriarchs chosen by God: first Abraham, then Isaac followed by Jacob, whose name was changed to Israel. It was one of Jacob's sons, Joseph, who, in his role as a high Egyptian official, invited the entire family (the Bible says about seventy people in Genesis 46:26-27) into Egypt for refuge. When they had entered Egypt the people of Israel were just one extended family with a big promise from God. The land of Canaan had been given to their fathers, Abraham, Isaac, and Jacob, by God, but that promise had never been realized in the lifetimes of the patriarchs.

After the deaths of Joseph and the pharaoh who had befriended him, the people of Israel became slaves of the Egyptians for about four hundred years. As slaves they grew into a people group roughly divided into the twelve tribes of the sons of Jacob. At the time of the Exodus, the men of Israel numbered around six hundred thousand (Exodus 12:37). That would have been men of military age, so if you count the women, children, and elderly, the total number could have been as many as three or four million people.

Every year in Egypt along the banks of the mighty Nile River, a rainy season with floods brought new fertile soil into the fields. Every year, the Egyptians planted and harvested with water from the Nile and drew their drinking water from it. Having an abundance of water was normal to them.

Once the people of Israel had passed through the Red Sea, they were in the Sinai desert, one of the hottest and driest places on earth! Anyone who has been there in the summer months can tell you that just finding shade during the day can mean the difference between life and death. They were helpless. Moreover, the people of Israel had never owned their own land and had never governed themselves. They had never been a nation before.

Now, after the exodus, the people of Israel in the desert were hopelessly disorganized. They had been slaves for centuries and had no national infrastructure or consciousness. At that stage, without a government, legal system, established religion, or national culture, they would surely have been classified as dysfunctional in terms of nationhood.

However, this is when and where God met them. After the deliverance from Egypt, under the leadership of the prophet Moses, God made a divine covenant with the people of Israel. Through that covenant, for the first time, they became a single nation and God became their King. Thus, Israel is portrayed in the Bible as a prototype, an early but inspired picture of the kingdom of God on earth. Here is what God spoke to the people of Israel through Moses: "Now then, if you will indeed obey My voice and keep My covenant, then you shall be My own possession among all the peoples, for all the earth is Mine; and you shall be to Me a kingdom of priests and a holy nation. These are the words that you shall speak to the sons of Israel" (Exodus 19:5-6).

Many people think that Moses was king of Israel, but this was never the case. He was called to be God's prophet, the servant of the Lord. God said, "You shall be *to Me* a kingdom of priests and a holy nation." God Himself became King of Israel and there in the desert, He began forming the extended family of Abraham through Isaac and Jacob, twelve separate tribes, into a nation for the first time. Becoming God's kingdom of priests meant that Israel's role as a nation was to serve all other nations and to be their example.

Some Christians today read "kingdom of priests" and think Israel was chosen to be a completely religious nation. This cannot be true because later, God only chose one out of twelve tribes for a specifically religious function. Only the members of the tribe of Levi were priests by profession. So what did God mean by calling Israel a "kingdom of priests"?

The function of priests is to stand before God on behalf of the people and also stand before the people on behalf of God. The priests take that "middle" position between God and man. They are expected by God to be spiritual models or examples for the public. This captures the calling of Israel as a kingdom of priests. It was to take the middle ground as God's chosen example or model nation.

It is as if God said, "I will work with you, my chosen people, and all the rest of the world must watch and learn!" Is this favoritism? Let me explain it this way. When I was born, my sister was already almost four years old. She was my older sister from my birth and now after all these years, she is still my older sister. I tried everything I could think of but I never caught up! However, when we were small children, there some things I learned never to do by watching my sister interact with our parents. In some ways she received a stricter upbringing than I did. I suppose it was just natural. We would get into trouble and Mom and Dad would say to her, "You should have known better!" Sometimes, I would be simply ignored and expected to watch and learn.

In God's family of the nations, He has many, many different children and He loves us all with the same eternal love. Actually, only someone who is a father or mother can fully understand that. Whether their children are gentle and sweet or independent and difficult, most parents have deep love for all their children. This is just a reflection of God's love.

In God's family, He loves all people and nations because He created everyone in His image. However, in this family there is still only one firstborn nation and that is Israel. History bears out that in many ways Israel received a stricter upbringing than the rest of the nations. They were chosen as the example, the model of God's kingdom, and they are that model in obedience as a shining example of blessings and in disobedience as a symbol of sorrow and chastisement. All the nations are called to honor, respect, and learn about God's kingdom from Israel.

The name *Israel* is mentioned more than twenty-three hundred times in the Bible while most of our nations and people are not to be found in the Bible at all. My ancestors are from Japan and that nation is not mentioned even once. The Japanese are people of honor and their culture is developed and beautiful. Why aren't they the chosen ones? I checked the Scriptures carefully and finding no trace of them, earlier in my life I was a little upset by that! But whenever I prayed about it, God seemed to be saying to me something like, "Well, Peter, you're just going to have to get over it. I chose one nation, Israel, as an example of My kingdom and everyone must accept My choice if they want to enter and learn."

In a way, it is similar to God's choice of His Son, Jesus, as the way of redemption for every human. If we accept God's choice of Jesus and make Him Lord, salvation is ours! Jesus is God's chosen model for every human and Israel is God's example of His kingdom for every society, culture, and nation.

God became King of Israel in the desert after the exodus when they were disorganized and had never governed themselves before. This was purposeful in that it should give hope to any society today, no matter how dysfunctional, that God's rule can transform a crowd of former slaves into a truly great nation.

Discussion Questions:

1. If Moses was not king of Israel, who became King and led the people through the wilderness?
2. Can I see the relationship between the kingdom of God preached by Jesus and Israel of the Bible?
3. Why does God use human examples like Jesus and Israel to reveal His intentions to us?

Prayer Point:

Lord, grant me revelation to see that the people of Israel were designed to be Your picture and Your example of the kingdom of God. Help me to connect Israel in the Bible with the gospel of the kingdom preached by Jesus.

Chapter 16

God's Kingdom Rejected

For almost four hundred years, after entering the land that God had promised, Israel was led by judges and later by the prophet Samuel. At that time, the people of Israel became secure in their own land and began being envious of the nations around them. Perhaps it was embarrassing to have no capital city, no royal palace, no honor guards, and no human king to impress the foreign visitors. They must have wondered, “Why do we have to be so different from everyone else? Other nations have a physical supreme leader or at least the image of a god in their temples; our God and King is invisible!”

According to the Bible, the people of Israel complained

Having a human king as the sole and sovereign ruler of Israel was never God's design.

to Samuel and demanded that he ask God to give them a human king. Because of their desire to be like other nations, the people of Israel rejected God as their King and therefore also rejected the kingdom of God. "But the thing was displeasing in the sight of Samuel when they said, 'Give us a king to judge us' and Samuel prayed to the Lord. The Lord said to Samuel, 'Listen to the voice of the people in regard to all that they say to you, for they have not rejected you, but they have rejected Me from being king over them'" (1Samuel 8:4-7).

Having a human king as the sole and sovereign ruler of Israel was never God's design. In God's plan, human kings were meant to rule on His behalf. In the years that followed, many men ruled over God's people, but only one of them was ever known as a truly great king. David, the son of Jesse, was superior to all the other kings because he saw himself as a small king compared to God, who was always the greater King. In his psalms, David repeatedly referred to God as his King, and he considered himself subject to God's laws. When David's warriors fought their way into Bethlehem to get him a drink of water from the well he had known as a child, David poured the water out as an offering to God. He declared that only God was worthy of his men's sacrifice. David was called a man "after God's own heart." Sadly, after David, the people of Israel were increasingly ruled by kings who led them away from worship of the true God and away from obedience to

His laws. David's son Solomon eventually turned from following the Lord and after him, the kingdom was divided by civil war, with ten tribes in the north and two in the south.

In the northern kingdom, called Israel, there was never a single good king. One evil king followed another and idolatry, corruption, political intrigue, and murder became rampant. In 722 BC, the weakened northern kingdom was conquered by the Assyrians and the people were taken into captivity.

The southern kingdom, known as Judah, had a few good kings who actively sought reform, but there were many bad ones, and in 586 BC their Babylonian enemies overcame them. Israel as God's nation and the example of His kingdom on earth was destroyed and the people taken into captivity. This was all because of the failure of human kings to rule the nation according to God's plan and His Law.

God's outrage and sorrow over the plight of His people Israel are evident in the words of the prophet Ezekiel, who prophesied from captivity in Babylon. "What you have in your mind shall never be, when you say, 'We will be like the Gentiles, like the families in other countries, serving wood and stone.' As I live," says the Lord God, "surely with a mighty hand, with an outstretched arm, and with fury poured out, I will rule over you" (Ezekiel 20:32-34).

For seventy years what had been God's kingdom on earth ceased to operate. After that time, a remnant of the southern tribes returned to the land of Israel under Nehemiah and Ezra. The walls of Jerusalem were rebuilt and a small temple reconstructed. This was not really a triumphant return. Only a few of the survivors from the southern kingdom returned. Some of the older people, who remembered the glory of the earlier temple, wept in disappointment when they saw the foundations of the new temple (Ezra 3:12).

In the years that followed, the nation was never completely free again. The Jewish people were ruled by the Persians and then the Greeks. For a short period under the Hasmonean kings, after a revolt led by Judas Maccabeus, there was a small, independent, Jewish kingdom. It lasted for only about a century and then the Romans conquered and dominated the region. Israel was an unimportant nation under the thumb of powerful empires considered pagan by the Jews.

During the centuries between the Old and the New Testaments, the people of Israel longed for a visitation from God as in the earlier days of their history. Probably many faithful people in Israel prayed to God during this time and repented for their forefathers' decision to follow human kings.

It was at this spiritual, political, and cultural low point that a voice was heard crying in the wilderness "Prepare the way of the Lord!" John the Baptist came to herald the coming of someone greater than he. Then Jesus appeared in the power of the Holy Spirit, preaching "Repent, for the kingdom of God is at hand!" and teaching the principles of the kingdom of God. His ministry was accompanied by powerful miracles and He was welcomed by many in Israel as a great prophet, a possible deliverer, and by some, as the Messiah.

This is the point where most Christians today come into the movie! Of course, the people of Israel knew they had been God's chosen kingdom. They also knew that choosing human kings in place of God had been a bad and sinful decision. When Jesus appeared with such power to perform miracles proclaiming the kingdom of God, the people wanted to make Him King.

Discussion Questions:

1. Why was it a sin for Israel to demand human kings?
2. What happened to Israel after rejecting God as King?
3. Why is understanding the kingdom of God important to me as a Christian?

Prayer Point:

Lord, put in me a heart that loves to be ruled by You. Make me a person who will always keep Your kingdom as my first priority.

Chapter 12

The Disciples' Last Question

Imagine if you were given five minutes alone with the Lord Himself. What a privilege that would be, and what if you could ask Him one question during that meeting? What would you ask Him? It would have to be a very important question! The disciples' understanding of God's kingdom is revealed in the question they asked in their last five minutes with Jesus before His ascension into heaven in Acts 1:6: "So when they had come together, they were asking Him, saying, 'Lord, is it at this time You are restoring the kingdom to Israel?'" The disciples asked Jesus when He was going to restore God's kingdom, that is, to bring God's rule back to their nation.

Over the centuries, Christian scholars have wondered why the disciples asked the Lord such a strange question. Didn't they realize by then that God's kingdom is spiritual, not earthly, and for all nations, not just theirs? Were they carnally nationalistic or just not thinking?

But the reason we may not understand the importance of this question is that we have come into the "movie" late, that is, long after the beginning of the story. God's kingdom has always been about establishing His rule on earth. Moreover, since the Exodus from Egypt, in obedience as a shining light and in disobedience as an object of sorrow, Israel was God's example of His intended and lawful reign over every area of society and culture.

Jesus replied to His disciples, "It is not for you to know times or epochs which the Father has fixed by His own authority; but you will receive power when the Holy Spirit has come upon you; and you shall be My witnesses both in Jerusalem, and in all Judea and Samaria, and even to the remotest part of the earth" (Act 1:7-8). He did not deny that the kingdom of God would be restored to Israel, but He deliberately avoided saying when. Jesus knew His disciples expected God's kingdom to appear immediately (Luke 19:11). If He had said it would take more than two thousand years, they would have been confused and discouraged! Instead Jesus directed their attention to the power of the Holy Spirit to make them His "witnesses" not only locally but also throughout the world.

John Calvin was one of the most brilliant and influential theologians of the Protestant Reformation. He was born over five hundred years ago in France and his preaching and writing form the basis of today's Reformed, Presbyterian, and Congregational theological understandings. In his commentary on the first chapter of Acts, Calvin examined the last question asked of Jesus by His disciples ("Lord, is it at this time You are restoring the kingdom to Israel?") and wrote, "There are as many errors in this question as words." Calvin went on to write that the disciples were foolish, ignorant, and poor scholars of the Bible because they longed for an earthly kingdom that God would rule among their own people. He wrote, "They are also greatly deceived herein, in that they restrain Christ's kingdom unto the carnal Israel."

Wait a minute! Didn't Jesus teach us all to pray that His kingdom would come *on earth* just as it is in heaven? Now that God has brought the people of Israel back to their own land and is restoring the good news of His kingdom to Jewish people everywhere, we can see that the disciples were wise and not foolish in the question they asked the Master. Leaving this aside for a moment, let's examine the attitude that lies behind Calvin's statements about Christ's original Jewish apostles. Calvin lived fifteen hundred years after they walked the soil of Israel with Jesus and he thought they were ignorant about God's kingdom. For three years, these men woke up each morning and looked at the face of God incarnate! They were the personal students of the Son of God.

Among those disciples who asked Jesus such an "erroneous" final question were men personally inspired by God to write parts of the New Testament. How could they have been poor students of the Bible? Among that group of men were Peter, Matthew, and John. They wrote the Bible! They knew Jesus not only as their Lord but as their own countryman, and friend and they had access to His emotions and His personal habits. They lived in the presence of the perfect life and knew the small details.

Jesus' disciples' understanding of God's kingdom was correctly focused on the culture and society of Israel.

When Jesus turned to the bleeding woman in Capernaum who had pushed through the crowd, and said, "Daughter, take courage. Your faith has made you well" (Matthew 9:22), the disciples saw even the look on His face and heard the tone of His voice. They listened to *all* His teachings. Not just the few we have recorded in the New Testament, but even the teachings He gave that were not written down. (According to the apostle John there were a great many). These men had seen all the many miracles Jesus performed. They witnessed His death on the cross as well as His physical resurrection. He breathed on them and said, "Receive the Holy Spirit" (John 20:22) and then He appeared to them over a period of forty days, speaking about the kingdom of God (Acts 1:3).

They were truly New Testament believers by the time of His ascension and spiritual giants because of His ministry to them. John Calvin thought they were ignorant and grossly mistaken. The truth is that it is we who today need a new reformation and the disciples' apostolic vision of God's kingdom restored to us.

John Calvin's comments reveal that Protestant Christians have been "coming into the movie late" for centuries and missing Israel as the foundational element in God's kingdom. Why should we be surprised that the result has been to "spiritualize" God's kingdom to the extent that we relegate it to a future age or reduce it to something that can be measured solely by church growth figures?

Jesus' disciples' understanding of God's kingdom was correctly focused on the culture and society of Israel. These men and their contemporaries were not ignorant of God's Word and His purposes. We know that the divine inspiration in the words of the New Testament is what the authors understood from God rather than how we, centuries later, interpret what they wrote. Therefore, our modern understanding of the kingdom of God must be rooted, as theirs was, in the reality of Israel as God's chosen nation.

Israel of the Bible is the picture, prototype, and example of what God wants and what He does not want among all societies on this earth. Jesus came to inaugurate a new covenant between Israel and God, but the concept of God's rule as King was not foreign to the people of Israel. The Jewish followers of Jesus understood that God's kingdom, that is, His rightful rule of their nation, was uniquely part of Israel's heritage, and they hoped it would be a reality again in their own time.

Being King is God's nature and part of His identity. This means loving God is the same as loving to be ruled by Him. His kingdom is simply His domain or the realm over which He rules. It may be in your heart, your family, or community, or in a Messianic age coming in the future, but God's kingdom is found at any time and anywhere He rules. In this way God's kingdom can be an inner spiritual reality and a future expectation at the same time.

God's reign as King was His intention from the time of creation. The Bible describes God as the Creator of the universe and of our world. When He made the first humans, they were created to be like Him and made to rule over the rest of creation. Jewish people of Jesus' day understood the concept of God's rule as King. They knew from the Scriptures and the history of their own nation that God had once been their King, and they longed for His rule to be restored. The Jewish understanding was then, and still is today, that the Messiah will come from God and rule Israel as King. This belief was deep in the hearts of Jesus' own disciples throughout their years with Him and even after His resurrection from the dead.

During His ministry on earth, Jesus was teaching His disciples that the kingdom of God would, from that time on, include all nations. We know now that God's purposes were not limited to Israel and the task of reaching the world would take centuries. Bringing the transforming power of God's kingdom into every culture requires even more than powerful evangelistic meetings and miracles of healing. It also takes supernatural power from God's Spirit on a personal level to make the life of each believer a witness that testifies to the sovereign rule of God. Developing a character and lifestyle that point to God is a process that starts in the heart of each disciple and extends outward into the culture of each nation. Jesus was prophesying that making disciples of God's kingdom through the power of the gospel would spread throughout the world and eventually return to the nation of Israel. We are seeing this in the lives and daily witness of Israeli believers who honor Him today in modern Israel as Messiah and King.

Discussion Questions:

1. Why did Jesus' disciples want Him to restore God's kingdom to Israel?
2. Does the disciples' final question have meaning for me today?
3. Did Jesus tell His disciples when the kingdom would be restored to Israel?

Prayer Point:

Lord, please reveal Yourself to me like You did to the disciples of Jesus. Show me why Your sovereign rulership in my personal life, society, and culture is so important to your plan.

Part 3

Faith and Works

Even so faith, if it has no works, is dead, being by itself. (James 2:17)

Chapter 18

Faith + Works = Salvation

If the gospel of the kingdom, which was entrusted to the apostles in the days of Jesus, is going to be restored to the end time church, the balance between faith and works must be biblically realigned. According to the Bible, saving faith and good works are not in opposition to one another but, like law and grace, they are two components of the same truth. The more holistic Hebrew mind does not see a division between faith and action, or between trust and obedience. The first question we have to ask is why does the apostle Paul emphasize faith over works in most of his epistles?

To answer that question we need to understand Paul and remember the kind of people Paul was writing to in Greek-speaking cities like Ephesus, Philippi, and Thessaloniki where he ministered and planted the first churches. We also have to get the timeline correct. The Gentile believers were first called "Christians" in Antioch, a Roman city with Greek culture outside the borders of Israel. This is recorded for us in Acts chapter 11. It was nine chapters earlier, in Acts chapter two, that the Holy Spirit was poured out on the almost entirely Jewish crowd in Jerusalem, and the movement of what we today call Messianic Jews began. If you have any questions about whether the crowd was almost 100 percent Jewish in Jerusalem on the day of Pentecost, you only have to read the chapter carefully.

Acts 2:5 says, "Now there were *Jews* living in Jerusalem, devout men from every nation under heaven." Why were they there? Because Pentecost is the Greek name for the feast of weeks (*Shavuot*) celebrated fifty days after Passover and one of the three annual "pilgrimage" feasts of Israel when all the men of the nation, wherever they were living, were commanded by God to come together to sacrifice and worship (Deuteronomy 16:16, 2 Chronicles 8:13).

During his address to the assembled people, the apostle Peter repeatedly used the terms *men of Judea*, *men of Israel*, and *brethren*. He knew he was speaking to a primarily Jewish crowd. Gentile believers only came into the picture eight chapters later in Acts 10 when the same apostle Peter, because of a vision from God, obediently went to preach in the home of Cornelius, a devout Roman soldier in the Roman headquarters city of Caesarea.

After the outpouring of the Holy Spirit on the Gentiles in the home of Cornelius, according to Acts chapter 11, Peter explained to the other Jewish apostles why he had gone to Gentiles in the first place and why the believers among them were now to be considered brothers. The other Jews, who like Peter, had walked personally with the Lord, after some discussion, accepted the authority of his words perhaps because they remembered it was to him personally the Lord gave the "keys" to His kingdom! They agreed and said, "Well then, God has granted to the Gentiles also the repentance that leads to life" (Acts 11:18).

After that, the Jerusalem apostles sent Barnabas to Antioch because of reports that a large number of Gentiles were turning to the Lord there. Barnabas found a zealous new Jewish believer named Saul to accompany him to Antioch. Maybe he chose him because Saul, who was later called Paul, was a native of Tarsus, a Greek-speaking, Roman-administered city in the area of Antioch who knew the local language and culture. Barnabas was originally from Cyprus and a Levite who had probably spent much of his life in Jerusalem.

Paul was chosen by God before he was born (Galatians 1:15-16) for his special role in revealing the "mystery" of the gospel to the Gentile world (Ephesians 3:1-7). Of course, Paul's birthplace, family history, religious training, and childhood background were all a part of God's meticulous plan. It is to Gentiles, like the ones he grew up among, that Paul was writing most of his epistles. He knew that they were almost entirely ignorant of God's laws in the Bible.

At the same time, Paul knew that some Gentiles were seeking after God and truth and that they had godly traits like honesty and courage, which were honored in Greco-Roman culture. Paul knew by revelation that the Gentiles he met were part of God's creation and had a place in His redemptive plan. They were in darkness and needed God's grace to begin lives of faith and obedience.

Paul's emphasis on God's grace to the Gentiles was meant to show them that they did not need to become Jews to have a saving covenant relationship with the God of Israel. The Jews were a people specially created by God from the line of Abraham, Isaac, and Jacob. The Bible describes them as the chosen people, the "cultivated olive tree" (Romans 11), God's model of His kingdom. They were first entrusted with the "oracles of God" (Romans 3:1-2) and therefore had a unique history with God that went back over a thousand years by the time of Paul.

The pagan Gentiles will never catch up with the Jews by trying to embrace their religious identity, but they can enter God's kingdom without becoming Jews simply by faith in the Messiah. This is the grace of God! Paul wrote to his Ephesian converts: "Remember that you were at that time separate from Christ, excluded from the commonwealth of Israel, and strangers to the covenants of promise, having no hope and without God in the world. But now in Christ Jesus you who formerly were far off have been brought near by the blood of Christ" (Ephesians 2:12-13).

Paul reminded the Ephesians that as Gentiles they knew nothing about the God of Israel. They needed only God's grace to begin new lives with God. Grace is the free divine gift that allows outsiders and strangers to enter God's kingdom without any previous religious achievements. They don't need to know the right way to sacrifice, bring offerings, pray, serve in God's sanctuary, or anything required in the laws of Moses.

To enter the kingdom of God, the only thing required is faith in His Messiah. So in the days of Paul, the Gentiles needed grace without works to enter God's house. The Jews had been living in God's house for a thousand years by the time of Paul but, according to the New Testament, God had a contention with them. The Jewish people, God's chosen nation, were not doing what they should do. Both Jews and Gentiles need salvation, but a different kind of guidance and correction is given to each.

Before we go further, let me tell you a true story and ask you a question. Some years ago I was traveling for ministry in one of the countries of the former Soviet Union. My host was a responsible and respected evangelical pastor leading a network of ministries in the region. We spent many hours together driving from meeting to meeting and he told me his story. During the dark days under Communism, before he was saved, this man was an assassin for the KGB. His profession was to hunt down people marked by the Kremlin as enemies of the state and eliminate them.

Then, through a series of miracles, he had an encounter with God and became a disciple of Jesus. Here's my question: After he gave his life to Jesus and entered God's kingdom by faith, could my friend have kept practicing his former profession of murdering and intimidating people on assignment and expect to make it into heaven? If he died while still planning and carrying out cold-blooded assassinations, could he expect to hear the Master say, "Well done, good and faithful servant"?

I think we would all say, "No!" Practicing murderers will not be found in heaven. So then, we also agree, it matters what you do as well as what you believe if you want the gift of eternal life. God's grace to enter His kingdom by faith must be combined with His grace to do the right things while we are alive if we want to be saved. Paul emphasized God's grace and salvation by faith alone to the spiritually blind Gentiles of his day because they couldn't find the door to the kingdom to enter it.

But preaching only faith when it comes to salvation is like selling someone a beautiful house and then delivering only a very fine front door. The buyers might then say, "Nice door. Where's the rest of the house?"

You could answer, "Well, what good is a house if you can't get in? You need a door if you're going to enter the house!"

"Yes, of course," they say, "but I still thought I bought the whole house! How are my family and I going to live with just the door?"

The fact is that after we believe and enter God's kingdom, most of us still have complete and challenging lives to live.

This is the problem with preaching the gospel using only Paul's epistles as the primary basis. A humorous way to look at it is like this: Faith without any works would be sufficient if every evangelist was immediately followed by an assassin like my Russian-speaking friend. As soon as anyone believes, we immediately shoot him or her so there are no backsliders. Everyone makes it into heaven after a single decision to believe.

The fact is that after we believe and enter God's kingdom, most of us still have complete and challenging lives to live. How do we find God's will, make good decisions, and finish our earthly race well? How do we overcome the sins that are still active in our lives? Is it necessary to live a good life or are we simply expected to believe the doctrines we are taught and help convince others to do the same?

Bible teacher David Pawson wrote, “I believe and preach salvation by faith, by continual faith and by continual works of faith, thus ensuring a continual supply of saving grace.” The apostle Paul wrote to his greatly loved disciples in Philippi, “So then, my beloved, just as you have always obeyed, not as in my presence only, but now much more in my absence, work out your salvation with fear and trembling for it is God who is at work in you, both to will and to work for His good pleasure” (Philippians 2:12-13).

Discussion Questions:

1. Is my salvation a life that I must live or simply a set of beliefs?
2. Is it possible for me to deliberately commit gross sins and still be welcomed by God after I die? What part does repentance play?
3. How important is my behavior when it comes to salvation?

Prayer Point:,

Lord, I need Your grace in my life every day if my behavior is ever going to meet Your standards. Please help me to do and say the things You would if You were living my life on earth.

Chapter 19

Gospel to the Jews

To restore the fullness of the gospel of the kingdom we have to rediscover what would have to be called the "gospel to the Jews." Several books in the New Testament were specifically written with a Jewish audience in mind. The book of Hebrews, as the title suggests, was written to Messianic Jews in the first century. The book of James begins in the first verse with the salutation, "James, a bond-servant of God and of the Lord Jesus Christ, To the twelve tribes who are dispersed abroad: Greetings."

Most scholars agree that Matthew's gospel was written with a Jewish audience in mind. Several clues point in this direction. The detailed genealogy in the first chapter showing that Jesus is not just of the tribe of Judah but is also the descendent of Abraham, that is, truly a Jew, is one such clue. The fact that Matthew quotes more frequently from the Hebrew Scriptures than any of the other gospels and focuses on the fulfillment of biblical prophecy is another.

If we examine the words of our New Testaments in the parts written specifically for a Jewish audience, another emphasis quickly emerges. In contrast to Paul's gospel to the Gentiles, these Scriptures strongly emphasize the value of actions, that is, our words and deeds, in determining whether the King will offer us a place in His eternal kingdom. Let's look at a well-known part of the New Testament, the parable of the Good Samaritan. According to Luke, Jesus was questioned by a lawyer, a young Jew who would have been someone studying to be an expert in the law of Moses, a Torah scholar. The man asked Jesus a question about finding salvation, eternal life. Jesus answered his question with another question. In effect, He said, "You're the Torah scholar. You tell Me, what does God's law say?" The lawyer chose two of the commandments found in the first five books of the Bible. One is from Deuteronomy 6:4 and the other from Leviticus 19:18.

"And a lawyer stood up and put Him to the test, saying, 'Teacher, what shall I do to inherit eternal life?' And He said to him, 'What is written in the Law? How does it read to you?' And he answered, 'You shall love the Lord your God with all your heart, and with all your soul, and with all your strength, and with all your mind; and your neighbor as yourself.' And He said to him, 'You have answered correctly; do this and you will live" (Luke 10:25-28).

We know that in Matthew 22, Jesus quoted these same

two commandments and it is recorded that He said, "On these two commandments depend the whole Law and the Prophets" (Matthew 22:40). So in Luke 10, the lawyer gave the same answer that Jesus would have given. Then Jesus answered His question about how to find eternal life. He said, "You have answered correctly; do this and you will live" (Luke 10:28). Please take note, Jesus did not say, "Believe this and you will live." He expected the lawyer, a Jew, to have faith in God. The lawyer's problem was that while he was pursuing the knowledge of God he was not doing what God commands.

But the lawyer still had questions. Luke wrote that he was trying to justify himself (Luke 10:29). Jesus' emphasis on his actions, decisions, and behavior struck at the root of this lawyer's religious beliefs. The lawyer knew that the Scriptures were God's inspired Word given specifically to the people of Israel. He was also aware that God has chosen him personally to be a Jew. He was studying Jewish tradition and working on understanding his religion's interpretations so he should be "safe." He wanted to say to Jesus, "I answered your question correctly, so I'm on the way to heaven. Right?"

Jesus, of course, is "the way, the truth and the life" (John 14:6) so He answered by telling the young man a story.

> Jesus replied and said, "A man was going down from Jerusalem to Jericho, and fell among robbers, and they stripped him and beat him, and went away leaving him half dead. And by chance a priest was going down on that road, and when he saw him, he passed by on the other side. Likewise a Levite also, when he came to

> the place and saw him, passed by on the other side. But a Samaritan, who was on a journey, came upon him; and when he saw him, he felt compassion, and came to him and bandaged up his wounds, pouring oil and wine on them; and he put him on his own beast, and brought him to an inn and took care of him. On the next day he took out two denarii and gave them to the innkeeper and said, 'Take care of him and whatever more you spend, when I return I will repay you.'" (Luke 10:30-35)

In Jesus' story, it seems understood that the traveler was a Jewish man and that after he was robbed and beaten, two religious Jews passed by his unconscious body without helping him. From Jesus' story, we can imagine that these religious men were not just callously indifferent to human suffering. They saw the motionless figure lying by the road but were probably thinking, *What is the right thing for me to do in obedience to God's commandments? If I touch the body and it turns out to be a corpse, according to the Scriptures, I will be unclean for seven days* (Numbers 19:11). *As a member of the high priestly family or even as a Levite, my entire week is wasted. I will be useless in my service to God! I should pretend that I didn't see it and pass as far away from that body as possible!*

The prohibition against touching a dead body is clear in the Bible. God's intention in giving this law to Israel was to prevent disease and reinforce the special value of life as a gift from God. According to Alfred J. Kolatch's *The Jewish Book of Why*, even today, in Jewish tradition, "A *Kohayn* (member of the Priestly Family) is not permitted to attend a funeral unless it is that of a member of his immediate family. If a *Kohayn* wishes to attend a funeral service, he usually stands away from the area where the service is being conducted."

Then, according to Jesus, along came a Samaritan. Jesus' choice of a Samaritan is surprising, not just because they were hated by the Jews. They were hated because they had the wrong beliefs. The Samaritans only considered parts of the Bible inspired and they thought God should be worshipped on Mount Gerizim in Samaria rather than in the Holy Temple on Jerusalem's Mount Moriah. We also know that Jesus did not endorse Samaritan beliefs. When He met the Samaritan woman at the well in John chapter 4, she had a theological question for Him and He answered, "You [Samaritans] worship what you do not know; we worship what we know, for salvation is from the Jews" (John 4:22).

Even though He did not agree with the Samaritan doctrines, Jesus deliberately used a Samaritan man, the man with wrong beliefs, in His parable to teach the Jewish lawyer.

According to Jesus' parable, the Samaritan man saw the body and immediately had compassion for the wounded man. He went to him and, discovering he was still alive, applied first aid and took him to the nearest inn. There he stayed with the man, caring for him through the night and left him in the morning telling the innkeeper he would be responsible for all costs incurred. Then Jesus asked the Jewish Torah scholar, "Which of these three do you think proved to be a neighbor to the man who fell into the robbers' hands?" (Luke 10:36). When the man said, "The one who showed mercy toward him," Jesus said to him, "Go and do the same" (Luke 10:37).

Please take note again that at this point, Jesus did not say to him, "Go and *believe* the same." Jesus did not want the Jew to believe what the Samaritans believed, but He wanted him to do what the Samaritan did. God's contention with Israel was that while believing correctly, they were failing to produce the fruit of saving faith. Remember that this conversation, according to Luke, began with a question about finding eternal life (Luke 10:25).

Jesus was saying that the kingdom of God is not subject to anyone's traditional or religious interpretation.

Jesus was saying that the kingdom of God is not subject to anyone's traditional or religious interpretation. While it is important to interpret God's Word correctly, being in the kingdom of God is more about having faith and enough strength by the grace of God to do what He commands us to do.

In the famous New Testament chapter about faith, Hebrews 11, the majority of the "heroes of faith" are mentioned because of their actions. Faith and good works are two sides of the same saving truth. This is the original New Testament "gospel to the Jews" and now, of course, it is meant for all believers everywhere.

Discussion Questions:

1. Why does the New Testament have a stronger emphasis on good works when addressing Jewish people?
2. If I have faith in Jesus is it necessary for me to act in obedience to God's word in order to be saved?
3. Can I recognize the connection between faith and good works in my own life?

Prayer Point:

Lord, give me love and respect for my older brothers and sisters in Your kingdom, the Jewish people. Help me to learn about You from their example.

Chapter 20

Three Teachings about the End

Toward the end of His ministry, Jesus answered His disciples' questions about the signs of His return in Matthew 24. Following that, Matthew records that Jesus gave three powerful teachings found in Matthew 25. All of these teachings are about judgment and eternal reward and it seems like the Lord was beginning to complete His training of the twelve disciples, preparing them for final events. The first of these three teachings is called the parable of the ten virgins.

In this parable, Jesus told a story of ten young women who wanted to attend a wedding banquet. They went out intending to meet the bridegroom at night with their oil lamps lit. It was understood that if they met Him with their lamps lit, he would invite them to accompany Him into the banquet.

Clearly, this is a teaching about the return of the Lord and the wedding supper of the Lamb. We, who believe, are expected to identify with the young women. In His parable, Jesus said that five of the ten women were wise and took extra oil because they prudently thought the bridegroom might be delayed for one reason or another. The other five foolishly took only whatever oil they had on hand and went out thinking the bridegroom would surely come right away.

The night grew late and at midnight the cry was heard, "The bridegroom is on His way!" By that time, the lamps of the foolish young women were flickering and about to go out, so they begged for more oil from the wise ones, who refused, saying there might not be enough to go around. Without other options, the foolish ones went into the town to buy oil and, while they were gone, the bridegroom appeared. Jesus ended His parable with these words, "And while they went to buy, the bridegroom came, and those who were ready went in with him to the wedding and the door was shut. Afterward the other virgins came also, saying, 'Lord, Lord, open to us!' But he answered and said, 'Assuredly, I say to you, I do not know you.' Watch therefore, for you know neither the day nor the hour in which the Son of Man is coming" (Matthew 25:10-13).

An important thing to notice is that in this teaching about the Lord's return, judgment, and eternal reward, all of the young women had the same basic beliefs. They all knew they should be there with lit lamps when the bridegroom arrived. They all wanted to accompany Him into the wedding supper. There was not a cynical unbeliever or rebel among them! The difference between those who went in and those who were refused is found in what they did. The wise ones made better decisions than the foolish ones.

Jesus followed this teaching with the parable of the talents. In this teaching, as in the previous one, all the people mentioned had the same basic beliefs. All three servants respected the authority of the master of the house and wanted to please him. They all desired to receive his commendation and a reward for their stewardship. The first two servants returned their talents each with a handsome profit and heard the master's words. "Well done, good and faithful servant; you were faithful over a few things, I will make you ruler over many things. Enter into the joy of your Lord" (Matthew 25:21, 23). The third servant, who didn't waste or steal or lose his talent, restored to the master exactly what was originally given to him.

According to Jesus, the master's response was this:

> But his Lord answered and said to him, "You wicked and lazy servant, you knew that I reap where I have not sown, and gather where I have not scattered seed. So you ought to have deposited my money with the bankers, and at my coming I would have received back my own with interest. So take the talent from him, and give it to him who has ten talents. "For to everyone who has, more will be given, and he will have abundance; but from him who does not have, even what he has will be taken away. And cast the unprofitable servant into the outer darkness. There will be weeping and gnashing of teeth." (Matthew 25:26-30 NKJV)

Clearly, this is another teaching about the return of the Lord, judgment, and eternal reward. The third servant, who was fearful and inactive, was thrown out! It was the wise and practical actions of the first two servants that caused the master to say to them, "Well done, good and faithful servant." The emphasis in Jesus' teaching is on what we do with what we are given in life. The master did not say to any of them, "I admire your beliefs . . ."

Finally, at the end of this incredible chapter, Jesus teaches about God's coming judgment of all the nations.

> When the Son of Man comes in His glory, and all the holy angels with Him, then He will sit on the throne of His glory. All the nations will be gathered before Him, and He will separate them one from another, as a shepherd divides his sheep from the goats. And He will set the sheep on His right hand, but the goats on the left. Then the King will say to those on His right hand, "Come, you blessed of My Father, inherit the kingdom prepared for you from the foundation of the world: for I was hungry and you gave Me food; I was thirsty and you gave Me drink; I was a stranger and you took Me in; I was naked and you clothed Me; I was sick and you visited Me; I was in prison and you came to Me." (Matthew 25:31-36)

According to Jesus, God's judgment and the reward of eternal life will be based on the actions of the "sheep" nations toward the poorest, weakest, most vulnerable and rejected people in their society. He said that in reaching out and serving "the least of these," they were unknowingly serving Him.

Then Jesus taught about God's judgment on the "goat" nations.

> Then He will also say to those on the left hand, "Depart from Me, you cursed, into the everlasting fire prepared for the devil and his angels: for I was hungry and you gave Me no food; I was thirsty and you gave Me no drink; I was a stranger and you did not take Me in, naked and you did not clothe Me, sick and in prison and you did not visit Me." Then they also will answer Him, saying, "Lord, when did we see You hungry or thirsty or a stranger or naked or sick or in prison, and did not minister to You?" Then He will answer them, saying, "Assuredly, I say to you, inasmuch as you did not do it to one of the least of these, you did not do it to Me." And these will go away into everlasting punishment, but the righteous into eternal life. (Matthew 25:41-46)

It goes without saying that in this third teaching in Matthew 25, both the sheep and goat nations have the same basic theology. They believe in God and want to be rewarded. The goats, like the priest and the Levite in Jesus' parable of the good Samaritan, found excuses not to serve those around them who are in need. Jesus taught that this is unacceptable to God. Serving the poor, the sick, prisoners, and refugees (who are

The epistles are just as emphatic in their emphasis on the value of right actions when it comes to salvation.

called "strangers" in the Bible) is not optional for disciples who desire to be among those chosen by God for eternal reward.

Some Bible teachers over the years have found ways to negate the authority of Jesus' words in the gospels. I have even heard it taught that everything Jesus said before the cross is under the old covenant and therefore not binding for Christians today! That kind of teaching would have been rejected by Jesus who taught, "If you abide in My word, you are My disciples indeed" (John 8:31). He also said, "Heaven and earth will pass away, but My words will by no means pass away" (Matthew 24:35).

In any case, the epistles are just as emphatic in their emphasis on the value of right actions when it comes to salvation. Let's look at the epistle of James who writes this in the second chapter, "What does it profit, my brethren, if someone says he has faith but does not have works? Can faith save him? If a brother or sister is naked and destitute of daily food, and one of you says to them, "Depart in peace, be warmed and filled," but you do not give them the things which are needed for the body, what does it profit? Thus also faith by itself, if it does not have works, is dead" (James 2:14-17 NKJV).

James writes that faith alone without works is useless. Inspired by the Holy Spirit and chosen by God to be among the writers of New Testament Scripture, James writes, "You see then that a man is justified by works, and not by faith only" (James 2:24 NKJV). James also makes the point in verse 19 that the demons even have correct beliefs about God but they are not going to heaven! Certainly, the devil has better theology than most of us. He knows God and he has seen God. He served God in heaven before he was cast down because of pride. The devil has personal knowledge that Jesus is God's Son. He knows that the Scriptures are true and accurate. But for all his correct beliefs, we are not going to see the devil in God's kingdom because he consistently acts against God's will and in opposition to His holy and lawful rule.

In case we should begin to think that the gospel as written to the Jews is not for Gentiles today, don't forget that the apostle Paul wrote that everyone who believes becomes a son of Abraham (Galatians 3:7) and that Gentile Christians are "grafted into" the Abrahamic tree of covenant (Romans 11:17-18). Eventually, all believers, Jews and Gentiles from every nation, will be joined together as one holy bride for the wedding supper of the Lord. Here is how John the apostle described his vision of this beautiful bride. "And I heard, as it were, the voice of a great multitude, as the sound of many waters and as the sound of mighty thunderings, saying, 'Alleluia! For the Lord God Omnipotent reigns! Let us be glad and rejoice and give Him glory, for the marriage of the Lamb has come, and His wife has made herself ready.' And to her it was granted to be arrayed in fine linen, clean and bright, for the fine linen is the righteous acts of the saints" (Revelation 19:6-8 NKJV).

The garment that adorns this spotless bride, the garment that shines with awesome beauty, according to John, is the righteous actions, all the good deeds done by the people of God while they lived here on earth. Jesus once said to His own Jewish brethren, "If you are Abraham's children, do the deeds of Abraham" (John 8:39). Doesn't that now apply to all of us who believe as Abraham did and have been "grafted in" to the Abrahamic tree of covenant?

Discussion Questions:

1. If all the ten young women in Jesus' parable had the same beliefs, why did only five of them go to the wedding banquet?
2. Why was the servant who hid his talent punished by the master upon his return?
3. According to Jesus' teaching, what should I do to be counted among the sheep and not among the goats?

Prayer Point:

Lord, when you judge the world please give me the grace to be among those you welcome with the words, "Well done!" Would You help me to become rich in good works?

Chapter 21

God's Amazing Plan for Our Lives

We know that faith without works is dead faith. Even if our church doctrine is not always clear on this point, the Bible is clear enough. Faith without the right kind of works is not saving faith. The question we must ask then is the same question the young Jewish Torah scholar asked Jesus in Luke 10:25. "Teacher, what shall I do to inherit eternal life?" Jesus' answer to the young man is the same as His answer to us. We must act on the commandments, not just believe them.

We learn from the Bible that God puts a strong emphasis on "good works" and that there is a difference between good works as in Matthew 5:16 and dead works that are found in Hebrews 6:1 and 9:14. In the New Testament, the word for works or deeds is *ergon* and the word for good is either *kalos* or *agathos*. Both *kalos* and *agathos* mean something beneficial, honorable, beautiful, and right.

Paul makes it clear that we are not saved just by doing good things. You must have faith in Jesus in order to be saved. Without faith, it is impossible to know God or please Him. However, James makes it clear that belief alone, if it does not produce good works, is dead and useless, that is, unable to save. Faith and good works are two sides of the same truth. One cannot be separated from the other.

Some people say the good works that complete our salvation have already been done in the actions of Jesus when He walked the earth so nothing more is required of us. I think this interpretation does not do justice to the words of the Scriptures or common sense. We are obviously expected by God to do something good in our lives. John wrote in his gospel, "Do not marvel at this; for an hour is coming, in which all who are in the tombs will hear His voice, and will come forth; those who did the good [works] to a resurrection of life, those who committed the evil [works] to a resurrection of judgment (John 5:28-29). The apostle Paul wrote to His spiritual son, Timothy, to teach wealthy people to be "rich in good works" (1 Timothy 6:17-18). Jesus taught that we, His disciples, are the light of the world. He said, "Let your light shine before men in such a way that they may see your good works, and glorify your Father who is in heaven" (Matthew 5:16).

I believe that the following passage from Paul's letter to the Ephesians illustrates the relationship between faith, good works, and dead works. The difference between good works and dead works is simply this: Works that arise from motives that are merely human are the ones that are dead. These are words and actions initiated by selfish ambition, religious obligation, or the expectations of family, friends, or culture. On the other hand, our good works have their origin in God's plan for our lives that He prepared for each of us before we were born! "For by grace you have been saved through faith; and that not of yourselves, it is the gift of God; not as a result of works, so that no one may boast. For we are His workmanship, created in Christ Jesus for good works, which God prepared beforehand so that we would walk in them" (Ephesians 2:8-10).

There are numerous examples of people in the Bible who at some point were directly told by God or otherwise came to the conclusion that there was nothing accidental about their lives. The prophet Jeremiah began his powerful ministry when he was a young man and we know his message was not a popular one. Perhaps in order to encourage him, God spoke these words about his calling in Jeremiah 1:5, "Before I formed you in the womb I knew you, and before you were born I consecrated you; I have appointed you a prophet to the nations." Jeremiah was told that God already knew who he was going to be before he was born and that his calling as a prophet had already been decided. But Jeremiah was far from alone in this realization. Let's go on to another example, King David.

King David was a multi-talented man who ruled as king in Israel and wrote many inspired and prophetic songs. Still, his greatest gift was that of a warrior. David was the greatest fighter ever to appear in Israel. He won every important battle he fought in his lifetime. If he hadn't been a successful fighter, he probably would never have survived to become king and if he hadn't been king, it is very possible that we would not be singing his songs today.

As a warrior, David lived most of his life in danger. Think how many times he arose in the morning and strapped on his sword, not knowing if he would return home in the evening. But late in his life, David realized that God had designed him for his unique calling and it had been divinely planned out carefully on a daily basis before he was born. Thinking about this kind of divine foreknowledge is deep, mysterious, and exciting. David sang these inspired words to God: "For You formed my inward parts; You wove me in my mother's womb. I will give thanks to You, for I am fearfully and wonderfully made; wonderful are Your works, and my soul knows it very well. My frame was not hidden from You, when I was made in secret, and skillfully wrought in the depths of the earth. Your eyes have seen my unformed substance and in Your book were all written the days that were ordained for me, when as yet there was not one of them" (Psalm 139:13-16).

What about the prophet Samuel? His mother, Hannah, could not bear children and it made her the object of ridicule within her own family. It might even have been considered a sign of God's disfavor upon her, but she wept bitterly, prayed, and eventually made a vow to the Lord. Hannah promised that if God would give her a son she would not be the one to raise him. He would be dedicated to the Lord's service throughout his life. Apparently, God liked that offer and so Hannah quickly became pregnant with Samuel.

Hannah kept her vow. Samuel was raised in the house of God and what a man he turned out to be! Samuel became a great servant of God and a spiritual giant in Israel, the last of the judges, and a forerunner of the great prophets. During his tenure, the entire nation changed. He chose and anointed the first kings of Israel and walked in God's authority and integrity throughout his days.

Can anyone doubt that all this was planned by God before Samuel's birth? By initially refusing to give her children God was saying to Hannah, "Precious woman, be patient. I have a special plan for your son!" God waited until she was ready to dedicate her first child to His service before giving her Samuel. Later, Hannah and her family saw that her earlier years of barrenness were not a sign of God's disfavor but actually the reverse!

John the Baptist is another example of a spiritually powerful man chosen by God before he was born for a specific vocation. John's mother, Elizabeth, was barren and also advanced in years, but Gabriel, an angel of God, appeared to Zacharias, John's father, in the holy place of the temple where he was serving as a priest. The angel announced the birth of a son, who like Samuel, would serve God all his days. His chosen name, as well as the nature of his unique calling, were also foretold by the angel. Clearly, John the Baptist's life was planned by God before birth.

If we go on into the New Testament, we come to the apostle Paul. Inspired by the Holy Spirit, Paul wrote to the Galatians, "But when God, who had set me apart even from my mother's womb and called me through His grace . . . ." (Galatians 1:15). Late in his life, Paul realized that before he was born God already knew what he would become. Before he was born to a Jewish family in Tarsus, before he studied under Gamaliel in Jerusalem and became a "Pharisee of

God designs all of us before we are born.

the Pharisees," before he became a persecutor of the early believers, before he encountered Jesus while traveling to Damascus—before any of that happened, God had already designed and chosen him for his unique apostolic calling.

Then, of course, we have the example of the Lord Jesus Himself. He has always been the only begotten Son of God, loved by the Father from before the "foundation of the world" (John 17:24). Jesus is and has always been "the image of the invisible God, the firstborn of all creation" (Colossians 1:15). There is absolutely nothing accidental about His existence and life on earth. He said, "I and the Father are one" (John 10:30). Everything about Jesus is perfectly aligned with God's eternal plan.

Faced with this amount of biblical evidence concerning people whose lives were planned by God before they were born, I think there are only two possible conclusions we could make. The first conclusion is something like, "I suppose God obviously has some 'elite' or 'designer' saints. These are the chosen individuals He personally designs and handcrafts in a luxury workshop in a reserved part of heaven. And then there are the rest of us who are basically stamped out in a factory in the industrial part of heaven!" This is meant to be humorous, but it describes the commonly held attitude that God creates at least two classes of people in His kingdom—the specially called, chosen, and gifted, and then the vast unenlightened majority.

The second possible conclusion is that God designs all of us before we are born. The biblical examples of so many people known and designed by God before their birth are in the Scriptures to show us what is true about everyone. We know God to be a Creator of infinite variety and intense creativity. On every tree that has ever grown or will ever grow, from the trees in the garden of Eden to the Tree of Life alongside the heavenly river described in Revelation chapter 22, every single leaf is different from the next. Every wave on the ocean, every cloud in the sky, every blade of grass, every grain of sand is unique.

When it comes to humans, the crown of God's creation, the only part of His creation that is made in His own image and likeness (Genesis 1:26-27), how much more attention does God give to each one of us? This means that when God created you, before you were born, He designed you with a good plan for your life in His mind and, out of love, a beautiful dream just for you in His heart.

Discussion Questions:

1. Do I believe that God created me and knew me before I was born?
2. Am I thankful to God for my unique design?
3. Have I discovered my destiny - God's purpose in creating me?

Prayer Point:

Lord, thank You that You created me to be unique in all the world and in all eternity. Help me to live out Your good plan for my life with humility, faith and courage.

Chapter 22

Hearing His Call

I think most of us would agree that the Bible overwhelmingly supports the conclusion that all humans are created and personally loved by God. We were made to be like our Creator, but sin has fragmented His image in us. We still bear the image of God but in broken condition, reflecting His beautiful design, love, and glory in the way a shattered mirror will still, but imperfectly, reflect the light of the sun.

So many lives are wasted through drugs, crime, and suicide, not to mention those swept away by accidents, war, famine, natural disasters, and illness. How many people live out their days without purpose, in anger or bitterness, or in loneliness and poverty, never tasting the joy of love or achievement? God's heart yearns for His lost creation to be redeemed from futility and despair, so He calls to us.

God's call to lost humanity is especially intense in the preaching and teaching of His words in Scripture, but His call is not in any way limited to this. He is calling all the time to everyone. God calls through the love of a mother or a father, through the faithfulness of a wife or husband, through the loyalty of a friend, through the beauty of nature, through the precision of science. David, the inspired psalmist sang: "The heavens are telling of the glory of God and their expanse is declaring the work of His hands. Day to day pours forth speech, and night to night reveals knowledge. There is no speech, nor are there words; their voice is not heard. Their line has gone out through all the earth, and their utterances to the end of the world" (Psalm 19:1-4a).

We are born into this world as a three- or four-kilogram "package" of life, but we don't know anything about God's plan for us. Right away, two people usually become like gods to us, that is, Mom and Dad. Most parents treasure their children and try their best to give them a loving home environment and pass on to them their highest values. However, whether they try to or not, in the months and years that follow, parents succeed in placing their dreams, ambitions, expectations, and hopes, along with all their broken dreams and thwarted ambitions, upon the little shoulders of their children.

Because we all live in a sinful, unjust world, there are some children who tragically do not survive that process. After these early years, most of us go to school. There, our classmates, friends, siblings, and teachers do their best to convince and sometimes force us into accepted patterns of behavior. They teach us how much it hurts to not measure up, to be left out, to be rejected.

Then, if we survive those years, we go on to our marriages, jobs, professions, or national service. Here we learn how to talk and dress and carry ourselves if we want to be successful, and how awful it is to fail. As a result, society is filled with adults who have reached maturity by learning to stay alert and adapt quickly to the expectations of other people. At the same time, we may have no idea what the divine plan for our lives is. We may at that point wonder, *Is there any real meaning to my time here on earth?*

By the grace of God, often through anguish and desperation, some of us become aware of our need for God. We may begin consciously searching for God or crying out in prayer. We may have never known God or read the Bible, but somehow, in our inner being, we begin to hear His "voice" calling out to us. But Jesus said, "Many are called, but few are chosen" (Matthew 22:14). Out of love, God calls to everyone, but some of us hearing His call begin making decisions, usually a series of small decisions, that together become a big decision and begin turning our lives toward God. No one can say exactly when or where, but it is in the making of those inner decisions that we pass from being among those called by God to those who are among the chosen. In other words, God calls but we choose to be chosen.

The Bible has a word for those who have heard the call of God, responded by deciding to turn towards Him, and have become among His chosen. The word is *ekklesia* and it means "called out." One way to understand "called out" is that those chosen are ones in whom God's call has become effective. They are called to move out of darkness into light, out of death into life, out of futility into purpose, out of their old lives

God's grace can lead you to the place where starting over with Jesus as your Lord becomes what you deeply desire.

into something totally new. In English, the Greek word *ekklesia* is translated "church." So the church is not a religion, building, or organization. It is the people who have chosen to belong to God.

Overall, why do so many people reject God's call? I think it is mostly because answering His call means having a ruler in your life. You are not on your own anymore. God's call means giving up your other ambitions and accepting a lifestyle of sacrificially loving other people. It means starting over. That's not attractive to everybody, even if it means finding the reward of eternal life. But God's grace can lead you to the place where starting over with Jesus as your Lord becomes what you deeply desire.

When you decide to answer God's call and start to walk down that path in life, things begin to change. You make believing friends and start to attend a fellowship where God is worshipped and His Word is taught. Soon you learn the basics: God is a loving God. The Bible is His Word. What it means to worship God. How to begin getting free from sin. How to start living in faith. But perhaps most importantly, how to pray. You learn God delights in His relationship with you and you can build that relationship through dialog with Him. Experience in prayer begins to teach you that God is committed to your good and has promised to answer your prayers in wise, generous, and powerful ways.

After a while, you learn that God, with whom you now have a growing relationship in prayer, is not only your loving

Father, Lord, Savior, King, and best friend ever, but He is also your Creator. You discover that He had a plan for you before you were born and He designed you uniquely for that plan. Because you have now learned how to pray, when you want to know God's plan, you begin to talk to Him about it. At this point what you hear from the Spirit of God and what you do about it will make the difference between having good works or dead works in your life forever.

Discussion Questions:

1. Have I already answered God's call to believe and follow Him?
2. Do I want to know why He created and called me?
3. Have I begun to speak to God in prayer about His plans for me?

Prayer Point:

Lord, please open my spiritual ear so I can hear Your call clearly. Remove obstacles, false goals and distractions from my life. Awaken my heart to leap up to obey at the sound of Your voice.

Chapter 23

The Path to the Plan

I have talked to a lot of people over the years, particularly young people, who reach this point in their spiritual walk and then seek out a pastor like me and say, "The Bible says God created me in His image and I believe He has a unique plan just for me, but whenever I ask Him in prayer to tell me the plan, He doesn't say anything to me!"

Usually, when this happens, I know what the problem is. Most of the time, it is simply that they are not ready or not yet willing to do what God wants to do with their lives.

God, of course, knows everything He wants to know. He knows what is in your heart before you even begin to speak with Him. If He knows that you are not going to do what He wants you to do, then it is actually more merciful for Him not to say anything to you. Because if He tells you what He wants you to do, knowing you are not going to do it, doesn't that just increase your guilt? So I think God often chooses to remain silent out of love. This may be one reason why He also chooses to be invisible. That way He can be silent and we think He is not there!

How can you get God to tell you His plan? Sometimes, it is not easy. Remember that God didn't give an answer to Samuel's mother Hannah until she made a very special commitment, a promise, to Him. This is something we all can do, but it is a serious step. The Bible says it is better not to make a commitment than to make a false promise to God (Ecclesiastes 5:5). However, if you are ready to make a sacrificial promise to God, here are some things to consider. In the Bible, there are dozens of instructions about sacrifice and offerings that are an acceptable and required part of our worship. I think, these may be summed up in a single sentence, "Never go before God with nothing in your hands, but always come to His house with a gift" (Exodus 23:15, Deuteronomy 16:16). Many people around the world understand because of their culture that you should never visit anyone's house without a gift. So why would you go to God's house empty-handed, especially if you want to receive something very valuable from Him?

I know what you might be thinking now. What can I give to God that is meaningful to Him? Isn't He the person who already has everything? Well, no. There is something that God does not have until you give it to Him. That is your solemn promise that whatever good work He tells you to do, you will do it to the best of your ability! So take time to prepare your gift for God before you talk with Him in prayer.

God created every human with a passion for something that has eternal value.

You will realize it is a precious sacrifice. It could change your whole life! You place it carefully on the altar and then say something like, “Lord, it’s me again. I made up my mind. Whatever you tell me to do, I will find a way to get it done for You. I will make it my business to accomplish whatever You say!”

So you pray that prayer privately and from your heart and then when things are quiet you may sense in your spirit that the Lord is saying, “Okay. Good. Do this!”

And a moment later you may say, “That? Oh, no, Lord! That’s not what I had in mind. Not that. I was afraid You were going to say that!” This is often true because at the time you brought your precious gift to the altar of sacrifice, you were ready to attempt any grand, glorious, and impossible thing. Now, what God is saying to do is something small, obscure, seemingly insignificant, lacking in any apparent glory or honor. How could this be the voice of God? He’s telling you to do something like visit a recovering alcoholic, cook a meal for a sick neighbor, lead singing in a home for the elderly, or volunteer to help problematic teens acquire new job skills. You are ready to write it off as an experiment in hearing God’s voice that didn’t work out, but then you remember what you promised.

Yes, you promised God that whatever He said you would do. So in obedience, you begin to serve others and to do what you know the Scriptures and the inner voice of His Spirit are urging you to do.

Maybe not immediately but soon, two things begin to happen in you. The first is a feeling of deep inner pleasure and joy whenever you begin to do the good work God assigned to you. You may not even want to admit this to your closest friends at first because what you are doing is so humble, but when you do what God said you should do, you feel wonderful! You are sensing the presence and joy of the Lord. You would do this if no one noticed, if no one applauded, and if no one paid you a single dollar! This feeling of joy and strength is called your passion and God created every human with a passion for something that has eternal value.

The next thing that happens to you is that after a while you realize, "This is unexpected, but I'm really *good* at this!" A skill, an innate ability, begins to emerge from you that enables you to accomplish whatever God commanded you. You're not just good at it. You are better than most of the others. When you start to work, you simply know how the job should be done. The way to do it successfully is obvious to you. Other people begin to notice it too. This ability is called your gift.

The New Testament is emphatic that each and every person is given a gift by God's grace (1 Corinthians 7:7, Ephesians 4:7, 1 Peter 4:10). The lists of gifts given in the New Testament are only partial. The spiritual gifts listed in Paul's epistles are the gifts needed for planting new congregations of believers among Gentiles where they had never existed before. We still need these special gifts today, but not everybody has them. In the rest of the Bible we find a multitude of people with gifts from God serving in many different ways and areas of society.

The first person mentioned in the Bible who is said to have a skill given by the Holy Spirit is Bezalel, an artist and craftsman (Exodus 31:2-5). Many others with nonreligious gifts are mentioned in the Bible. Abraham's great grandson Joseph was a national level administrator in Egypt; Daniel was a statesman in Babylon; Nehemiah was a government official; King David was a political leader, psalmist, and warrior. The list goes on and on. God's gifts and calling for every individual must be understood in the context of His kingdom as a nation, that is, an entire society in which each person has a chosen and assigned place.

Israel's calling was to be the nation chosen as God's example of His kingdom to the world. This calling started with God's promise to Abraham. Israel was organized into a society under Moses and the national calling was never revoked. In fact, the apostle Paul in the New Testament book of Romans confirms that God will not even allow Israel's opposition to the gospel to change His chosen plan.

God will never change His mind about the purposes He had in calling Israel and He will never take back the gifts He gave to accomplish His plan. In the powerful eleventh chapter of Romans, Paul explains, "From the standpoint of the gospel they [Israel] are enemies for your sake, but from the standpoint of God's choice they are beloved for the sake of the fathers; for the gifts and the calling of God are irrevocable" (Romans 11:28-29).

This biblical truth may explain something that has baffled the greatest minds of the modern world and has become the source of numerous false conspiracy theories. The mystery of why Jewish people have been so successful wherever they were scattered cannot be explained simply by cultural factors like an emphasis on education or the value of working hard. Other cultures have similar values and have not achieved as much. The Nobel Prize was established in the will left by Swedish scientist Alfred Nobel in 1895. It is a series of international awards given each year in recognition of academic, cultural, or scientific advances.

According to Wikipedia, as of 2017, Nobel Prizes had been awarded to 892 individuals, of whom 201 or 22.5 percent were Jews, although the total Jewish population comprises less than 0.2 percent of the world's population. This means the percentage of Jewish Nobel laureates is at least 112.5 times or 11,250 percent above average.

The inspired words of the New Testament reveal the secret of Jewish brilliance evident over a broad spectrum of human areas of achievement. It is a divine gifting that God bestowed by covenantal promise on the descendants of Abraham, Isaac, and Jacob. It is a sign to the Jewish people and rest of the world of God's faithfulness to keep His promises.

Discussion Questions:

1. Can I think of a time when God spoke to me about His plan for my life?
2. Have I ever made a solemn promise to God?
3. Am I ready to do whatever He tells me to do?

Prayer Point:

Lord, I promise that if You would speak to me and begin telling me Your plan, I will find a way to do whatever You say. Hear my prayer and help me find the path to my eternal purpose!

Chapter 24

Your Gift —Your Anointing

Even without the benefit of biblical faith, it is possible to recognize God's gifting in certain people. For example, in many nations, if a child can play Mozart on the piano by the age of five or kick a football really hard and accurately, someone is going to notice and probably try to help the child develop in that area of talent. Physical beauty, academic achievement, singing, playing the violin, piano, or guitar, or excelling in a game like chess are other gifts easily noticed, and there are many more such areas.

However, the Bible reveals that human ability should point to the Giver of every good gift. Faith in God that produces persistence, love, humility, and a heart of gratitude for

> Your gift becomes a part of your identity and a part of your lifestyle.

abilities and their rewards in life are essential character qualities to help the gifted young person through the intense heat of competition and the often ugly and corrupted struggle for success.

In some parts of the Christian world, on the other hand, the emphasis is strongly focused on spiritual gifts that are used in the church. It is hard for some Christians to accept that people are gifted by God in an infinite variety of human endeavors. After Israel was chosen by God as the example of His kingdom, only one out of the twelve tribes was specifically set aside for the professionally religious function of priests. This is less than 10 percent of the complete nation. I think this ratio is still in effect.

As a young pastor, I thought everyone in my congregation needed to become a minister like me. I was disappointed that so few people over the years showed an interest or aptitude and I was sure that I was failing to lead them properly. Finally, I realized that it was never God's intention for everybody to serve Him by working in the church or as professional ministers. Godly, biblical religion is vitally important but it is only part of God's kingdom. Why did it take me so long to understand what was so clearly written in the text of Scripture?

In Ephesians 4:7 Paul wrote, "But to each one of us grace was given according to the measure of Christ's gift." Then, a few verses later he wrote: "And He gave some as apostles, and some as prophets, and some as evangelists, and some as pastors and teachers, for the equipping of the saints for the work of service, to the building up of the body of Christ; until we all attain to the unity of the faith, and of the knowledge of the Son of God, to a mature man, to the measure of the stature which belongs to the fullness of Christ" (Ephesians 4:11-13).

People who are gifted by God to serve Him in a ministry calling have the responsibility to identify and then help develop the calling and gifting of everyone else! Spiritual gifts that have a religious application and are used in gatherings of believers are meant to "equip" others for the use of their own gifts. The "fullness of Christ" is His kingdom, which extends over all things, not just the church.

I have a friend who is called as and has the gifting of an accountant. I am a Bible teacher and accounting is not a gift that God in His wisdom gave to me. When I examine a multi-page spreadsheet, the little numbers look just like ants running around on my desk! But my friend with his special gift can gaze at the same document and chuckle. He is likely to say something like, "Well, it's perfectly clear to me. You have some financial problems to solve! And actually, you have three main problem areas and my advice is to address this one first."

If you are someone like me, you should seek friends who are called and gifted like that.

Let's say that you have identified your main gift from God and you are committed to using that gift for His purposes in your life. You have found a God-given ability that enables you to serve God and others in an effective way and it is evident that other people are benefitted by your service. Of course, you realize that there are others who have similar, though not identical gifts, to yours. Some of them have developed their gifts far more than you. Some have powerful, efficient and beautiful aspects to their gift that help you recognize unseen dimensions of your own gift. You study those people and learn from them. You dedicate yourself to the discipline of practicing your gift and being accountable for its use.

Isn't this why a professional athlete submits to a good coach? Like any top athlete, you desire to become a champion for God! Proverbs 18:16 (NKJV) says, "A man's gift makes room for him and brings him before great men" and Proverbs 22:29 says, "Do you see a man skilled in his work? He will stand before kings; he will not stand before obscure men." Your gift becomes a part of your identity and a part of your lifestyle.

Your gift is holy. John the Baptist said, "A man can receive nothing unless it has been given him from heaven" (John 3:27). It is also true that what is given to you from heaven will never be taken away but it can be wasted. You should treat your gift with respect and use it for pure purposes. However, holy also means it is set apart, reserved for you by the Lord. Your gift was designed by God to be a part of you. It is uniquely and eternally yours. No one gets to use your gift except you and no one has a gift, or will ever have a gift, exactly like yours.

I used to think that God's gifts were not already determined in His sovereign plan and whether I got one was dependent on how "good" I acted or how faithful I was in prayer. I thought that if I fasted enough, stayed alert, and sat on the front row in worship services, the Holy Spirit might just appear and start handing out gifts. I desperately wanted to become a person gifted by God but all my efforts failed. Finally, I began to realize that my gift was part of God's design in me. There is nothing random about my gift or yours. God designs and creates our gifts to match our unique calling. We need that particular gift to accomplish His plan for us.

Using your God-given gift in an effective way makes God very pleased. When our first grandson was just a toddler, adult members of the family, in a loving way, tried to give him the one gift he would enjoy and play with more than his other toys. Successfully giving the most used toy of the month or week made some of us feel good and even inwardly boast, "See, he's using *my* toy! That's the one *I* got for him."

I think it gives God a lot of pleasure to watch His children find their gifts and use them with dedication and joy. It pleases the fatherly heart of God so much that every once in a while He might just reach out His mighty hand and touch the use of your gift with supernatural power!

For instance, let's say you love children and know that raising them is your calling. Others in your family see it in you as well and say you are an excellent mother. Eventually, you become in charge of a kindergarten and for several days a week the children of fifteen or twenty families are your responsibility. You always pray quietly over every child and sometimes at home you pray for their families.

One day, one of the mothers calls you and says, "I know there is something different about your class. My son's asthma attacks have disappeared since I enrolled him. What are you doing there that is so special?" You didn't do anything to heal the boy but you know that God did. That is called "the anointing" of God's Spirit.

Your anointing, like your gift from God, is holy, that is, set apart for God's service, and something very special between just God and you. Supernatural empowerment from God never originates with us, but it is given according to the Lord's sovereign grace and favor. When God's anointing is given to anyone, it is personal and specific. Because it is God's grace on you personally, you cannot have the anointing that belongs to someone else. I know that some people believe they can give you their anointing and I have also stood in those prayer lines over the years. It never worked for me and I don't think it works for anyone. A person who uses their gift in an anointed way can encourage you, inspire you, stir you up, spark in you a holy jealousy, but you can't have what belongs to another person. You have to seek and find your own anointing from the Lord.

Some people point to the biblical example of Elisha, Elijah's disciple who received a double portion of his mentor's anointing. If you read the Scripture carefully though, you will see that it was God who selected Elisha and commanded Elijah to anoint him as a prophet in his place (1 Kings 19:16). When Elijah was taken into heaven and Elisha began his prophetic ministry, the sons of the prophets said, "The spirit of Elijah rests on Elisha" (2 Kings 2:15). But it was not God who proclaimed that Elisha received Elijah's anointing. After the departure of Elijah, Elisha received his own personal anointing from the Lord. John the Baptist, who later came to minister in the "spirit and power of Elijah," said, "A man can receive nothing unless it has been given him from heaven" (John 3:27).

Using your gift with diligence and being anointed by God are important because this produces the impact for good your life will have on the people around you. The influence you exert for God and His kingdom on the lives of others determines the fruitfulness of your calling. Your fruitfulness is vital because the good works that God prepared for you before you were born are the works that complete your faith. Without these, your faith is useless (James 2:14 and 20).

These good works also determine your eternal reward. The apostle Paul made the point that there will be some who misuse their gift or otherwise fail to become fruitful and still receive eternal life from God but with no reward (1 Corinthians 3:13-15). I have heard some people say they plan to wait until they are on their deathbed to repent and be saved. That is a very dangerous decision since hardly any of us know the exact time when our lives will end. There are also Christians who say, "I hope to just make it into heaven and don't want any reward!" Around us the entire world is groaning spiritually and seeking help and salvation. There are so many opportunities to use our gifts and God's anointing. Why would anyone alive today with access by faith to God's amazing grace and the power of the Holy Spirit desire to be saved without eternal reward from God?

Discussion Questions:

1. Do I know what my main gift from God is?
2. Have I experienced God's anointing on the gift He has given to me?
3. Is the promise of heavenly reward something that is attractive to me?

Prayer Point:

Lord, please help me identify and use the gift You have designed for me. Give me humility, dedication, and Your anointing as I use what You gave to me.

Chapter 25

Where's the Fruit?

Fruitfulness is the impact for what is good in the eyes of God that your life has on the others around you. Bearing fruit is important because the day will come when each of us will stand before our King and give an account for what we have done. Years ago, I was asked by a ministry to drug addicts and alcoholics to come and give a Bible teaching. I agreed to come and the leader assigned a topic for my session. The theme he chose for me was "Judgment and Eternal Reward."

The truth was that I had never taught a message on God's judgment before. The reason was that such a message did not normally fill more seats in our worship service! I was dedicated to church growth and thought that attracting people to sit in the weekly meeting was my way of advancing God's kingdom. Nevertheless, for those humble and spiritually hungry guys in the rehab program, I was ready to teach whatever was necessary and prepared the study. I was shocked! Almost all of the Scriptures I found about God's judgment in the New Testament were about our behavior and not our beliefs.

Jesus said, "For by your words you will be justified, and by your words you will be condemned" (Matthew 12:37) and also, "For the Son of Man is going to come in the glory of His Father with His angels, and will then repay every man according to his deeds" (Matthew 16:27). Revelation 20:12 reveals that the dead will be judged according to their deeds or works. When our final day comes, if we want to hear the Master say, "Well done, good and faithful servant," it is a good idea to have done something that pleases Him by then!

But what is required? How can we have the confidence of faith that our works will be acceptable on that day?

For many years, I never wanted to preach or teach about God's judgment because I thought it would be frightening to my congregation and involve "heavy" issues of condemnation and guilt. Now, however, I think that properly taught, the subject of God's judgment is liberating. If I am required to faithfully "run the race" with spiritual endurance (Hebrews 12:1) and in such a way that I will win (1 Corinthians 9:24), I need to know where the finish line is located!

Here is another way to think about judgment. Imagine we are all in school together and the end of the term is approaching. We know that in order to graduate we have to pass the final examination. But then, before the end of the term, the school administration makes an announcement. Any student who requests can receive the questions that will be on the exam in advance. As one of the students, would you ask to see the questions? Of course, you would. And if you know what is going to be on the exam, you also know something liberating. You know what is *not* going to be on the exam. If you are not going to be asked about it, you can ignore that material. Now that you know what you are responsible for, you can focus your attention and concentrate your strength! As God's student, His disciple, you only need to study and produce the work that is required by Him.

God will ask you about the plan He made for you before you were born.

When it comes to judgment, we know that it is important to have lived a sanctified life. That means we all must struggle with our own carnal natures and selfish motives each day to become progressively free from sins caused by our fleshly bodies and minds. When we fall short, we rely, by faith, on the mercy of God through the sacrificial love and grace of Jesus to cover our failures and get us back in the fight! Sanctification is practical and progressive. Over time, if we do not give up, our thoughts, motives, and habits change. This builds our relationship with God and increases our usefulness to other people. When we help others succeed in life, we are an instrument of God's goodness. Jesus was not only pure, but He also did things that produced godly change in the lives of others. His work of atonement and redemption broke the power of sin, making it possible for us to do what we must while here on earth.

Many people would like to know what they are responsible for in life, and I am sure there are a great many teachings and theories available, but I think this is what you are most likely to be asked by God on your day of judgment. God will ask you about the plan He made for you before you were born. The plan that was in His mind when He designed you and the dream He had in His heart for you when you were uniquely created.

On the day you stand before Him to give an account, God will speak to you about His original purpose for your life. How could He hold you responsible for what He did not design you to do? Your good works are the actions that are "written" in His good plan. Everything else is dead works. "For I know the plans that I have for you," declares the LORD, "plans for welfare and not for calamity to give you a future and a hope. Then you will call upon Me and come and pray to Me, and I will listen to you. You will seek Me and find Me when you search for Me with all your heart" (Jeremiah 29:11-13).

Out of love, God's plan for every person is a good plan. We are given the freedom and responsibility to choose how we will live our lives, but God reveals His good will to those who seek Him with all their hearts. Some of us have been given something small to do and others something big. To the one much is given, more fruit will be expected by God.

In the end, it is not so important how much God gave you but whether you did what He told you to do! May God help each of us to hear the voice of God and grasp, by faith, our holy calling that is according to His eternal will for us (2 Timothy 1:9).

Discussion Questions:

1. How can I know that I am producing spiritual fruit in my life?
2. If I ask Him in prayer will God give me guidance to find my calling and place of fruitfulness?
3. Do I have confidence now that God is pleased with my life?

Prayer Point:

Lord, I want to be very fruitful for You in my life. Please build my faith with the assurance that You are committed to my spiritual success, guiding me and looking at me with love.

Chapter 26

Down Is Up

The Sermon on the Mount is considered by many to be the most comprehensive of Jesus' teachings. Some say it is the greatest moral teaching in history. Here is the greatest teacher who ever lived speaking inspired words that have made a life-changing impact on people without number for two thousand years. This incredible teaching begins with what is called the Beatitudes because of the nine blessings that Jesus describes in the first verses.

> When Jesus saw the crowds, He went up on the mountain; and after He sat down, His disciples came to Him. He opened His mouth and began

> to teach them, saying, "Blessed are the poor in spirit, for theirs is the kingdom of heaven.
> Blessed are those who mourn, for they shall be comforted.
> Blessed are the gentle, for they shall inherit the earth.
> Blessed are those who hunger and thirst for righteousness, for they shall be satisfied.
> Blessed are the merciful, for they shall receive mercy.
> Blessed are the pure in heart, for they shall see God.
> Blessed are the peacemakers, for they shall be called sons of God.
> Blessed are those who have been persecuted for the sake of righteousness, for theirs is the kingdom of heaven.
> Blessed are you when people insult you and persecute you, and falsely say all kinds of evil against you because of Me." (Matthew 5:1-11)

Please notice that this teaching began as a private session for the disciples of Jesus. We have already seen that Jesus continually retreated from the crowds and sought time with just His disciples. Whenever He taught them privately, away from the crowds, truth in powerful clarity was the result. Matthew chapters 24 and 25 are two of many examples. The great teaching of the Sermon on the Mount began with the disciples, but other people must have followed them and joined in because by the end of the teaching it says, "the crowds were amazed at His teaching" (Matthew 7:28).

Our eternal impact does not start by looking up to those who have more than we do, but rather by looking down and noticing those who have less.

In these nine blessings, Jesus was turning the world that the disciples knew, and the world that is also familiar to us, upside down. He was saying what you think is the top is really the bottom and what you consider down is really up. What you think is lowly and debased is actually where you will find the glory, the power, the influence, and the presence of God. If you want your life to have an eternal impact, it is not going to be found by clawing and scratching your way to the top of the human pyramid! It is not by searching for people of political power, financial wealth, or cultural influence that we gain good and lasting influence for God's kingdom. Our eternal impact does not start by looking up to those who have more than we do, but rather by looking down and noticing those who have less.

In Matthew 5:3, we don't know exactly what is meant by "poor in spirit," but it certainly does not refer to a person who is self-satisfied, feeling personally powerful, and full of pride. It may refer to someone who is brokenhearted, experiencing inner emptiness, and sorrowful about his or her shortcomings. We don't really want to be poor in spirit. It doesn't seem like a blessing to us, but the Lord thinks otherwise. He says that those who are "poor in spirit" are the ones who receive His kingdom, which means the fullness of His presence and power.

Someone who is mourning has just lost a close relative or loved one. We don't think that mourning is such a blessed thing and we don't look forward to being in that state. However, the Lord says mourners are blessed by God and it is with them that His comfort is going to be found.

We don't really think that gentle people are going to end up with the wealth of the earth. Warplanes and tanks are needed to defend our borders and fierce legal struggles often characterize our disputes over real estate. Nevertheless, the Lord said people who are genuinely gentle and meek will be given the earth and its resources by God. He went on to say that the people who today suffer because of injustice, corruption, and oppression will be satisfied in the presence and protection of the righteous judge of all the earth.

Jesus' teaching turns the world upside down and He reveals to us where the opportunities lie to make an important and lasting impact with our lives. It is not by climbing up in society but rather by learning to climb down and help somebody who has a need we can meet. Most inspiration for ministry, as well as a great many sustainable businesses, began when somebody noticed another person in need and did something practical to help them. We find freedom and the blessings of God when we look down, take the low road of service, and begin to help others.

Some years ago, we began a ministry to help women in need of refuge in one of our buildings on Mt. Carmel. After a while, our director of the shelter received a call from the immigration police, asking if she would take a Sudanese woman and her daughter who had walked from the Sinai desert into Israeli territory seeking asylum. At the time, genocide was being reported in Darfur (a region in the west of Sudan), and Sudan was officially at war with Israel. The woman and her daughter were going to be treated as enemy aliens unless we took them in and gave them shelter. After a quick prayer, she said, “Yes.”

That began a flood of Sudanese refugee women and children coming to our shelter who were fleeing the horrors of war in their own country. After escaping Sudan to Egypt, where many had faced persecutions and killings, some paid Bedouins to take them into the Sinai where they walked across very dangerous territory into Israel seeking refuge. As we accepted them into our shelter, we were soon facing difficult problems. We didn’t understand their languages or their tribal identities or customs. Nothing had prepared us to care for traumatized and wounded African women and their children. There were fights between the women in the shelter and difficulties that arose because of the attitudes of our neighbors. Our ministry staff became busy dealing with disputes and caring for strangers who had no homes and whose families had been torn apart by war.

Pressures began to build up in our ministry and I worried that we had allowed a terrible distraction to take our focus away from serving the people of Israel. Eventually, Israeli newspapers heard about the shelter and suddenly began contacting us for the story. We do not often receive positive or even fair coverage of our Messianic community in the Israeli press but for the sake of this story, they promised to write about our faith accurately. Soon, the articles began to appear on the front pages of the Hebrew language daily papers. They not only told the stories of how these women and children were being cared for and rehabilitated, but they also wrote that we are a community of Messianic Israeli Jews and Gentiles who are taking care of foreigners in accordance with God's commands.

When I saw the articles about the women and their pictures in our nation's newspapers and even on television, I realized that these simple refugees, without money or status in our society, had lifted up the Lord's name among His own Israeli people in an unprecedented way. Although they were among the weakest and most rejected people in our country, they had given Jesus publicity in Israel that could never have been purchased with money or acquired using political influence. Surely, down is up in God's kingdom and the bottom always eventually moves the top.

Discussion Questions:

1. Why did Jesus want His disciples to look down for opportunities to serve?
2. Who are the people at the bottom of our society?
3. If I think about the people in my daily life, is there someone I know who is now in need of help that I can provide?

Prayer Point:

Lord, teach me to look down and not up to find the glory, power, and influence of Your kingdom. Help me to notice the many who have needs that I can meet right around me.

Chapter 27

Freedom from Striving

During the days of Moses in the book of Exodus, the people of Israel had become slaves in the land of Egypt. It happened because after the death of Joseph, who had risen to the level of prime minister, another pharaoh came to power who "did not know Joseph" and the people of Israel were persecuted and forced into slavery. Egypt had grown into an empire exercising power over people groups that stretched across northern Africa and into the Middle East.

The people of Israel were a collection of different tribes, a small ethnic group that had little or no power in Egyptian society. They were not accepted in the cultural mainstream and were forced into manual labor at the lowest level of the economy. This Egypt in the Bible becomes a picture and symbol of a sinful political and religious system characterized by injustice and slavery, everything that the God of the Bible stands against in His kingdom.

Ten times in the book of Exodus, God used the same phrase when He spoke to the pharaoh of Egypt through the prophet Moses. Moses said, "The Lord, the God of the Hebrews, sent me to you, saying, 'Let My people go, that they may serve Me in the wilderness.' But behold, you have not listened until now" (Exodus 7:16). Pharaoh wanted God's people to serve him as slaves, but God wanted Israel to worship and serve as free men and women.

In this confrontation, we see two worlds in contrast and collision. The earthly system as symbolized by Egypt (and later, by Babylon) in the Bible is driven by ambition and disregard for the suffering of others, and is characterized by competitive striving to get to the top position of power.

The kingdom of God, on the other hand, is about pressing forward in faith to lay our lives down in worship and service in obedience to God's command to love. Laying down our lives in service and bowing down in worship mean taking the lowest place, relying on God for everything, and helping those who are most needy. As in the days of the Exodus, our inner motives are revealed by fiery trials and hardship. The question is, are you here to serve or be served? Answering this question requires truth of the kind that can set you free. It also helps us define the nature of true freedom.

The apostle Paul, although he came from a very religiously restrictive background, became known as the apostle of the "heart set free." He found freedom in reaching down to help others. Paul's motive was love, not personal ambition.

He laid aside his religious privileges as a Jew and social advantages as a Roman citizen to go to common people in the Gentile world, many of whom were slaves. In his powerful book, *Paul: Apostle of the Heart Set Free*, Bible scholar F. F. Bruce wrote this about Paul: "Where love is the compelling power, there is no sense of strain or conflict or bondage in doing what is right: the man or woman who is compelled by Jesus' love and empowered by his Spirit does the will of God from the heart. For (as Paul could say from experience) 'where the Spirit of the Lord is, there the heart is free'" (2 Corinthians 3:17).

The question is, are you here to serve or be served?

Paul himself wrote to the Corinthians, "For though I am free from all men, I have made myself a slave to all, so that I may win more . . . To the weak I became weak, that I might win the weak; I have become all things to all men, so that I may by all means save some. I do all things for the sake of the gospel, so that I may become a fellow partaker of it" (1 Corinthians 9:19, 22-23).

The motive of love and service calls us to look downward in society and this becomes the light of a godly example the world needs in time of darkness. The will to gain power and the motive to climb up the social ladder is so easily corrupted by sin. Satan was the one who said, "I will ascend, I will make myself like God." Isaiah's words are thought by many to contain a biblical description of Satan himself: "How you have fallen from heaven, O star of the morning, son of the dawn! You have been cut down to the earth, you who have weakened the nations! But you said in your heart, 'I will ascend to heaven. I will raise my throne above the stars of God and I will sit on the mount of assembly in the recesses of the north. I will ascend above the heights of the clouds. I will make myself like the Most High'" (Isaiah 14:12-14).

Human ambition says, "It is right for me to climb up the ladder of success, whatever the cost to myself or others. I will rise to take the top position in the organization's power structure and do whatever it takes to come in first and not last!" The Egyptians built massive pyramids as symbols of what they considered divine and eternal. It was a picture of their society—a few people at the top with power, money, and other privileges, and a great mass of poor people and slaves at the bottom. The more people at the bottom, the greater the pyramid. Many governments, business organizations, and even some churches today are shaped like those pyramids.

The way of God's kingdom and the way of freedom say, "I will not seek to climb the pyramid but continue to walk on the level ground like a simple man or woman who is there to serve. Moreover, I will bow down to worship the true God. I will lay my life down every day in ordinary ways to serve God and others. In service, I find my gift, my passion, my inheritance, my destiny, and my reward. In worship and bowing down I discover God's power and goodness everywhere!" The inspired psalmist sang: "Where can I go from Your Spirit? Or where can I flee from Your presence? If I ascend to heaven, You are there; If I make my bed in Sheol, behold, You are there. If I take the wings of the dawn, if I dwell in the remotest part of the sea, even there Your hand will lead me and Your right hand will lay hold of me" (Psalm139:7-10).

Down is up in God's kingdom, but Jesus too was tempted to climb up. The gospel writer and disciple Matthew wrote, "Then the devil took Him into the holy city and had Him stand on the pinnacle of the temple, and said to Him, 'If You are the Son of God, throw Yourself down; for it is written, "He will command His angels concerning you" and "on their hands they will bear You up so that You will not strike Your foot against a stone"''' (Matthew 4:5-6).

The great temple in Jerusalem was the highest building in the land, and it was built on top of Mount Moriah and nestled among the hills of Judea. It was not only a topographically high place, but it also represented the highest religious point in the nation. Satan tempted Jesus to make His ministry into a huge religious spectacle that would make people gasp in amazement and then swear they had witnessed God's hand of redemption. Jesus refused.

Then the devil tempted Jesus with political power and the influence of money. "Again, the devil took Him to a very high mountain and showed Him all the kingdoms of the world and their glory; and he said to Him, 'All these things I will give You, if You fall down and worship me.' Then Jesus said to him, 'Go, Satan! For it is written, "You shall worship the Lord your God, and serve Him only."' Then the devil left Him; and behold, angels came and began to minister to Him" (Matthew 4:8-11).

Instead of seeking the highest point, Jesus took the lowest one. He chose the road of love and service, a road that led through humiliation, suffering, and death to the brightness of His kingdom. No human eyes were watching when Jesus made those decisions that set us free from sin. But the angels saw and came to serve Him. Freedom requires commitment and struggle, but it is the destiny of true disciples. For those who choose to follow Jesus, the same Spirit who raised Him from His grave is given to each of us as a down payment of our inheritance. Paul the apostle wrote,

> Do nothing from selfishness or empty conceit, but with humility of mind regard one another as more important than yourselves; do not merely look out for your own personal interests, but also for the interests of others. Have this attitude in yourselves which was also in Christ Jesus, who, emptied Himself, like a bond-servant, humbled Himself becoming obedient to the point of death on a cross. For this reason, also God highly exalted Him, and gave Him the name which is above every name, so that at the name of Jesus EVERY KNEE WILL BOW and that every tongue will confess that Jesus is Lord, to the glory of God the Father. (Philippians 2:3-11)

Looking back after reading the inspired stories of the Bible, who would you rather be, Joseph or the Pharaoh of Egypt at the time of the famines mentioned in Genesis? The Pharaoh was considered a god by his people and was arguably the most powerful man in the world of his era. But today, billions of people know Joseph's name and story and hardly anyone can name that pharaoh.

What about in the days of Moses and the exodus? Who would you rather be, Moses or the Pharaoh he confronted in

Egypt four hundred years after Joseph? Would you rather be the prophet Daniel or Nebuchadnezzar in Babylon? Jesus, the Son of God, or Pontius Pilate, the Roman governor? Of course, we would choose Joseph, Moses, Daniel, and Jesus. Each of these men took the low road and spoke truth to the powerful people of their world. But Joseph was a slave and a prisoner for thirteen years. Moses was a fugitive for forty. Daniel was a foreign captive and endured the lions' den and, of course, Jesus washed His disciples' feet and then went to the cross. The low road is the path to freedom from bondage and striving.

Discussion Questions:

1. Do I know any people who are like slaves to the drive for success?
2. How can I find and walk the lower path to freedom in my life?
3. Will God help me through difficult areas where I cannot help myself?

Prayer Point:

Lord, please guard my heart from selfish ambition even in ministry. Jesus, You are the way, the truth, and the life for me and for us all who seek to be Your disciples.

Chapter 28

Other People Hold the Keys

Because we are all made in God's image, after God, people represent the highest value in heaven and on earth. Setting aside the eternal value of a human soul, all of the things that are considered valuable in our world, like food, shelter, security, money, political power, family, fame, even human love are controlled by and can be supplied by other people. After God's grace and favor, it is recognizing the value of other people that determines earthly success or failure in our lives.

The apostle Paul emphasized the importance of others in our pursuit of Christlikeness. He wrote, "Do nothing from selfishness or empty conceit, but with humility of mind regard one another as more important than yourselves. Do not merely look out for your own personal interests, but also for the interests of others" (Philippians 2:3-4).

Jesus said that loving others and working to meet their needs is the way to greatness in God's kingdom (Matthew 20:25-28). This is the way to greatness in our modern societies as well. Loving and serving your neighbor in practical ways is the secret of effective politics. Take the example of Mahatma Gandhi, who led his nation, India, to independence from Britain using nonviolent means. These statements are attributed to him: "You must be the change you wish to see in the world. The best way to find yourself is to lose yourself in the service of others." Gandhi, a Hindu, learned much from reading the Bible and wrote, "What does Jesus mean to me? To me, He was one of the greatest teachers humanity has ever had," and "Jesus lived and died in vain if He did not teach us to regulate the whole of life by the eternal law of love."

During the 1960s, the Reverend Martin Luther King mobilized millions of both black and white Americans to march in nonviolent support of civil rights in the United States. These powerful demonstrations touched the conscience and changed the culture of a nation. In his now famous "I Have a Dream" speech in 1963, Reverend King said, "I have a dream that my four little children will one day live in a nation where they will not be judged by the color of their skin but by the content of their character." Reverend King became a courageous voice speaking out for parents and children across America. He also became an example worldwide of the power in a leader to bring change by giving people without political power a movement and a voice.

Nelson Mandala in South Africa is another example of a leader who brought change for the good to his nation through sacrifice and by serving uneducated and ordinary people. Mandela spent twenty-seven years confined as a political prisoner and then was released to lead his African National Congress party to an election victory that ended apartheid in South Africa.

It is not necessary to agree with all the beliefs and practices of these men to see that they achieved something great for their people. All of them (like the Good Samaritan in Jesus' teaching) produced powerful results by tirelessly helping poor and relatively powerless people. The great prophet Isaiah urges all of us to consider how God empowers the poor. "Trust in the LORD forever, For in GOD the LORD, we have an everlasting Rock. For He has brought low those who dwell on high, the unassailable city; He lays it low, He lays it low to the ground, He casts it to the dust. The foot will trample it, the feet of the afflicted, the steps of the helpless" (Isaiah 26:4-6).

Of course, apart from the Lord, there are no perfect people and even great leaders have "feet of clay." There are countless ways to distort and corrupt the truth that power in politics comes through sacrificially helping others. But the fact that parts of our cities have tawdry neon lights and garish LCD displays does not negate the beauty and power of the sun that rises every morning. God's Spirit radiates truth to all, saint and sinner alike, in an imperfect, broken world. Jesus Himself said, "He [God] causes His sun to rise on the evil and the good and sends rain on the righteous and the unrighteous" (Matthew 5:45).

Many notable business successes have resulted from

the motive of practically loving and serving your neighbor. It has been said that the unprecedented success of the American free-market economy in the last century or two is the result of a system that encourages even unrepentant sinners and atheists to act like "Good Samaritans." That is, if you see people around you with legitimate needs and if you make good decisions and work hard to provide what they need for a reasonable price, the economy will reward you with money and even fame. God's divine command to "love your neighbor" can also result in businesses that are blessed.

When automobiles were invented in 1886 by Karl Benz in Germany, Henry Ford was a young man with a passion for engineering from a farming background in the middle of America. Twenty years later, automobiles were still, for the most part, hand-built playthings for the rich. Henry Ford was an extraordinary leader but may not have been the most likable person. He had an abrasive personality and held strongly anti-Semitic views that were an early encouragement to Adolf Hitler's political rise in Germany. But Ford saw in the automobile an invention so useful that he thought every American family should have one. His ambition to provide an affordable family car led to the invention of the assembly line and introduction of the Model T in 1908. Its incredible success changed the world and made Henry Ford one of the wealthiest and best-known Americans of his day.

The McDonald brothers, Richard and Maurice, opened their first California hot dog stand in 1937. Their vision, which developed over the next few years, was to provide affordable restaurant meals to working-class families who were pouring into California after the Second World War. They switched to hamburgers and, after streamlining production, began franchising their growing business in 1953. In 1954 they partnered with Ray Kroc, who later bought them out and made McDonald's the most successful restaurant business in history with branches and a brand name known around the world. It all started when the McDonald brothers worked hard to create a better way to literally serve their neighbors.

Because of God's love for the whole world, helping to meet the needs of other people will always be the key to fruitfulness.

Henry Ford with automobiles and the McDonald brothers with hamburgers are two examples of American entrepreneurs who found successful ways to provide valuable products to American families living on limited incomes. More recently, computer scientists, business leaders, entrepreneurs, and academics, along with thousands of others, developed technology that enabled computing power to move out of costly specialized laboratories into the daily lives of working people and even into the hands of school children. This resulted in the present-day economic explosion of the internet, enabling e-mail, video streaming, online shopping, and social media that changed the modern world. Will these advances be used to bring faith and a better life to millions or as tools of exploitation and control?

Because of God's love for the whole world, helping to

meet the needs of other people will always be the key to fruitfulness. Discipleship includes the discipline of keeping our motives pure, especially when our best efforts begin to reap positive results. With success in the eyes of the public, whether in ministry or business or any other endeavor, comes the temptation to control or manipulate others in order to serve ourselves.

True disciples recognize that our gifts and the strength to use them come only from God and we are always accountable to Him. Love for God and love for our neighbor are His two most important commands. Paul wrote that "the love of God has been poured out within our hearts through the Holy Spirit who was given to us" (Romans 5:5). We may tend to interpret that love as an emotion or something related to Christian faith and to de-emphasize God's intended expression of His love through an almost infinite variety of talents, skills, and professional callings. Some people have been given ministry gifts that are for use in the church. However, God's love for the world means every person's God-given gift can be used to serve others. That is the kind of divine love that releases God's purposes for all and ultimately changes nations.

Discussion Questions:

1. How can I, by trying to meet the needs of other people, make progress toward building my own relationship with God?
2. Why does God put such a high value on how I treat other people in my life?
3. Will God show me particular people I should love and help me develop Christlike attitudes and actions toward them?

Prayer Point:

Lord, after loving You with all my heart, help me to love the people You have placed around me and seek to help them in spiritual as well as practical ways.

Part 4

Law and Grace

Lovingkindness and truth have met together; Righteousness and peace have kissed each other. (Psalm 85:10)

Chapter 29

The Value of Law

In Romans chapter 3, the apostle Paul makes the point that the Jews and Gentiles fall short of God's requirements so that the entire world is under sin and will be judged by God. We know from other New Testament scriptures that all of God's lawfulness is embodied in Jesus, who is the exact representation of God in human form. However, the truth of God's lawfulness is not just for those who are spiritually inclined but for everyone, since He governs the entire universe. God created the heavens and the earth so all of His creation, even in sin and rebellion, ultimately is witness to His lawful and righteous rule.

First of all, everywhere we look, we find law. There is

an order that underlies all of the vast and seemingly chaotic world we live in. While scientists are still learning the laws that govern the natural world and the universe, both the nature of our planet and that of the universe beyond it are lawful. This consistent orderliness is what creates the possibility of scientific investigation. Technological development is impossible without a lawful universe.

All of creation declares the lawfulness of its Creator.

Having worked in the computer industry since the early days before personal computers, I witnessed the rise of computer science, software engineering, and artificial intelligence. An entirely new rules-based world emerged based on mathematical logic and the predictability of electrons moving through highly complex "hardware" microprocessors. Today's smartphones are very sophisticated machines based on complicated mathematical algorithms, but they are designed to appear simple and easy to use! Modern medicine is much the same. We thank God for blood tests, X-rays, ultrasounds, CT, PET, and MRI scans. These vital medical procedures are based on laws of physics and other laws that govern the proper functioning of the human body as an entire system. We know these laws go right down to the molecular and even subatomic level. Music is also lawful. Sports are lawful. All of creation declares the lawfulness of its Creator.

What if you developed persistent pressure and pain in your chest and were taken to a hospital emergency room? Would you accept a physical examination conducted by one of the cafeteria cooks instead of a trained cardiologist? Of course not! What's the difference? The cardiologist has been required by civil law to study for years in order to learn thousands of other laws that govern the functioning of a human body and especially the heart. That doctor uses an understanding of the laws of medicine to determine what is wrong with you and prescribe appropriate treatment.

Our freedom to live healthy lives is helped by medical professionals who take the time and effort to learn those laws. Because there are a seemingly endless number of laws to learn and some of them are very subtle, research scientists are continually studying and experimenting to extend the frontiers of human knowledge. With that knowledge comes the power to stop epidemics and conquer deadly diseases that still take the lives of millions.

In our home congregation on Mt. Carmel, worship of God in the form of music and singing is very important. We have musically talented singers and songwriters in our community and a gifted worship director. The guiding vision is to restore Hebrew language worship to Israel using contemporary sounds and modern instruments.

One Sabbath, a guest musician from another country was invited to sit in during the weekly worship celebration meeting. His instrument that day was the soprano saxophone. Unfamiliar with the other musicians and not knowing most of the songs, he played along in the background for a while. However, at a certain point, he stood up and soloed for about four or five seconds. In those few moments, the feeling in the entire room changed. People's hearts were touched. Around me, I saw hands raised toward heaven, even tears on some faces. He elevated the spiritual atmosphere for everyone by playing less than twenty musical notes on his instrument!

Afterward, I went to him and asked, "How were you able to do that?" Realizing I was asking about his short solo, he answered, "Oh, after about thirty years of study and practice!" It turned out that as a boy he and his brother were tested by a local music professor invited by their parents to determine if they had an "ear" for music. After that, he spent decades in private music lessons, music academies, orchestras, jazz bands, studio sessions, and worship groups. In short, he knew a lot about the rules of music. So when it came time to improvise and play a few notes to help worshippers touch heaven, he knew which notes to play. Music is defined by multitudes of musical laws, and freedom results when we master enough of them to play what is needed.

In the year 1215, King John of England signed the "Great Charter," called the *Magna Carta*, which established that even the king would be subject to the law of the land. It also guaranteed the rights of individuals to justice and a fair trial. Since the days of the Magna Carta until now, the rule of law has proven to be the single most important political factor in the relative success and prosperity of nations.

Imagine that you are a businessman who wants to establish a manufacturing company and the two locations available to you are in Somalia and Singapore. Let's say you choose Somalia, which has a modern history as one of the most lawless countries in the world. You build the manufacturing plant, purchase resources, hire and train your staff, and then the day comes when it is time to go into

Good law matters when it comes to business and prosperity.

production. You arrive to cut the ribbon and begin work and at that moment the local warlord arrives in his pickup truck with several AK-47-toting "assistants." He says, "I'm the law around here and I say, 'Your factory is now my factory!'" As a result, you can leave but your investment is lost.

However, if it was Singapore and a local gangster or corrupt official tried to force you to pay "protection" or a heavy "facilitation fee" for your business to open, you have recourse to the law, the courts, and law enforcement agencies. None of this is perfect in Singapore but good enough to ensure that in the end, your company will be able to go into business. The overall effect is that more businesses and services want to be based in Singapore and so the standard of living is considerably higher there than in Somalia. Good law matters when it comes to business and prosperity.

I once read a book titled *12 Books That Changed the World*. According to the author, one of those great books is *The Rule Book of Association Football*, which contains the rules of the game that eventually gave birth to other games like rugby, American football, and Australian-rules football. It is what Americans call soccer. This game is played and watched by more people in the world than any other sport in history.

I was told that when the World Cup is being played, the majority of humans on earth either watch or participate in some way. Football is something that almost every nation on earth shares and it is all based on a handful of simple rules.

If you change even one of the rules, you change the entire game for everybody! The "laws" of football bring intense enjoyment to billions of people every year. My conclusion is that there is no freedom without law. Bad laws restrict freedom; good laws mean more freedom. Does that mean the perfect laws of God's kingdom bring perfect freedom? In the following chapters of this section we will see how God rules His kingdom with perfect law.

Discussion Questions:

1. How does law affect my daily life as a citizen?
2. Can I think of an example of good laws that provide and protect freedom?
3. Are there some laws in our society that should be changed? Why?

Prayer Point:

Lord, please reveal the lawfulness of Your character to me through Your word. Show me evidence that You originally intended our world to be lawful and designed it as a place for us to thrive.

Chapter 30

Lawful or Lawless?

In Exodus 19, God became King of Israel in the wilderness of the desert. He called the great prophet, Moses, to Mount Sinai and in the next chapter, Exodus 20, God gave him the law of the kingdom, including the Ten Commandments. Virtually the first thing God revealed about His way of being King is that He chooses to rule lawfully. In the days of Moses, all the nations were ruled by kings and God's kind of lawfulness would have been a radical departure from the standard procedure of most of them. Even if codes of laws existed, the king himself was outside of that system and essentially lawless. The human king of most tribes and nations not only made the laws, he *was* the law. If Pharaoh in Egypt or Nebuchadnezzar in Babylon liked you on Monday, you were in a good position; your family and your business were also in a good position and you had a future in the nation. However, if one of those kings for any reason did not like you on Tuesday, everything changed. You, along with your family and your business, had no future in the nation.

Virtually the first thing God revealed about His way of being King is that He chooses to rule lawfully.

At Sinai, God's actions expressed to Israel, "That is not how My kingdom operates. In My kingdom, I will tell you in advance what is required and then I will always honor My word. I won't change. Therefore, you always know where you stand with Me. No need to flatter Me. Don't try to manipulate Me. You cannot buy My favor. Just do as I say and it will be well with you!"

Later, Moses wrote in the book of Deuteronomy, "The Lord will make you the head and not the tail, and you only will be above, and you will not be underneath, if you listen to the commandments of the Lord your God, which I charge you today, to observe them carefully" (Deuteronomy 28:13).

In the New Testament era, the apostle Paul emphasized the point that the new Gentile believers were not required to obey the laws given by God to Israel but needed only faith in Jesus to enter the kingdom. Paul wrote that the Gentiles did not need to first become Jews to find the path to eternal life. However, this did not change the fundamentally lawful quality of God's kingdom. Once Gentile Christians entered the kingdom by faith, they were still required to understand and submit to the framework of God's laws.

In the Christian world today, we still read Paul's epistles to new Gentile believers as if they contain everything we need to know about God's kingdom. Many Christians want to skip the laws of the Old Testament but the apostle Paul, who wrote much of the New Testament did not feel that way. Paul said of himself, "Circumcised the eighth day, of the nation of Israel, of the tribe of Benjamin, a Hebrew of Hebrews; as to the Law, a Pharisee; as to zeal, a persecutor of the church; as to the righteousness which is in the Law, found blameless" (Philippians 3:5-6). He saw in Jesus Christ the divine example of the perfectly lawful life, the embodiment of all that God requires in His law. Paul taught all his new Gentile Christians to know and believe the Hebrew Scriptures so that they would understand God's laws and abide in the lawfulness that Jesus embodied. Remember, in Paul's day, the New Testament as we know it had not been completely written and was therefore not considered part of the Bible.

Because we Christians tend to overemphasize the New Testament today and put special weight on Paul's letters, our tendency when confronted with God's laws in the Bible is to say, "We are not under law but under grace." This seems like a way to solve the issue of the law. We simply cut the Bible into two parts and say that only the New Testament has real authority for us. But the New Testament was written by Jews (including Paul) who deeply understood that God rules a lawful kingdom, so it has much to say about God's laws. Let's look at what is written in the New Testament about the lack of law.

We will start by following a word in the original Greek language of the New Testament, *anomia,* which means the lack of law. In the *Septuagint*, the Greek language Old Testament used by some of the New Testament writers, the word used for Torah, or law, is *nomos,* from which the word *anomia* (literally, the lack of law) is derived. *Anomia* or lawlessness in the New Testament is a serious offense that strikes directly at the foundations of God's kingdom. Jesus taught His disciples that the days preceding His return would be marked by an increase in *anomia*.

In Matthew chapter twenty-four, Jesus described the times before His return: "Because lawlessness [*anomia*] is increased, most people's love will grow cold" (Matthew 24:12). Jesus didn't say that people's love in the end times would grow cold for lack of kindness or mercy from God. Jesus taught that people who have some love for God will lose it because they are not sufficiently protected by the structure of divine law.

When he wrote about the end times, the apostle Paul described the coming world leader called the Antichrist as a man of *anomia,* or "lawlessness" (2 Thessalonians 2:3). He wrote that Jesus' return will not occur before the lawlessness of the Antichrist is revealed. Paul did not write that the Antichrist would be characterized by oppression, deception, or violence. He wrote that the Antichrist will be a man who embodies rejection of God's lawful reign and said that this "mystery of lawlessness is already at work" (2 Thessalonians 2:7).

Those who consider themselves followers of Jesus will not be immune from practicing lawlessness. Jesus made this clear in His Sermon on the Mount: "Not everyone who says to Me, "Lord, Lord," will enter the kingdom of heaven, but he who does the will of My Father who is in heaven will enter. Many will say to Me on that day, "Lord, Lord, did we not prophesy in Your name, and in Your name cast out demons, and in Your name perform many miracles?" And then I will declare to them, "I never knew you; depart from Me, you who practice lawlessness [*anomia*]" (Matthew 7:21-23).

According to Jesus, the abilities to work miracles and to prophesy are not the ultimate signs of acceptance by God. Living under God's reign is what it means to be known by God in His kingdom. According to Jesus' disciple John, lawlessness is another word for sin. He wrote, "Everyone who practices sin also practices lawlessness; and sin is lawlessness" (1John 3:4). If lawlessness is another word for sin, then righteousness would be a way of describing life under God's lawful reign. The following chapters focus on what disciples need in order to live lives of freedom, joy, and fruitfulness within the structure of God's kingdom. God's amazing grace and life-giving Spirit encourage us and guide our steps as we walk the lawful path that leads to eternal life.

Discussion Questions:

1. What are some examples of lawlessness I could point to in the society where I live?
2. Is rejection of God's lawful reign a sin?
3. Can I point to examples of lawlessness among Christians?

Prayer Point:

Lord, help me to recognize the spirit of lawlessness that is at work around me. Guard my heart and mind from being drawn into lawlessness so that my attitudes and actions will direct others to your kingdom.

Chapter 31

Jesus' Law

Many consider Jesus' Sermon on the Mount, which begins in Matthew chapter five, to be His most important teaching. There is an interesting parallel in the Bible between what is written in Exodus chapters nineteen and twenty and the New Testament gospel of Matthew chapters four and five. In Exodus nineteen, God met the twelve tribes of Israel in the desert and chose them as His kingdom, His covenant nation. In the following chapter, God called His servant, the prophet Moses, up to Mount Sinai in the desert and gave him the law for the nation of Israel.

In Matthew four, Jesus chose his twelve Jewish disciples, who (because of Israel's twelve tribes) were meant to represent a new redeemed people of Israel. In Matthew five, Jesus called the chosen twelve up to a mountain near the Sea of Galilee and gave them the law of His kingdom. He directly addressed the issue of God's kingdom and Torah in His most famous sermon. He said: "Do not think that I came to abolish the Law or the Prophets; I did not come to abolish but to fulfill. For truly I say to you, until heaven and earth pass away, not the smallest letter or stroke shall pass from the Law until all is accomplished. Whoever then annuls one of the least of these commandments, and teaches others to do the same, shall be called least in the kingdom of heaven; but whoever keeps and teaches them, he shall be called great in the kingdom of heaven" (Matthew 5:17-19).

According to Jesus, God still rules His kingdom lawfully. Jesus said He did not come to destroy or take away God's law, but to fulfill it. The Greek word for fulfill is *pleroma,* which in other places in the New Testament is used to describe the totality or fullness of God that is found in Jesus Christ. Some Christians today think that Jesus meant to finish with the law by saying He had come to fulfill it. This would have the same effect as abolishing or destroying it. When Paul writes in Colossians 1:19 and 2:9 that Jesus is the *pleroma* of God, he is not saying that now we can do away with God because we have Jesus. Paul's position was that Jesus does not replace God's law but He is the full embodiment, a perfect model for our benefit, of what God intended in the law.

From Jesus' Sermon on the Mount, it is clear that His teaching on the law was meant to establish principles of interpretation of the Torah rather than to just add new commandments. Jesus' teaching in Matthew chapter five is not an exhaustive commentary on every statute of the law. His intention was ultimately to reveal God's *purposes* in giving the law. Jesus' teaching described not a different law but rather a new and higher way to approach the living God who is our reigning King in God's kingdom.

He taught and demonstrated to His disciples a manner of living in greater holiness and obedience to God than the way of the legalistic Pharisees who had substituted their religious traditions and interpretations of God's laws for God's direct authority. The Pharisees were intent on literally keeping all 613 of the commands in the Torah but Jesus was teaching and demonstrating a life that fulfilled God's commands and purposes using the power of faith. He said to His followers, "For I say to you that unless your righteousness surpasses that of the scribes and Pharisees, you will not enter the kingdom of heaven" (Matthew 5:20).

However, surely Jesus' disciples had questions in their minds after the first portion of Jesus' teaching that day. Did they think He was reinforcing biblical laws concerning permitted foods, forever outlawing pork and seafood for His followers? What did Jesus mean by speaking about "fulfilling the law?" No doubt knowing that everyone would have questions, Jesus continued with six illustrations about what He meant regarding God's law in His kingdom. In most of them, Jesus quoted the Torah and then said "but I say unto you . . .," giving His interpretation.

In these six examples, Jesus was not adding six new commandments to the existing commandments in the Torah. In this, His most famous sermon, He was teaching His disciples New Testament principles for interpreting the whole of God's law. Perhaps one could say that He chose six illustrations, one illustration short of seven, the perfect number, to show His followers that the list was meant to be incomplete. It should be completed as His disciples lived out the intention, purpose, or spirit of His teaching.

In the Sermon on the Mount, Jesus' words are more than just His good recommendations for a happy life. They are foundational to our understanding of God's kingdom. Jesus' first illustration had to do with murder, something almost all societies view as unlawful and a criminal offense. "You have heard that the ancients were told, 'You shall not commit murder' and 'Whoever commits murder shall be liable to the court.' But I say to you that everyone who is angry with his brother shall be guilty before the court; and whoever says to his brother, 'You good-for-nothing,' shall be guilty before the supreme court; and whoever says, 'You fool,' shall be guilty enough to go into the fiery hell" (Matthew 5:21-22).

Here, Jesus quoted from the Ten Commandments. Often spoken of as universal moral laws for all humanity, these commandments are part of God's law for Israel, and the sixth commandment is against murder. The purpose, or the spirit, of the law according to Jesus is to quench the inner fire of anger and hatred before it becomes the act of murder. Jesus was teaching that the sin of murder does not begin when we pick up a weapon in our hand. The sin begins with anger that is harbored and nurtured in our hearts. The law of Jesus' kingdom deals with sin at its root, at the source of transgression. God's ultimate purpose is reconciliation and peace, the healing of wounded and broken relationships, replacing anger with love.

In His second of six illustrations, Jesus said: "You have heard that it was said, 'You shall not commit adultery'; but I say to you that everyone who looks at a woman with lust for her has already committed adultery with her in his heart" (Matthew 5:27-28).

The purpose of this law is purity of heart. God's plan is to cleanse His people from sexual sin, starting deep within the heart. Jesus had previously taught in the same sermon that the pure in heart are blessed with the ability to see God. Anyone who has ever wrestled with the sin of pornography or sexual addiction will testify that it takes a continual outpouring of God's grace to be free. In the Bible, Job said, "I have made a covenant with my eyes; How then could I gaze at a virgin?" (Job 31:1). Jesus said that this kind of purity in the inner man of the heart is the law of His kingdom.

Jesus' Sermon on the Mount continued with His laws concerning marriage, divorce, and the keeping of promises. God hates divorce and His covenant with Israel was compared in the Scriptures to marriage. One of the primary values in God's kingdom is faithfulness. God knows that in marriage, a bedrock of mutual commitment to resolve hurts and differences is essential. In most cases, when a husband and wife decide together to deal with the issues that are destructive to their marriage, reconciliation will result. Jesus forbade divorce except when there was sexual unfaithfulness, and He said that remarriage for anyone wrongly divorced is a sin that will harm God's blessings (Matthew 5:32).

Jesus also taught that God is a God of truth and that He hates lying, but the devil is a liar by nature and the "father of lies" (John 8:44). The principle in Jesus' Sermon on the Mount is that in God's kingdom, the standard is honesty. In some nations today, before testifying in a court of law, you are required to publicly swear an oath of honesty, sometimes with your hand on a Bible. After swearing that oath, if you then lie, it is considered a crime called perjury and it is punishable by a fine or imprisonment.

In the days of Jesus, people swore by many things considered sacred and Jesus condemned the practice. He said, "But I say to you, make no oath at all . . . let your statement be, 'Yes, yes' *or* 'No, no'; anything beyond these is of evil" (Matthew 5:34, 37). Jesus taught that in His kingdom it is not necessary to swear at all; honesty and integrity should be the norm.

From the teaching of Jesus, it is easy to see how deeply His sayings have become embedded in the language and culture of the English-speaking world. Phrases like "turn the other cheek" and "the meek will inherit the earth" and "salt of the earth" and "light of the world" are familiar to many. However, it is important to see them in their proper biblical context. "You have heard that it was said, 'An eye for an eye, and a tooth for a tooth.' But I say to you, do not resist an evil person; but whoever slaps you on your right cheek, turn the other to him also" (Matthew 5:38-39).

Jesus was opening the door to understanding one of the central pillars of God's reign in His heavenly kingdom. This is the nature and value of God's mercy and mankind's universal need for it. The relationship between justice and mercy is what Jesus described as being among the "weightier provisions of the law" (Matthew 23:23). The question is do we want justice or mercy? Are we seeking the satisfaction of revenge or the peace of reconciliation? If we want mercy for ourselves and those we love, how can we receive it without giving it to others as well? However, giving mercy requires the strength to overcome personal pain and loss. Jesus was also teaching that your endurance, the strength to "absorb" pain, is almost always stronger than your enemy's power to afflict you. Any boxer who gets into a ring expecting to be hit only once will never become a champion. The trophy goes to the fighter who is still standing when the final bell rings. The strength to turn the other cheek is the power we all need to be victors in life.

The Master taught us, "You have heard that it was said, 'You shall love your neighbor and hate your enemy.' But I say to you, love your enemies and pray for those who persecute you" (Matthew 5:43-44). Jesus' law to love your enemy must be among the greatest truths of His kingdom. The principle is that it is preferable and more powerful to win the heart and mind of your enemy than to defeat him in war. Which of the two, in the end, will bring real and lasting peace? In times of conflict and war, the resulting harm is deeper than wounds in the flesh. Even after violence subsides, the survivors on both sides bear inner pain and dysfunction that continue to destroy lives. Justice must be diligently sought after and rigorously applied to the guilty.

Still, in a multitude of cases, complete justice will never be achieved. The only solution in places like Northern Ireland, South Africa, Rwanda, and Syria is to seek peace and reconciliation through the recognition of shared grief and pain. Hatred and genocide become possible when we dehumanize members of another group. Love begins with the recognition of our shared humanity. Only godly love and forgiveness can break the evil cycle of revenge and retribution.

After His six illustrations, Jesus summed up this part of His greatest sermon with the words, "Therefore you are to be perfect, as your heavenly Father is perfect" (Matthew 5:48). This statement connects to the words He used to begin His discourse on the laws of God. He started by telling His disciples that unless their righteousness surpassed that of merely religious people, they would never enter His kingdom. Still, there is a big difference between simply being "better" and being "perfect." Jesus was telling us to keep our minds fixed on things above because God's standards and, therefore, the goal of all Christians cannot be defined by even the best solutions this world has to offer.

I have always enjoyed watching world-class athletes compete in track and field. They train so hard and make feats impossible to most other humans look easy. One of my favorite sports to watch is high jumping. They start at the incredible height of close to two meters and jump backward! The way it works is when everyone has had a chance to jump at a certain level, the bar is raised and all the successful ones try again. This process is repeated until finally there is only one jumper who is successful, and that person is declared the winner. Then in some cases, they raise the bar again to see if there a new world or Olympic record is achieved. As a result, the bar is finally raised until no one is successful.

Reading in the Bible about God's laws, it seems to be a lot like high jumping. Let's say that God's requirement in the Torah is represented by placing the bar at a certain level. In the Ten Commandments, God said, "You shall not commit murder." Now we all have to try to jump that bar. Those who fail are punished. Although some do fail, most of us have learned to jump at least that high. When Jesus said that having a heart free of murderous anger (Matthew 5:22) was the law for His disciples was He saying that since He has fulfilled the laws of God there is to be no more "jumping" in God's kingdom? Was He saying that now we have unlimited grace and mercy guaranteed in the New Testament, so we can remove the "bar" of God's lawful requirement against murder? No, Jesus did not say that. What He did teach in His Sermon on the Mount was that rather than removing the bar, He was raising it to the level of perfection! However, faced with these requirements, we are not only all guilty before God's laws, but we are destined to fail. Even if we love Jesus and want to serve Him with all our hearts, most of us simply cannot "jump" high enough to win the prize of righteousness and our King's approval. If we have to successfully obey these perfect laws to live in Jesus' kingdom, who will save us from our failure? It is exactly at this point that we discover our desperate need for and the truly amazing quality of God's grace.

Discussion Questions:

1. Did Jesus do away with the laws of the Old Testament?
2. Does Jesus as the Son of God rule God's kingdom lawfully?
3. Since I am now a Christian must I seek to obey the words of Jesus as King of God's kingdom here on earth?

Prayer Point:

Lord, give me clarity and courage when I read the words of Jesus in His Sermon on the Mount. Help me reach out in faith toward obedience that seems beyond my human abilities.

Chapter 32

Grace is Amazing

King David, the inspired psalmist, sang, "The law of the Lord is perfect, restoring the soul; the testimony of the Lord is sure, making wise the simple" (Psalm 19:7). God's lawful nature is expressed in His creation and His sovereign rule of the universe. But we live below heaven on the earth in an imperfect, fallen world. The nations and economies where we live always need better civil and tax laws. Our societies and cultures have moral laws, religious laws, and traditional laws that define "good" or acceptable behavior but even these laws can be sometimes cruel and unfair.

We are constantly surrounded by law made by other humans. Laws in general are essential and valuable. We all need the protection, authority, and freedoms they define and guard. But laws made by humans can never be perfect. The very best our political leaders and legal systems can do is make laws and rules that somehow reflect or point to God's perfect rule. Much of the time, laws created by humans do much less than point to God's wisdom and justice.

God's perfect laws, combined with His amazing grace, mix with each other like the different ingredients of a divine "concrete."

Laws may be essential to our lives, but a world that knows only law is cold and impersonal because justice, by necessity, is impartial. A world governed only by law eventually becomes unjust because people who are skilled in law will take advantage of those who don't understand it. A world with only law is also unforgiving. Think of the laws of nature. Animals kill and devour other animals mercilessly. Nature's law is survival of the fittest and strongest. Yes, nature is essentially ruthless and we should all be aware that humans can be crueler to each other than animals are.

Also, laws alone do not and cannot give meaning to our lives. Just knowing the rules of football does not explain why billions of people find the game so interesting, exciting, and emotionally refreshing. The laws of music don't explain why music moves us so powerfully and can even allow us to sense the presence of God and worship Him.

The truth is that law does not stand alone in God's kingdom. It is part of a truth that draws its strength from actually being two truths held together in tension. God's perfect laws, combined with His amazing grace, mix with each other like the different ingredients of a divine "concrete," to create one of the central "pillars" in the house of God's kingdom.

On the one hand, we have God's eternal justice. He will always reward the righteous and punish the transgressor. God is lawful and His rule extends over everything, but alongside of His lawfulness, God is loving, gracious, and merciful by nature. The Bible says that "God is love" (1 John 4:8). God's character overflows with grace, lovingkindness, and mercy. He is always looking for a new opportunity to show His redeeming love.

God's lawfulness defines the rules of life and should convince us that not one of us is able keep all the rules. If you drive, you will probably get a parking or speeding ticket at some time. Even great athletes are given penalties on the playing field. Accomplished musicians will play a wrong note in the middle of a symphony. Unfortunately, your doctor may make a medical misdiagnosis. You're going to lose a friend, forget your wife's or husband's birthday, have trouble with your taxes, or worse. That's life.

Even when we try to keep the rules, we break them and pay the price. The lawfulness of God is there to guide us and humble us, but there is a silver lining to that dark cloud of humiliation. The Bible says that God opposes the proud and gives His grace to the humble and God's grace is simply amazing.

Award-winning author Philip Yancey wrote in his book, *What's So Amazing About Grace?* the following about that special word *grace*. "The many uses of the word in English convince me that grace is indeed amazing—truly our last best word. It contains the essence of the gospel as a drop of water can contain the image of the sun. The world thirsts for grace in ways it does not even recognize; little wonder the hymn 'Amazing Grace' edged its way onto the Top Ten charts two hundred years after composition. For a society that seems adrift, without moorings, I know of no better place to drop an anchor of faith."

When we transgress God's laws in ways that are small or great, we must know several things: God notices everything. Our transgression is never hidden from Him and justice is always due. However, when we humble ourselves before God and by faith reach out for His mercy, we find an unending fountain of His favor freely given to cover the things we did wrong. God has the ability and the authority to wipe our worst sins away! Only God can clean our record so thoroughly that it is as if our sin never happened (Psalm 103:11-12).

But God's law and His grace are two sides of the same great truth. Together, they are essential to the structure of His house. We enter God's house by faith, that is, by believing and trusting in Him. By faith, we do what is humanly not possible, that is, we can go beyond the laws and appeal to the writer of the laws, the Judge Himself. The apostle Paul explains this in biblical language. "But now apart from the Law the righteousness of God has been manifested, being witnessed by the Law and the Prophets, even the righteousness of God through faith in Jesus Christ for all those who believe; for there is no distinction; for all have sinned and fall short of the glory of God, being justified as a gift by His grace through the redemption which is in Christ Jesus" (Romans 3:21-24).

Paul writes in Romans 3:21 that "apart from," that is, *alongside* His law, God displays His righteousness through faith in Jesus and in verse 24 that we are justified, that is, saved as a gift of grace apart from trying to keep God's laws. This points away from God's lawfulness to other parts of His nature, His love and mercy. Faith allows us to follow the path of God's justice into the realm of His tenderness and fatherly love. Our eyes of faith are able to discern the importance of God's law as it defines our need for grace. Paul concludes, "Do we then nullify the Law through faith? May it never be! On the contrary, we establish the Law" (Romans 3:31).

All humans are deeply flawed, and this is why we so desperately need God's grace. When Jesus died on the cross for our sins, the requirement of God's laws did not change. What did change was that for the first time, God's requirements were satisfied—not by us, but by the atoning sacrifice of His own Son. Jesus was the only human to ever fully keep the laws of God. In doing so, He opened the way for us, through belief in Him and *identification with Him,* to be declared righteous by God. Through slow and sometimes painful spiritual growth, we begin to appreciate the meaning and truly amazing quality of God's grace. God loves you and me. He created us to be moral and spiritual champions and believes that is what we all can eventually become.

I have been walking on the path of faith for many years now and hope I'm becoming a more "gracious" person, but God's grace goes far beyond human grace. Most of us start the day out with some grace in our hearts. We give it freely to those whom we love; we give some grace to those who can help us; we give less to those who hurt us; we give none to those who betray us. By the end of the day, we are sometimes completely at the end of our grace. We have used it all up! But God's grace never ends. Like an eternal fountain of life, it keeps pouring and pouring. Alongside His lawfulness, God is eternally gracious by nature.

The gospel message says that when we realize God's standards are not optional, it means an agonizing death to our human efforts to please Him. The good news is that if I put my trust in Jesus and "die" in pursuit of His goals, the same Spirit that raised Jesus from His grave will begin to live in me (Romans 8:11). The power of faith then rises in my heart from the ashes of my human inability. It's no longer me who is alive but God's Spirit who is alive inside of me. I start to believe I can do anything He requires through His power working in my new life. I say with the apostle Paul, "I can do all things through Christ who strengthens me!" (Philippians 4:13).

God is not only the judge of my life's efforts; He is also my spiritual coach, mentor, and loving Father! He is committed to my success so that if I don't give up, I will begin meeting His highest standards (Philippians 1:6). God's grace is more than His mercy, which forgives my sin and failure. His grace is also the enabling power of the Holy Spirit in me to overcome the personal challenges of life and succeed spiritually in a broken world.

Discussion Questions:

1. Why is God's grace so amazing?
2. When have I experienced God's grace in my life?
3. How would I explain the connection between law and grace in God's kingdom?

Prayer Point:

Lord, I want to sing the words to the song "Amazing Grace" with new joy and conviction. Please pour more of Your grace into my life.

Chapter 33

Law and Freedom

God's grace is free, but it is not cheap. "Cheap grace" is a message that lowers the standards of God's laws or casts scorn on the value of divine law as the way God governs His eternal kingdom. There are preachers today who say that the Old Testament is concerned with law, but the New Testament is about grace, and we have to choose between the two. In forcing us toward this false choice, they teach that law means legalism, judgment, and condemnation, but grace is all about love and mercy. Their message is that Jesus paid the entire price for all of our sins once and for all; therefore, we are forever freed from the requirements of God's law by the gift of grace.

What's wrong with that? Didn't Jesus die to give us His salvation as a gift? Doesn't the New Testament teach that we are justified (made righteous before God) by faith in Him? Yes, this is true, but if we stop listening there, we might come to the wrong conclusion about God's reason for saving us by grace.

It is God's moral requirements in His laws that define sin and convict me as a sinner. Before we knew God's laws, we didn't feel a need for divine grace at all. If God has high standards, then we need great grace to be declared by Him as righteous. But if God has low standards, His grace does not need to be that amazing or precious. Any message that overtly or subtly by suggestion reduces the requirements of God's laws cheapens grace.

One fact about human nature is that we all love finding bargains. Like the crowds swarming to a half-price sale in a shopping mall, a pastor or Bible teacher who cheapens grace will find that at least initially a lot of people will be interested in attending his church. However, they may not be ready to go on to become disciples of Jesus.

It is true the Bible teaches that "mercy triumphs over judgment" (James 2:13), but mercy should never *replace* judgment. Mercy only has real value to me when I know I deserve judgment. We receive mercy as a free gift of God's grace and should appreciate it all the more because the Bible teaches that God always has and always will rule His kingdom by law. Mercy always must be the *exception* to the law's unwavering justice.

What if there was a judge in a city who always decided in every case to show mercy? Soon every serial killer, rapist, child molester, and professional gangster would be lining up outside that judge's courtroom. No one would be punished. No one would be compelled to change, and all would go free. Is that God's kind of mercy or simply injustice?

Dietrich Bonhoeffer was a Christian pastor in Germany during the 1930s when Nazism was rising to power. He wrote in *The Cost of Discipleship* that God's mercy is not meant to be applied to everyone as a doctrine, but as a gift given personally and individually by God Himself to those who put their trust in His Son, Jesus.

People are not only saved but also liberated and transformed by the power of God's truth in the process of discipleship.

When God gives mercy, He does not nullify or change His own laws; thus, the one who receives mercy must afterward seek to remain "hidden in Christ," which means to live in a way that meets the demands of God's righteousness. This process is called sanctification and results in discipleship. Bonhoeffer pointed out that justification by faith means that God justifies the sinner but not the sin. When we fall into sin and then turn to God through faith in Jesus, we receive grace to be forgiven, and we are justified, which means restored to righteousness. God says, "You are okay now. Go and sin no more." He isn't saying to us, "Your sins are okay now. Don't worry about it anymore."

The laws of God's kingdom define His character as well as the way He rules. God's intention is to mold us as disciples into the image of His Son, Jesus. God's laws give disciples moral authority and spiritual guidance to be personally changed and then to begin restoring God's purity and love to the world around us. When we live as disciples of the kingdom, deeply embedded sins like self-hatred, the bondage of addictions, unforgiveness, and other dysfunctions will yield to the power of God's lawful reign.

People are not only saved but also liberated and transformed by the power of God's truth in the process of discipleship. When Bonhoeffer served as a pastor in Germany, that nation was called the "cradle of the Reformation" and thought to be among the most "Christian" countries in Europe. However, the preaching of cheap grace had *Christianized* Germany but not transformed it. The majority of German Protestants believed they were saved but lacked the moral authority and personal integrity to resist Nazism. The devastation that resulted was one of the hidden costs of cheap grace.

The road to freedom is like a highway with two ditches, one on each side of the road. The highway is called "lawfulness." It means trusting God, obeying His Word and the leading of His Spirit. The ditch on one side of the highway is called "legalism." It describes a man-made system of rules that takes the place of God Himself. We can try to live by keeping the rules and end up ignoring the rule-giver! The ditch on the other side is called "lawlessness" and it is when we obey no law at all in the name of freedom, grace, or for any other reason. Personal freedom and growth in discipleship mean staying in our lane on the highway where God's protection, guidance, and authority are ours!

God's laws are meant to protect His people and to provide a framework for personal freedom. This includes the freedom to prosper in our work. Consider these first verses from Psalm 1 a portion of Scripture that must have been close to Jesus' heart. Loving and respecting God's laws leads to fruitfulness in life. "How blessed is the man who does not walk in the counsel of the wicked, nor stand in the path of sinners, nor sit in the seat of scoffers! But his delight is in the law of the Lord and in His law he meditates day and night. He will be like a tree firmly planted by streams of water which yields its fruit in its season and its leaf does not wither and in whatever he does, he prospers" (Psalm 1:1-3).

Discussion Questions:

1. What are some examples of lawfulness in my life?
2. What is the difference between lawfulness, legalism, and lawlessness?
3. How does lawfulness honor God's sovereignty and provide liberty?

Prayer Point:

Lord, keep me moving forward on the highway of Your lawfulness. Don't let me fall into either legalism or lawlessness in the pursuit of a spiritually fruitful and prosperous life.

Chapter 34

Is Freedom Independence?

The New Testament teaches that God's law is a perfect law and a law of freedom. The apostle James wrote, "But one who looks intently at the perfect law, the law of liberty, and abides by it, not having become a forgetful hearer but an effectual doer, this man will be blessed in what he does" (James 1:25).

I previously thought, as did most of my generation in the 1960s, that law meant restrictions and punishment, not freedom, and I struggled with understanding God's laws as being laws of liberty. It made me consider what it means to be truly free, and I began coming to a new definition of freedom in my own life. Earlier in my life, I would have defined freedom as independence. Freedom meant being unconstrained by outside restrictions. Growing up as an American, I had been taught to regard July 4th, Independence Day, as the symbol of American freedom. Later, I began to realize that independence from England alone had not made Americans free; rather it was the drafting of the Constitution and the creation of new laws that guaranteed American freedoms.

I was once told the story of a man who equated freedom with independence and wanted to find it. He was desperately poor and sought freedom from poverty, so he worked hard and eventually became wealthy. However, after becoming rich he found that he couldn't buy freedom from loneliness, and so he found a woman he cared for and decided to be married. Soon they had children, but the man felt trapped by his marriage relationship and the responsibility of raising a family. So he abandoned them, and then saw a newspaper advertisement for something called "space tourism." He could pay to be trained and sent beyond earthly restrictions into outer space! He enrolled in the program and once in space, he found himself painfully confined by the tiny size of his spacecraft, so he embarked on a spacewalk in just a spacesuit. Yet he was still tethered to the spacecraft by an annoying and short "umbilical cord" of tubes and cables. Seeking the freedom of complete independence, the man uncoupled his connecting cord and drifted off into space. Now, at last, he was totally independent and, of course, totally dead.

A better definition of freedom starts with having all your needs met while, at the same time, being protected from harm. After that, freedom means growing in a life that brings you closer and closer to God, who is the source of all freedom. If that is so, then your freedom began before you were born. When you were in your mother's womb, you didn't do anything wrong. All your needs were met, and you were completely protected and cared for.

Freedom is not an end in itself but rather God's way of bringing us to maturity.

In Hebrew, the word for womb is *rechem,* which is closely related to the word *rachamim,* meaning "mercy." It is a big challenge for anyone to leave the protection and contented freedom of the womb and start to deal with the harshness and injustices of life in this world. Maybe this is why every healthy baby cries as soon as it is born!

True freedom must serve our changing needs and the developing destiny of our lives. Freedom is not an end in itself but rather God's way of bringing us to maturity. We can't stay our whole lives in our mother's womb, but even after being born, we still need a loving, protective environment to grow into our full potential. The Bible actually says a lot about freedom. It has a very high value in God's kingdom. God wants His people to be free and He is willing to struggle and sacrifice His own Son to make us free.

The Messianic prophecy that Jesus read in His own synagogue is found in Isaiah sixty-one. Jesus read, "The Spirit of the Lord God is upon me, because the Lord has anointed me to bring good news to the afflicted; He has sent me to bind up the brokenhearted, to proclaim liberty to captives and freedom to prisoners."

Freedom is one of God's essential characteristics, and the Bible says all humans were created in the image of God. We are supposed to be like Him, and whether we believe in God or not, all of us have an inner longing for freedom. According to the Bible, God created us for freedom, but our sin shattered His image in us. We became slaves to sin. But when Jesus came, He told His followers in John eight, "You will know the truth, and the truth will make you free. Everyone who commits sin is the slave of sin. The slave does not remain in the house forever; the son does remain forever. So if the Son makes you free, you will be free indeed."

Of course, Jesus was teaching about moral freedom, that is, freedom of the heart. God's will is a heart set free from guilt, condemnation, regret, addiction, and self-destruction. God wants you to be free, to be exactly who He created you to be. Here is a deep and enduring truth about God and His kingdom: Freedom in God's kingdom is defined and protected by law. The Bible describes moral freedom as something that cannot be achieved or even understood apart from God's lawful reign.

The apostle Paul certainly knew the Torah better than most people of his day. As a young man, he was a disciple of Gamaliel, one of the leading rabbis in his generation. Paul was being groomed for the Sanhedrin, the top religious ruling council in the land. When he was later questioned by that same council, he proclaimed he was a "Pharisee, the son of a Pharisee" (Acts 23:6), that is, a religiously observant Jew who was zealous to observe all the 613 commands in the Torah. However, after He came to faith in Jesus, he ministered with powerful liberty and inspired many to follow his example.

Paul devoted much of his teaching to our relationship with God's laws. He deeply appreciated the Torah as God's Word but understood that the power of sin made pursuing obedience to the literal commands result in legalism, bondage, and ultimately spiritual death (Romans 7:8-13). On the other hand, life outside the bounds of God's law ends in lawlessness and separation from God's reign, a different but equally dangerous result. Paul applied himself to solving the problem of how believers can progress from the letter of the law that kills us through legalistic condemnation to the Spirit of the law that sets us free without losing the lawful reign of God in the process.

Paul's conclusion is that God Himself provided the answer to that question by sending His own Son, Jesus, to come to us as a man, that is, someone under the laws of God. Jesus was the only human to fully obey God by living perfectly in the spirit of God's law. Yet He was condemned and submitted to death on behalf of all of us who could not keep either the letter or the spirit of the law.

We understand that since Jesus died and rose from the grave, His Spirit can live in us and write the laws of God within our hearts while also giving us the power to obey them. God doesn't condemn me for stumbling while trying to please Him; rather He condemns the sin in me that is opposed to God's will for my life (Romans 8:1-3). Paul, who knew the Torah so well, wrote that by the power of God's Spirit in us, we can live in such a way that God's requirements are accomplished, that is, fulfilled in us. We struggle toward a freedom that is real and not found through an escape from God's laws. It is in pursuit of *mastering* God's laws, we begin to taste personal victory. The Holy Spirit does not lead us into a culture of lawlessness. Instead, it is the *lawfulness* of the Spirit of life that comes from Jesus, the King Himself, that sets us free to know God personally and begin a new life in His kingdom. We learn that whenever we yield to the Spirit of God that inspired His laws, we also find freedom and the power to begin living here on earth as we would in heaven!

When the disciples asked Jesus about restoring the kingdom to Israel in Acts 1:6, He told them about the power of the Holy Spirit to make them "witnesses." In Greek, the word *witness* is related to the word *martyr*, someone who gives up his life for God. When we pursue God's will to the end of our human resources, our hearts open in new ways to the power of God's grace. We discover freedom that liberates us from our own limitations. Developing a believing lifestyle is a process of first coming under the seemingly impossible standards of Jesus and then grasping by faith His truly amazing grace to begin meeting those perfect requirements one by one.

For all disciples, this is a lifestyle that consists of first dying to our personal selfish desires, and then rising again in new hope. This must be what Jesus referred to when He said, "If anyone wishes to come after Me, he must deny himself, and take up his cross daily and follow Me" (Matthew 16:24). The struggle may be longer and more difficult than we expected, but in the end, it is a path toward true freedom and life that is everlasting.

Discussion Questions:

1. What is the difference between freedom and independence?
2. Even as a believer, are there still areas in my life that are not free?
3. Does God define freedom as the ability to find my God-given destiny and then help me to achieve it?

Prayer Point:

Lord, I want to be free but never independent of You. Show me how to find true freedom of the heart that allows me to be the disciple you called me to become.

Chapter 35

Law of the Spirit

The Bible reveals that God rules His kingdom in a lawful way. God's good laws define and protect our freedom to live as disciples rather than by arbitrarily restricting us. The key to entering God's kingdom and enjoying its liberty, authority, and security is the Spirit of God. The apostle Paul makes the point that to help people function joyfully and fruitfully in God's kingdom, we must serve them not with a legalistic interpretation of God's Word, something he calls the "letter," but rather by serving in the Spirit of God. Paul wrote, "but our sufficiency is from God, who also made us sufficient as ministers of the new covenant, not of the letter but of the Spirit; for the letter kills, but the Spirit gives life" (2 Corinthians 3:5-6).

The key to lawful living is discerning and applying the "spirit" of God's laws.

God's laws are spiritual but they are also practical in the sense that they deal with real human situations. God's laws are also purposeful and were meant to define and mold Israel as a society that was ordained by God to be the model of His kingdom. If we begin to separate God's commands from their intended practical results and observe them for primarily religious purposes, we will misinterpret God's intentions and fall into the trap of sterile legalism like the Pharisees of Jesus' day. The key to lawful living is discerning and applying the "spirit" of God's laws.

Two people in the Bible help us enormously to understand and walk in the spirit of God's laws. The first person is Jesus Himself. When God's voice thundered above Mount Sinai and He came down to write His laws on the stone tablets held by Moses, where was Jesus then? Sometimes we think that only God the Father was there on Sinai, but of course, that was not the case. Jesus, the only begotten Son of God, is eternally one with the Father. That means He has always been and always will be in full accord with God's commands. Theologically, it could be argued that it was Jesus who with God wrote the Torah for the people of Israel.

Jesus is the inspiration behind all of the Old Testament. Therefore, when He walked the earth, would Jesus ever have broken God's commands? Never! If He had broken even one command, it would have been a sin and He could never have been the sinless Lamb of God, the perfect sacrifice for our atonement. Instead, we see Jesus continually teaching and demonstrating the spirit of God's laws.

Take, for example, the occasion found in the Gospels when Jesus healed a man in the synagogue on the Sabbath.

> Now it happened on another Sabbath, also, that He entered the synagogue and taught. And a man was there whose right hand was withered. So the scribes and Pharisees watched Him closely, whether He would heal on the Sabbath, that they might find an accusation against Him. But He knew their thoughts, and said to the man who had the withered hand, "Arise and stand here." And he arose and stood. Then Jesus said to them, "I will ask you one thing: Is it lawful on the Sabbath to do good or to do evil, to save life or to destroy?" And when He had looked around at them all, He said to the man, "Stretch out your hand." And he did so, and his hand was restored as whole as the other. (Luke 6:6-10)

The Pharisees were convinced that Jesus had broken God's command to cease from all work on the Sabbath by healing the man, so afterward they consulted together about how to stop or even kill Him. Today we should ask the same question asked by Jesus. What is lawful in the eyes of God to do on the Sabbath? God's intention for the Sabbath is to provide rest, to restore and refresh us from the labors of the week that is past and to prepare us for fruitful service in the six days ahead. The focus of the Sabbath is not on itself but on how it serves the rest of our week. What better day to heal a man from a crippling disability! That meant for the first time in years he would be able to take care of himself and serve his family usefully. Jesus didn't break God's command to rest on the Sabbath; rather, as the Son of God, He revealed its perfect intention. Jesus said, "The Sabbath was made for man, and not man for the Sabbath. Therefore the Son of Man is also Lord of the Sabbath" (Mark 2:27-28). This is the spirit and not the letter of God's law.

How did Messianic Jews understand the command to rest on the Sabbath in light of the teachings and example of Jesus? The book of Hebrews was written by a Messianic Jew to other Jewish followers of Jesus of His day. The third and fourth chapters are dedicated to an inspired interpretation of the Sabbath from a New Testament point of view. The writer makes the point (quoting from Psalm 95) that the people of Israel failed to enter into the Sabbath rest that God had given directly to them in His commands when they were at gathered at Mt. Sinai.

If there was any generation of God's people who should have obeyed the words of Torah, it was this generation! They had seen the holy fire fall on Sinai and received the commandments from Moses himself. The writer of Hebrews goes on to say that God's rest is entered by faith in God and by ceasing from our own self-initiated and self-directed work. As far as when the Sabbath should be observed, five times in these thirty-five short verses the writer uses the word *today*. His point is that Jesus might have taught in His Sermon on the Mount, "You have heard that the seventh day is holy as a Sabbath to the Lord, but I say unto you, today and every day should be holy to God and you should cease from vanity and ambitious striving to enter His rest *daily* by fully trusting Him."

Jesus' teaching in the New Testament raised the requirements of God's law to a perfect level and shifted the focus of obedience from outward behavior to inner commitment and obedience of the heart. Jesus taught that God's law was God ruling the inner man by a law of the heart or of the spirit. This teaching was radical but was not new to Israel. Centuries before Jesus, the prophet Jeremiah had written:

> "Behold, days are coming," declares the Lord, "when I will make a new covenant with the house of Israel and with the house of Judah, not like the covenant which I made with their fathers in the day I took them by the hand to bring them out of the land of Egypt, My covenant which they broke, although I was a husband to them," declares the Lord. "But this is the covenant which I will make with the house of Israel after those days," declares the Lord, "I will put My law within them and on their heart I will write it and I will be their God, and they shall be My people. They will not teach again, each man his neighbor and each man his brother, saying, 'Know the Lord,' for they will all know Me, from the least of them to the greatest of them," declares the Lord, "for I will forgive their iniquity, and their sin I will remember no more." (Jeremiah 31:31-34)

Interestingly, the words in the Hebrew text for "new covenant," *brit hadasha*, are the same words used in modern Hebrew for the New Testament. Most Jews today regard the New Testament as a book that is foreign to them and not Jewish. Many are surprised to read in their own Hebrew Scriptures that Jeremiah prophesied God would make a "new testament" with none other than the people of Israel and Judah. He said that it was God's intention to write His law on the hearts of His people, and this would mean that each individual would have personal accountability to the living God. Jeremiah's prophecy is a description of God's Spirit reigning inside each person.

Here is a story that illustrates the difference between the letter and the spirit of the law and also illustrates the process of coming to spiritual maturity. Think of yourself as a three-year-old child. Outside your house is a busy street that curves, and at that curve is a crosswalk and a traffic light. Your father takes you by the hand out to the sidewalk and tells you in his most serious voice that under no circumstances are you allowed to step out on the street when the light at the crosswalk is red. You will always wait until the light is green before beginning to cross. There are no exceptions whatsoever. If you disobey, you will be punished. It is your loving father's law.

Now fast forward to ten years later. You are thirteen years old and feeling very grown up. You no longer need your father to take you across the street. You go by yourself now, and no one needs to tell you not to step out on that busy street when the light is red. You come down to the corner, the light is red, so you stop and wait. You have internalized your father's teaching by now. What was once his law is now your own. Also, over the years, you have seen some very bad accidents at that same intersection so you agree with the wisdom of your father's instruction. Your obedience is habitual and automatic at an almost subconscious level. This is what the prophet Jeremiah referred to when he wrote about God's law being written on the hearts of His people.

Then one day while you are standing obediently at the curb waiting for the red light to change, something happens that tests your obedience to your father's law and your understanding of his character at the same time. You see an elderly woman walking unsteadily with a cane stepping off the curb and entering the crosswalk on the other side of the street. She is either partially blind or disoriented, and she evidently has not noticed that the light is still red. She is walking into danger.

Instantly, you know several things: In a moment, a car will come sweeping around that curve, and the driver will not have time to stop before hitting her. You know exactly how fast the cars are driven on that street! However, in the same instant, you also know something else. You know that if you immediately run out in the street, you could probably reach the woman in time to help her back to safety. But what should you do? The light is still red. Your father has always strictly forbidden you from even stepping into the street until the light changes, and now that law is written on your own heart.

On the other hand, even at thirteen, you are mature enough to realize that your father's intention in giving you his law about the red light was to protect your life and the lives of others. You know his character and that saving a human life is one of his highest values. So you immediately leap from the curb, run to the woman, and help her back to safety!

This is an illustration of the law of the spirit of life in Christ Jesus that Paul wrote about in Romans chapter eight. If you had stuck with the "letter" of the law, the woman could have been badly injured or killed. You appeared to break the letter of the law in order to fulfill the higher requirement in the spirit of the law. You did this in confidence that after saving the woman, your father, having seen all from his window and emerging from the house, would not scold you for transgressing his rule, but rather embrace you and congratulate you for a job well done. He might even say, "I can see that you are maturing, developing courage and good judgment. You're ready to take on greater responsibility!"

It occurs to me that living according to the spirit of God's laws is somewhat like learning to drive a car. Piloting a motor vehicle even at normal speeds is not a trivial task. Only a few seconds of bad driving can make almost anyone a mass killer! The fact is that when you drive, you are functioning within a highly complex matrix of laws. Laws of physics govern the way the car handles at different speeds, road conditions, and whether you are driving straight or turning a corner. Laws of engineering are applied to the design and construction of every car and its engine, while complex laws of chemistry and physics govern the production of its fuel.

While driving, we also have to be constantly aware of laws that govern human behavior. A child playing with a ball by the side of the road is likely to act differently from an elderly person or a young man on a bicycle. Then, of course, we have to obey the local traffic laws, including signs, painted lines, and traffic lights. Many laws converge on the driver of an automobile, and yet, after a few years of practice, we function safely within those laws, all the while listening to music or thinking about something else. Certainly, you have to be constantly alert to drive a car safely, but my point is that when you have mastered the skills needed to drive, most of it becomes nearly subconscious and automatic. This is another illustration of how we are meant to internalize the spirit of God's laws. The habitual lawfulness demonstrated in Jesus' own life is the goal of discipleship.

Discussion Questions:

1. What is the difference between the letter and the spirit of God's law?
2. Why is it important to understand the purpose and divine intention behind God's laws?
3. Can I think of an occasion when I obeyed the spirit and not the letter of a law in my life?

Prayer Point:

Lord, help me to love and respect all Your laws and to grow as a disciple in the spirit of lawfulness.

Chapter 36

Sons Ask "Why?"

The apostle Paul taught powerfully and repeatedly on the subject of God's laws. He was well qualified because before his miraculous meeting with Jesus on the road to Damascus, Paul was a zealously religious Pharisee. He wrote about his religious background to the Philippians: "[I was] circumcised the eighth day, of the stock of Israel, of the tribe of Benjamin, a Hebrew of the Hebrews; concerning the Law, a Pharisee; concerning zeal, persecuting the church; concerning the righteousness which is in the law, blameless" (Philippians 3:5-6).

However, after being confronted by the risen Lord on his way to persecute those he regarded as unrepentant violators of God's laws, Paul became a dedicated disciple of Jesus. His life and ministry thereafter demonstrated joyful freedom and power in God's Spirit that few have attained since his time. Paul's disciplined and lawful liberty in the Spirit of God provoked millions of people over the centuries to follow in his footsteps. He became the foremost apostle to the Gentile nations and authored almost one-third of the New Testament Scriptures.

The key is one word. It is the question, "Why?"

Paul gave us a key to interpret the letter of God's laws and understand the spirit of the law without losing God's lawfulness in the process. The key is one word. It is the question, "Why?" Let me explain by using what Paul taught in the fourth chapter of his letter to the Galatians. "Now I say that the heir, as long as he is a child, does not differ at all from a slave, though he is master of all, but is under guardians and stewards until the time appointed by the father. Even so we, when we were children, were in bondage under the elements of the world. But when the fullness of the time had come, God sent forth His Son, born of a woman, born under the law, to redeem those who were under the law, that we might receive the adoption as sons" (Galatians 4:1-7).

Paul wrote to the Galatians that a little child, even though he may be the heir of the house, is treated in the same manner as a slave until he is considered mature. According to Paul, we have become God's children by faith and the letter of God's law was like a guardian assigned to protect and rule over us while we were immature. He wrote that now, as God's heirs, we are being brought to maturity through faith in Jesus, God's perfect Son. We are no longer to act like slaves or like little children blindly obeying the commands of others who tell us what to do. The Torah, God's written law, which is our "guardian," deals with elementary and practical things regarding this earthly life, but we should mature to the point of discerning and walking in the spirit and intention of God's laws.

Because we are His children, we cry out to God "Abba!" which means "Father" or sometimes even "Daddy." When a father gives his child a command, a true and mature son or daughter is not only allowed, but expected to say, "Dad, please tell me why." Slaves and little children are not expected to question their father's laws. Their responsibility is to hear and obey. However, the mature child, who is an heir, is supposed to act with understanding because one day he or she will rule in the house. So we must ask God questions about all of His commands. For example, we should ask, "Abba, why do You command rest on the Sabbath?" As soon as we ask that question, God's answer, based on the pattern Jesus established in His Sermon on the Mount, seems obvious. I think He would say, "You don't give Me one day of the week and keep six for yourself. I command you to rest one day so you will be refreshed, strong, and healthy to serve Me the rest of the week!"

This shows us that the Sabbath should not be focused on whether you answer the telephone or drive your car or even conduct church services on a certain day of the week.

Sabbath is about honoring God with the discipline to rest enough regularly so we are strong and alert for service in His kingdom on a daily basis. Paul wrote that these laws are about "elementary" or basic things that everyone is expected to know. God's laws were not meant to bring us into a system of enforced observances that Paul calls bondage. We are called to freedom, but true freedom also carries with it greater responsibility.

Discussion Questions:

1. How are mature sons and daughters different from slaves and little children (Galatians 4:1-7)?
2. How can the question "Why?" become a key to freedom in the framework of God's laws?
3. Can I point to examples of Christian rules or traditions that should be questioned?

Prayer Point:

Father in heaven, I want to mature as a son or daughter in Your house. Teach me to respectfully ask, "Why?" and learn how to become more like You.

Chapter 37

Love Is the Greatest

All of God's law comes together in the expression of His redemptive, transforming, eternal love. God's perfect love is personal love that began before the world was created and will extend after it passes away. His love is unique because it takes into account your human design, your strengths, your faults, and your limitations. God's love is redemptive in that it touches your life at the moment you realize your destiny can never be achieved through your own abilities. It is transforming because God's love embodied in His Son, Jesus, is the power to help every disciple go beyond our weaknesses and receive indestructible eternal life.

As recipients of God's love, we find in Him the ability to

genuinely love others. God's love is meant to flow through us to other people. If we try to selfishly hold onto God's love for ourselves, it eludes us. But when we release His love to others, the flow increases. Sometimes when we feel the emptiest, it is the best time to show God's love to others. When we give a little love to those around us, we often end up being filled by God without seeking to be.

Love makes up what we lack. It can even make us courageous when we feel afraid. The disciple John wrote, "There is no fear in love; but perfect love casts out fear, because fear involves punishment, and the one who fears is not perfected in love. We love, because He first loved us" (1 John 4:18-19).

When you say "I love you" to another person, those words may have countless meanings and shades of meaning. But if you are sincere, there are two truths that are foundational to that statement. The first is that I recognize you are unique and I appreciate how special you are in my life. You don't really love someone if you think they are just like all the other people you know. The second truth is that I think that you are at least as important as I am. I'm saying that your feelings, needs, and rights are to be respected and defended as I would my own. This is the basis of true love.

The eternal uniqueness of every human and the right of every person to "life, liberty, and the pursuit of happiness" (from the United States Declaration of Independence, 1776) is something that comes from God alone. Science, politics, religion, or human sympathy cannot produce this kind of love.

The Bible says that true, pure love comes from God because that is His nature and our response to God's love is to love Him and the other people that He made. John, who is thought to have been the youngest of Jesus' apostles and the one He loved the most, wrote, "Beloved, let us love one another, for love is from God; and everyone who loves is born of God and knows God. The one who does not love does not know God, for God is love" (1 John 4:7-8).

Jesus said that the two greatest commandments given to Israel and through Israel to the world were about love. He quoted from God's law in Deuteronomy 6:5 and Leviticus 19:18. "And He said to him, 'You shall love the Lord your God with all your heart, and with all your soul, and with all your mind.' This is the great and foremost commandment. The second is like it, 'You shall love your neighbor as yourself.' On these two commandments depend the whole Law and the Prophets" (Matthew 22:37-40).

Paul the apostle wrote, "For the whole Law is fulfilled in one word, in the statement, 'You shall love your neighbor as yourself'" (Galatians 5:14) and, "Love does no wrong to a neighbor; therefore love is the fulfillment of the law" (Romans 13:10). The apostle James called God's commandment to love the "royal law." He wrote, "If, however, you are fulfilling the royal law according to the Scripture, 'You shall love your neighbor as yourself,' you are doing well" (James 2:8). Fulfilling the "royal law" starts among the disciples of the King. The apostle John records that Jesus taught, "A new commandment I give to you, that you love one another, even as I have loved you, that you also love one another. By this all men will know that you are My disciples, if you have love for one another" (John 13:34-35).

Love can have powerful political impact. Politics is about ordering people's lives for the good of society. It is concerned with right governing and involves the use of power to require people to act in a certain way and to punish people who refuse. Democracies and dictatorships alike make laws. The difference lies in why various laws are made and how they are enforced. Law lies at the heart of politics and we are all aware that even the best democratic governments constantly struggle and often fail to make good laws. No matter what kind of political government rules our nation the disciples of Jesus are always bound by God's laws of love.

No matter what kind of political government rules our nation the disciples of Jesus are always bound by God's laws of love.

Jesus said that His disciples are the "salt of the earth" and the "light of the world" (Matthew 5:13-16). Disciples sow the seeds of God's law of love in the heart of the general population and this law from God must be upheld and honored above civil law for any people to live in peace and freedom. God's love is essential in building strong nations where diverse peoples and different races forge an agreement to be governed as one. God's love must first, by individual faith and discipleship, fill the hearts and minds of political leaders and then the decisions they make regarding the lives of others will be for good and not for evil. These are leaders who, as disciples of Jesus, become a force for uniting people and building powerful and productive societies.

When God became King of Israel in the wilderness

(Exodus 19:5-6), His tent was erected in the middle of the camp. His pillars of cloud and fire led the people by day and night and He united the twelve tribes into a single nation for the first time. Years later, after entering the promised land, Israel rejected God's sovereignty and chose human kings. In the end, these human rulers were a disaster in terms of keeping the nation united against its enemies.

Only one human king was trusted enough by the leaders of all the tribes to unify the nation and that was David, the man whose heart was wholly devoted to the Lord. Perhaps it was David's promise to Saul not to destroy his family (1 Samuel 24:20-22) or maybe it was David's love for his friend Jonathan that continued even after his death, but when he had the political power, David and his tribe of Judah did not take revenge on Saul and Jonathan's smaller tribe of Benjamin. David became known as a man after God's own heart, and the other ten tribes came to him at Hebron and anointed him king over all Israel (2 Samuel 5:1-3). David sang to God in one of his inspired songs, "Blessed is the nation whose God is the LORD, the people whom He has chosen for His own inheritance. The LORD looks from heaven; He sees all the sons of men; From His dwelling place He looks out on all the inhabitants of the earth, He who fashions the hearts of them all, He who understands all their works" (Psalm 33:12-15).

In today's world, the role of the church is to be God's instrument in bringing His kingdom to the earth. However, this does not necessarily mean becoming *identified* with one political party or candidate against another. The primary calling of the church is to produce disciples of God's kingdom. These are men and women who have been spiritually equipped to represent God's love every place they are sent to serve in society. Governments change in a godly way when disciples who are called by God to serve in politics and civil service demonstrate God's love and integrity through their daily words and behavior. Every local church has a vital role in producing these redeemed and transformed lives.

What does God's law look like as it moves out of the church into society? Paul the apostle wrote, "Love is patient, love is kind and is not jealous; love does not brag and is not arrogant, does not act unbecomingly; it does not seek its own, is not provoked, does not take into account a wrong suffered, does not rejoice in unrighteousness, but rejoices with the truth; bears all things, believes all things, hopes all things, endures all things. Love never fails. . . . But now faith, hope, love, abide these three; but the greatest of these is love" (1 Corinthians 13:4-8, 13).

God's law of love rules the inner person, the hidden motives of the heart. Here is where the kingdom of God is rooted and from this root comes its power. Institutions and movements that are focused on what can be seen with natural eyes are destined to rise and fall, but truth imparted to others by God's love will never die. This love brings His kingdom to earth and never fails (1 Corinthians 13:8).

"Now having been questioned by the Pharisees as to when the kingdom of God was coming, [Jesus] answered them and said, 'The kingdom of God is not coming with signs to be observed nor will they say, "Look, here it is!" or, "There it is!" For behold, the kingdom of God is in your midst'" (Luke 17:20-21).

Discussion Questions:

1. Why does the Bible say the law of love is God's highest law?
2. How could God's law of love change my nation?
3. Why must true love contain both justice and mercy for everyone?

Prayer Point:

Lord, I believe that Your love is the highest law in the kingdom. Change my heart to love as You do and show me how to apply the sacrificial power of Your love in my life and work.

Chapter 38

God's Laws about Food

Years ago when I lived in Tokyo, one of my friends was the rabbi of the Jewish Community Center, whom I met when I attended services at the synagogue. On several occasions, I ate with him and his wife in local restaurants and I remember the difficulty in finding a place that could prepare food compatible with his dietary restrictions. Among other things, Jewish tradition forbids the eating of pork, or shellfish and the mixing of meat and dairy products in the same meal. He would scan the menus, looking for types of fish that were "kosher," which means considered fit to eat, and then instruct the chef to cook it on tin foil instead of on a grill that might have been used for non-kosher food.

I went to my Bible and sure enough, God forbade, among other things, the eating of pigs, reptiles, bats, birds of prey, rodents, and shellfish. This made me curious about the spirit of the biblical dietary laws. I went back to the Sermon on the Mount and tried to understand what Jesus would have taught concerning these laws. In His teaching on God's laws, Jesus repeatedly used the phrase, "you have heard . . . but I say." He would quote one of the commandments Moses had received on Sinai and then give His own ruling as Messiah and King. In each case, Jesus elevated the commandments from the law given to Israel to a higher, perfect level. What would He have said about eating pork?

First of all, three thousand years ago when God's laws were given, there was no refrigeration and no knowledge of viruses, bacteria, or microscopic parasites. We know that pigs in the wild will eat just about anything, including human feces. I previously thought that indigenous people in places like Borneo were immune to diseases from eating wild boars as well as pigs penned under the houses but later learned from local doctors that this is not the case. Whole villages have been known to become ill from eating contaminated swine. Certainly in the days of Moses, eating an undercooked pork chop, a wild bat, or a rat could have resulted in serious illness, death, or even have started an epidemic.

The other fish, birds, and animals forbidden to be eaten by God's law are the kind of creatures that feed off the bottom of bodies of water or eat the rotting flesh of dead animals. Again, this kind of wildlife is much more likely to cause health problems than animals like sheep, goats, chickens, cows, and fish with fins and scales, which are all allowed. God is very concerned about our physical well-being. Divine health is better than divine healing! I think that today Jesus would remind us that our bodies are "temples of the Holy Spirit" (1 Corinthians 6:19) and command us to do whatever we can to choose healthy foods and good eating habits.

> God is very concerned about our physical well-being. Divine health is better than divine healing!

Food seems to play a prominent role in religions around the world. Why didn't Jesus address it directly in His most important sermon on the Law? I think it's because while food is important, it is not that important in God's kingdom compared with other weightier moral issues. Dietary habits rank high among the surface elements of culture and not among its root issues. Jewish tradition has identified 613 commandments in God's laws given to Israel through Moses in the first five books of the Bible. Less than 5 percent of these commandments are about food.

Jesus scolded religious people for not understanding which of God's commandments are more important. He said, "Woe to you, scribes and Pharisees, hypocrites! For you tithe mint and dill and cumin, and have neglected the weightier provisions of the Law: justice and mercy and faithfulness; but these are the things you should have done without neglecting the others" (Matthew 23:23). The apostle Paul followed that up with this saying, "For the kingdom of God is not eating and drinking, but righteousness and peace and joy in the Holy Spirit" (Romans 14:17).

God's laws, including the ones about food, were originally given to Moses for the purpose of defining and building a society that honored God as King. This society, the people of Israel, was the prototype of God's magnificent kingdom on earth. Food, of course, is vital to every human society and culture. Regulating and protecting the food supply is usually a government responsibility and falls under the general category of public health. By His word, three thousand years ago, God molded Israel from a mass of former slaves into a lawful nation as an example for the whole world. From the start, as King of Israel, God demonstrated His good and loving rule by, among other things, giving commands about foods, public health and personal hygene.

For example, in the Torah, there are numerous instructions about washing with water. These commands were not intended by God to become religious rituals or simply traditions. Today, at many *kosher* (certified rabbinically as following Jewish dietary traditions) restaurants, there are metal pitchers and special taps for running water at the entrance so that religiously observant patrons can ritually rinse their hands before eating. In the same restaurants, there may be signs in the restrooms with words like, "Employees must wash their hands before returning to work." I think this second type of handwashing is more in line with God's original commandments. Among the first instructions given by public health authorities to help nations fight against the COVID-19 virus pandemic was frequent handwashing. Ancient wisdom from the Bible has powerful application in the modern world.

Eating or not eating certain foods is not what makes a person any more or less acceptable to God. However, out of love for our neighbors, we want to respect the customs and beliefs of others. Paul, the apostle wrote, "Do not tear down the work of God for the sake of food. All things indeed are clean [Greek: *kathara* — spiritually pure], but they are evil for the man who eats and gives offense. It is good not to eat meat or to drink wine, or to do anything by which your brother stumbles. The faith which you have, have as your own conviction before God. Happy is he who does not condemn himself in what he approves" (Romans 14:20-22).

Discussion Questions:

1. Why are the foods we eat important to God?
2. Are there some foods that I will or will not eat because of my faith?
3. Why should Christians respect the eating customs of others?

Prayer Point:

Lord, please help me to accept the discipline of a healthy diet and keep me from causing anyone in Your flock to stumble because of food or drink. Help us all to stay focused on the most important values in Your kingdom.

Chapter 39

Feasts of the Lord

God's laws for Israel contain an entire annual calendar. These divinely commanded seasons are organized around seven major holidays and other feasts, fasts, Sabbaths, and special days. The holidays and observances give the daily life of Israelis an orderly and meaningful rhythm and are part of Jewish culture even to this day. While the majority of the holidays are agricultural in origin or mark some biblical or historical event, all have an important spiritual component because God is honored in different ways during the entire year. In the Bible, these special days and seasons are not called the holidays of Israel but rather the "feasts of the Lord" (2 Chronicles 2:4).

As with the rest of God's laws, the commands concerning holidays are part of inspired Scripture and redemptive in their purpose. Christians must not ignore them as cultural trivia nor try to create a legalistic system of religious observance out of them. The feasts of the Lord are powerfully instrumental in establishing the culture of God's kingdom. They are commanded in the Bible and every disciple of the Lord, Jew or Gentile, should know and respect God's appointed times throughout the year. However, we all must learn to observe God's feasts in the spirit and not the letter of the law.

As with the rest of God's laws, the commands concerning holidays are part of inspired Scripture and redemptive in their purpose.

We know from history that less than three hundred years after Gentile believers were first called "Christians" in Antioch (Acts chapter 11), the first Christian emperor of the Roman Empire, Constantine, outlawed the "Jewish" holidays and moved the Sabbath from the seventh day (Saturday) to Sunday. The biblical holiday of Passover was banned and replaced by a Christianized springtime fertility celebration with pagan origins. It became known as Easter. No one is sure where this name originated but it may be traced to an Anglo-Saxon goddess of spring named *Eostre*. To this day, many Easter celebrations include painted eggs and rabbits, which remain from ancient pre-Christian fertility symbols.

Although removed from the Christian world almost two thousand years ago, of all the biblical holidays, the feast of Passover most clearly illustrates God's redemptive purposes. Passover celebrates the deliverance of Israel from slavery in Egypt. It begins on the evening before the seven-day "Feast of Unleavened Bread" (Leviticus 23:5-6). For one entire week, all the people of Israel are supposed to eat baked products without yeast. The reason, given in the Bible, is to remember that the Jewish people left slavery in Egypt in such a hurry they had no time to allow their bread to rise.

> Now the LORD said to Moses and Aaron in the land of Egypt, "This month shall be the beginning of months for you; it is to be the first month of the year to you. Speak to all the congregation of Israel, saying, 'On the tenth of this month they are each one to take a lamb for themselves, according to their fathers' households, a lamb for each household.'" (Exodus 12:1-3)

> Now you shall eat it in this manner: with your loins girded, your sandals on your feet, and your staff in your hand; and you shall eat it in haste—it is the LORD's Passover. For I will go through the land of Egypt on that night and will strike down all the firstborn in the land of Egypt, both man and beast and against all the gods of Egypt I will execute judgments—I am the LORD. The blood shall be a sign for you on the houses where you live and when I see the blood, I will pass over you, and no plague will

> befall you to destroy you when I strike the land of Egypt. Now this day will be a memorial to you, and you shall celebrate it as a feast to the LORD; throughout your generations you are to celebrate it as a permanent ordinance. Seven days you shall eat unleavened bread, but on the first day you shall remove leaven from your houses for whoever eats anything leavened from the first day until the seventh day, that person shall be cut off from Israel. (Exodus 12:11-15)

It may be said that the Lord's Supper, the Protestant observance of Holy Communion, and even the Catholic Mass, are all Christian expressions of the Passover that developed over the centuries. *Pascha Nostrum,* which is Latin for "Our Passover," is a hymn used historically by both Catholics and Protestants during the Easter season. The first words of the hymn are in the *Book of Common Prayer* of the Episcopal church and are well known in the English-speaking world: "Christ our Passover has been sacrificed for us; therefore let us keep the feast, Not with the old leaven, the leaven of malice and evil, but with the unleavened bread of sincerity and truth. Alleluia."

When I was a child, my parents were members of the Episcopal church, so I was baptized and confirmed in that Christian tradition. This was years before I had a personal spiritual encounter with Jesus and dedicated myself to becoming His disciple. While I was growing up and attending a local Episcopalian congregation, I served for a time as an "acolyte," which meant on Sunday I wore a special robe over my normal clothes and helped the congregational leader serve the communion. He would read the prayers and then people were invited to come forward and kneel where we would offer them wine from a large silver chalice and individual circular wafers of white unleavened bread stamped with an Episcopal cross. Even though I lacked real faith, I knew this was something holy and meant to be a way for people to connect with God.

As a young man, my life was transformed when I reached out to Jesus in prayer for salvation. After beginning a new life as a believer at the age of twenty-three, I married a Messianic Jewish woman and also began attending Bible school in preparation for ministry. I learned from my wife's family that Passover in the Jewish world is a big annual family celebration with roots in traditions that go back to ancient times and the Bible. Every year, relatives and close friends gather together to eat a festive meal with specially prepared dishes, recite Bible stories, read from a book called a *hagadah*, and sing traditional songs. This big event is called a *seder* and families spend all day cooking and preparing for the evening celebration in their homes. When the time comes, unleavened bread called *matzoh* is eaten, the story of Israel's deliverance from Egypt is told, and four cups of wine are lifted, two before the meal and two after it. Sometimes special pillows are even arranged so guests can recline as a symbolic statement, "Once we labored hard as slaves in Egypt but now as free people we can relax because of God's deliverance."

In those first few years as I celebrated the Passover holiday and learned more about the New Testament in my studies, a convergence began to take place in my mind between

Passover and the Lord's Supper. It occurred to me that, of course, Jesus and His disciples were all Jews who lived in the context of Jewish law and tradition. Passover was a big event and a special holiday for everyone in their culture too. All the synoptic gospels (Matthew, Mark, and Luke) record that the disciples asked Jesus where He wanted them to prepare the Passover. Jesus' answer is recorded in Luke's gospel. "And He said to them, 'When you have entered the city, a man will meet you carrying a pitcher of water; follow him into the house that he enters. And you shall say to the owner of the house, "The Teacher says to you, 'Where is the guest room in which I may eat the Passover with My disciples?' And he will show you a large, furnished upper room; prepare it there.' And they left and found everything just as He had told them and they prepared the Passover" (Luke 22:10-13).

I had learned that preparing the Passover is not a trivial task. There is shopping, cooking, and arranging the room that has to be finished before anything can start. Throughout the day, there is an excitement and an expectation about the evening celebration when everyone will be gathered in the house. This special holiday was close to Jesus' heart as it was to all His countrymen. Jesus' Passover meal would be a "last supper" with His dearest friends, who by that time, were even closer to Him than family. Luke's gospel records that, **"**When the hour had come, He reclined at the table and the apostles with Him" (Luke 22:14). Reclining on cushions at the Passover table was a custom for them as it is for some Jews today. "And He said to them, 'I have earnestly desired to eat this Passover with you before I suffer; for I say to you, I shall never again eat it until it is fulfilled in the kingdom of God'" (Luke 22:15-16).

In the course of a traditional Passover *seder*, the story of God's miracles in Pharaoh's court and at the Red Sea are recounted. Special foods represent the clay used by Hebrew slaves in Egypt to build Pharaoh's cities, the bitterness of bondage, and the salty tears that were shed by generations of people who were never permitted to be more than foreign laborers. It is a celebration of liberation and freedom! God commanded a lamb to be slain for each household and its blood brushed on the doorposts and lintels of each home so that death striking the Egyptians would "pass over" those homes. The people of Israel were instructed to eat the sacrificial lamb at sunset in family gatherings with bitter herbs and unleavened bread.

During the Passover meal, while retelling the story of God's judgments on the Egyptians and His miracles that saved the people of Israel, Jesus took up the unleavened bread. Luke records, "And when He had taken some bread and given thanks, He broke it and gave it to them, saying, 'This is My body which is given for you; do this in remembrance of Me'" (Luke 22:19). Everyone who was seated at the table with Jesus on that holy night understood that the bread He held up was not ordinary bread. It was the unleavened bread of freedom, the special bread that Israel was commanded to eat to remember the urgency of deliverance from slavery. Now Israel's Messiah was revealing the spiritual core and powerful truth hidden in God's commands regarding His holy festivals.

Four cups of wine are served during the *seder*. Each cup has a meaning derived from four promises God made to the people of Israel found in Exodus 6:6-7. God said, "I will bring you out. I will deliver you. I will redeem you. I will take you for My people." The third cup, taken immediately after dinner, is the cup of redemption. Although it is difficult to know for sure, there are Jewish sources that say this tradition goes back more than two thousand years. If so, it makes good sense why the New Testament records that it was this third cup that Jesus raised with His disciples that night.

In the course of a traditional Passover seder, the story of God's miracles in Pharaoh's court and at the Red Sea are recounted.

Luke 22:20 says, "And in the same way He took the cup after they had eaten, saying, 'This cup which is poured out for you is the new covenant in My blood.'" It was the cup of redemption, the third cup of the Passover *sede*r, that became the heart of the holiest Christian celebration, the Eucharist, Holy Communion, the Lord's Supper.

Jesus was saying in effect, "I am the Passover. My blood will be your sacrifice, your covering, your protection. Death will 'pass over' you because of Me and the giving up of My body will sustain you on your journey to spiritual freedom."

Jesus considered Passover to be a divinely ordained feast. He did not abolish the Passover law for Israel but rather revealed its inner spiritual meaning and God's original intention for His chosen people. Jesus said, "Greater love has no one than this, that one lay down his life for his friends" (John 15:13). Here the "greater love" was demonstrated as the perfect Man lay down His life at the center of the culture God had created for His people Israel. Far from erasing the meaning of God's feasts, He changed Passover and the biblical calendar forever, giving it new significance. Jesus' observance of Passover and the events that followed marked a spiritual revolution. It was the beginning of a "new and living way" first for the Jews and then also for the world.

Now I see that the biblical perspective I gained when Passover and the Lord's Supper converged in my mind should be given to every Christian throughout the world. This is part of restoring God's kingdom on earth and bringing the authentic gospel of the kingdom, which is rooted in God's commands to Israel, to every people. For some, it will bring a renewed depth to Christian or Jewish traditions we have been following for years. For others, the connection between Passover and Easter will be a fresh and startling revelation from God.

Practically speaking, if you are a Messianic Jew, *Pesach* is meant to be restored and renewed for you and your family as a way to honor the Lamb of God and give Him a central place in your annual celebrations. If you are from Western culture and a Christian tradition, holidays like Easter and Christmas, whatever their pagan roots, still may have redemptive value. Your culture, even in unbelief, accepts to a greater or lesser degree, that these special cultural seasons have Christian or biblical significance. When God calls us to serve other people, communicating God's truth requires engaging in their culture, not abolishing it. Having said that, I believe that all Christians should know, love, and respect the biblical feasts of the Lord. I urge Christian pastors to teach the meaning of Passover to their congregations and learn to celebrate a Messianic *seder* to make Jesus' words and sacrifice more real for all believers.

However, if you are from a people who are just receiving the truth of the Bible for the first time in your history and most Christians among you are first-generation believers, it is a different story! Now that you are Christians, you want holidays that honor the true and living God, the God of the Bible. Why should you import Western Christian holidays with pagan roots that did not grow in your cultural soil? Why not start with the feasts of the Lord given by divine revelation to Israel and adapt them in a way that honors God and suits your culture? Don't many of us today do this with worship songs? No one knows the inspired melodies that King David originally strummed on his harp. So, we use God-given creativity, filtered through our culture and modern musical tastes, to create new melodies using his words (most often in translation) to worship and praise God!

Western Christians ended up with holidays like Easter and Christmas by adapting biblical events to suit their own cultures. In spite of the distortions, commercialization, and misuses, these holidays served them well and helped turn Western culture toward Christ for over one thousand years.

In summary, all disciples of Jesus should know the biblical feasts of the Lord because of their place in God's inspired Word and their redemptive value. The feasts of the Lord are an integral part of the culture of His kingdom. Through the biblical holidays we understand so much more about the Bible. For instance, why was it important for Joshua and the people of Israel to celebrate their first Passover after crossing the Jordan into the Promised Land? Why was Jerusalem filled with Jews from all over the ancient world at the time of Acts chapter 2 when the Holy Spirit was poured out? Pentecost takes on deeper meaning when we understand it is another name for *Shavuot*, the biblical feast of weeks, one of three pilgrimage feasts commanded by God for the men of Israel to gather together for worship.

As valuable as they are, however, we approach the biblical holidays as we do all of God's commands, respecting and observing them in the spirit of obedience and not in the letter of the law. Here is what the apostle Paul wrote about the culturally significant behaviors of eating foods and observing holidays.

"One person regards one day above another, another regards every day alike. Each person must be fully convinced in his own mind. He who observes the day, observes it for the Lord, and he who eats, does so for the Lord, for he gives thanks to God; and he who eats not, for the Lord he does not eat, and gives thanks to God" (Romans 14:5-6).

Discussion Questions:

1. Why are the biblical holidays called the "Feasts of the Lord"?

2. What is the connection between Passover and the Lord's Supper?

3. Should all Christians study and know about the biblical calendar?

Prayer Point:

Lord, please give me a love for all Your holidays and feasts in the Bible. Even though I may not be accustomed to them, I know they are precious to You and teach us important truths about Your kingdom.

Chapter 40

Paul's Freedom

Paul was first and foremost a disciplined follower of the Messiah Jesus, who challenged all His disciples to deny themselves and lay down their own personal lives in order to serve others (Matthew 16:24). Paul's sacrifice, his "death" to his own religious identity and his familiar culture, opened the door for him to fulfill his unique calling. He was able to adapt to whatever culture he was in. Did this show a lack of integrity? Should we call Paul a "cultural chameleon"? No, he was obeying a higher unchanging truth, a divine law, being "obedient to the heavenly vision" (Acts 26:19). He was demonstrating the culture of God's kingdom.

Here's what Paul wrote about his liberty in Jesus:

> For though I am free from all men, I have made myself a slave to all, that I might win the more. And to the Jews, I became as a Jew, that I might win Jews; to those who are under the Law, as under the Law, though not being myself under the Law, that I might win those who are under the Law; to those who are without law, as without law, though not being without the law of God but under the law of Christ, that I might win those who are without law. To the weak I became weak, that I might win the weak; I have become all things to all men, that I may by all means save some. And I do all things for the sake of the gospel, that I may become a fellow partaker of it. (1 Corinthians 9:19-23)

No man except Jesus Himself brought the teaching of God's kingdom to as many as Paul did. His inspired letters still lead people into God's kingdom almost two thousand years after they were written. Trained as a rabbi, he knew God's biblical law better than most men of his day, yet through faith in Jesus, he experienced freedom few have attained since his time. Paul's freedom gave him the flexibility to represent the eternal kingdom of God and still embrace the cultural identity of the people to whom he was sent. Paul had the freedom and spiritual ability to become the servant of many, both Jews and Gentiles, and the result was his apostolic ministry bringing cross-cultural transformation.

For Paul, the sovereign rule of God by the Holy Spirit

in his personal life led to his discovery of powerful freedom. In Paul's heart, as a disciple of Jesus, the twin truths of God's law and grace found their meeting point. Freedom is where justice and mercy touch. The psalmist wrote, "Lovingkindness and truth have met together; Righteousness and peace have kissed each other" (Psalm 85:10). For Paul, God's law defined the eternal kingdom, but the amazing grace he experienced in God's Spirit enabled him to live in it. He poured out his heart to the church leaders of Rome in his inspired letter. Follow the progression of these five statements in which Paul explains his problem and then describes God's solution.

1. "So then, the Law is holy, and the commandment is holy and righteous and good" (Romans 7:12).
2. "For we know that the Law is spiritual, but I am of flesh, sold into bondage to sin" (Romans 7:14).
3. "For I joyfully concur with the law of God in the inner man, but I see a different law in the members of my body, waging war against the law of my mind and making me a prisoner of the law of sin which is in my members. Wretched man that I am! Who will set me free from the body of this death?" (Romans 7:22-24).
4. "Therefore, there is now no condemnation for those who are in Christ Jesus. For the law of the Spirit of life in Christ Jesus has set you free from the law of sin and of death" (Romans 8:1-2).
5. "So that the requirement of the Law might be fulfilled in us, who do not walk according to the flesh but according to the Spirit" (Romans 8:4).

If we follow the thoughts of this anointed man, his words become a roadmap to moral freedom—freedom of the heart liberated from sin, the freedom of God Himself. We don't get to this destination by ignoring the laws of God, discarding them (in the name of grace), or regarding them as annoying restrictions of our liberty. Rather, we struggle in our own lives with God's divine standards, like a bird caught in a trap, until our self-will dies. Then the Spirit of life in Christ Jesus, the same Spirit that raised Him from the dead, takes over and begins to fulfill the moral excellence of God in our lives. The apostle Paul wrote, "I have been crucified with Christ and it is no longer I who live, but Christ lives in me" (Galatians 2:20). This exchange of his life for the life of Christ gave Paul access to God's unlimited freedom and power. He wrote to the Philippians, "I can do all things through Him who strengthens me" (Philippians 4:13).

We struggle in our own lives with God's divine standards, like a bird caught in a trap, until our self-will dies.

This is the reason Paul could write these inspired words to the struggling Corinthian church, "All things are lawful for me, but not all things are profitable. All things are lawful for me, but I will not be mastered by anything. Food is for the stomach and the stomach is for food, but God will do away with both of them. Yet the body is not for immorality, but for the Lord, and the Lord is for the body" (1 Corinthians 6:12-13). "All things are lawful, but not all things are profitable.

All things are lawful, but not all things edify. Let no one seek his own good, but that of his neighbor" (1 Corinthians 10:23–24).

All who follow Jesus as Lord are walking on this same road through the wilderness from slavery and sin to freedom and life. The only truly holy person among us is the Holy Spirit. When we are in His presence, we taste freedom for a moment, enough to strengthen us to take another few steps. There are times to rest and other times to press on. There are battles to be fought and enemies that must be vanquished. Like Abraham, we see a city ahead in the distance whose builder and maker is God, so we do not lose heart. Along this sometimes difficult road, a remarkable thing occurs. We begin to experience joy.

Joy is God's gift to free people. It is not the same as happiness. Happiness has reasons. If you achieve a long sought-after goal, get married, have a child, buy a house or a new car, you have good reason to feel happy. But joy is a spirit and it is a gift from heaven. Joy comes upon us as we become free, for seemingly no reason at all. It is wild, untamed, and sets fire to something dry and waiting to burn in our hearts. When you feel this joy, you know you can do anything that is required by God! We all need to experience this kind of joy for as the Scripture says, "The joy of the Lord is your strength!" (Nehemiah 8:10).

The spirit of godly joy can make you laugh, or make you cry, or make you want to dance or shout aloud. In the lyrics of the worship song, "I Could Sing of Your Love Forever," songwriter Martin Smith of the band Delirious? included this verse,

Oh, I feel like dancing
It's foolishness I know;
But when the world has seen the light,
They will dance with joy,
Like we're dancing now!

Christian thinker and author C. S. Lewis wrote that joy is "an unsatisfied desire which is itself more desirable than any other satisfaction." In his book *Surprised by Joy*, Lewis clearly separates joy from both happiness and pleasure. He wrote, "I doubt whether anyone who has tasted it [joy] would ever, if both were in his power, exchange it for all the pleasures in the world. But then Joy is never in our power and pleasure often is."

Like the writer of a worship song that touched millions around the world and someone like C. S. Lewis, whose books are loved by generations of readers, servants of the Lord who use their gifts to communicate God's freedom and joy become influential. Other people quickly sense and respond to godly and joyful freedom because there is something in almost every human heart that deeply longs for it. "So the ransomed of the Lord will return and come with joyful shouting to Zion, and everlasting joy will be on their heads. They will obtain gladness and joy, and sorrow and sighing will flee away" (Isaiah 51:11).

Discussion Questions:

1. Can I describe the nature and source of Paul's freedom and joy?
2. Is spiritual freedom an important value for me in the kingdom of God?
3. Are we free now? Will we be free in heaven?

Prayer Point:

Lord, You said that the truth will make us free. Please, make me more and more into a free person who knows the feeling of Your joy in my daily life.

Part 5

All Over the World

This gospel of the kingdom shall be preached in the whole world as a testimony to all the nations, and then the end will come. (Matthew 24:14)

Chapter 41

The Worldwide Kingdom

Ultimately, God's strategy for the world goes beyond nations to the community of nations. God's plan starts with the individual, includes the family, and goes on to families of families, tribes or ethnic groups, and nations. The Bible shows that a nation emerges from the agreement of diverse tribes to unite, to be governed as one, and to interact with the rest of the world as a single entity. The kingdom of God includes God's plan at every level. We know that He rules over the whole universe, but it is not realistic to jump from God's plan for an individual straight to God's plan for the world.

Growth is always a process of steps. There are significant challenges and the possibility of failure at every stage of growth. Not every person builds a family. Not every family becomes a tribe. Not every group of tribes becomes a nation and there are many examples in history when nations have failed, broken apart, and even ceased to exist.

From the days of Genesis, it has been God's plan for all of humanity to be united as one kingdom under His Messiah, the Prince of Peace. There have been countless counterfeits of this international unity throughout history, including the many attempts of human leaders and nations to build empires by military force, political alliances, economic power, or religion.

After each of the two great wars of the twentieth century, attempts were made by the victorious states to form international bodies that could ensure peace. In 1920, after the First World War, the League of Nations was established and in 1945 the United Nations came into being. Each of these international bodies, launched with hope and idealism, failed to bring about peaceful agreement between the nations of the world.

In the future, the system of global control presided over by the Antichrist, as predicted in the book of Revelation, will be the final ambitious attempt of human leadership to unite the world. This attempt will be born of desperation and fear of worldwide war mixed with idealism but will ultimately end in a deceptive, despotic, and demonically inspired tyranny.

Jesus contrasted the people of God's kingdom with the people of the world in His parable of the wheat and the thorns.

> Jesus presented another parable to them, saying, "The kingdom of heaven may be compared to a man who sowed good seed in his field. But while his men were sleeping, his enemy came and sowed tares among the wheat, and went away. But when the wheat sprouted and bore grain, then the tares became evident also. The slaves of the landowner came and said to him, 'Sir, did you not sow good seed in your field? How then does it have tares?' And he said to them, 'An enemy has done this!' The slaves said to him, 'Do you want us, then, to go and gather them up?' But he said, 'No; for while you are gathering up the tares, you may uproot the wheat with them. Allow both to grow together until the harvest; and in the time of the harvest I will say to the reapers, "First gather up the tares and bind them in bundles to burn them up; but gather the wheat into my barn."'" (Matthew 13:24-30)

According to Jesus' words, godless society will develop in tandem and in conflict with the kingdom of God right up until the end of the age. At that time, God will make a distinction between those who, in trying to serve themselves, wittingly or unwittingly, served the "ruler of this world" (Jesus' term for the devil) and those who lived to serve God. The work of those who ignored God or considered Him an enemy will be destroyed, and an angel will proclaim, "The kingdom of the world has become the kingdom of our Lord and of His Christ; and He will reign forever and ever" (Revelation 11:15).

> Godless society will develop in tandem and in conflict with the kingdom of God right up until the end of the age.

In the meantime, as disciples we must engage in spiritual warfare. Paul wrote, "For our struggle is not against flesh and blood, but against the rulers, against the powers, against the world forces of this darkness, against the spiritual forces of wickedness in the heavenly places" (Ephesians 6:12). The great rivalry between God and the devil that began in heaven is being played out on earth in a multi-generational struggle for the hearts and minds of the human race. Global domination has been the grand prize since the creation of the world. Everyone and everything in our world is at stake. Because of technology and the availability of worldwide travel, today's world is shrinking rapidly so the totality of global spiritual warfare is easier to discern than in previous eras. The Coronavirus pandemic that began in 2019 and spread throughout the world also revealed how interconnected and vulnerable to disruption our international systems have become.

We are living in the age of globalization, which is linking the economies of the world into one vast "global village." This process is inevitable and will only accelerate in the end times. Sin, crime, corrupted governments, war, and disease are also being increasingly globalized. But God's plan for His kingdom to be worldwide started from the beginning of creation. Before modern nation states were even imagined, God said to Abraham, "In you and in your seed all the families of the earth will be blessed!" Almost two thousand years before there were world wars and a United Nations, Jesus already said to His disciples, "Go into all the world and make disciples of all the nations!"

How will God's plan for making disciples succeed in the context of the power structures of our world? The business, political, and military organizations of the world that stand in opposition to the kingdom of God resemble pyramids in structure. They have a few powerful and highly rewarded individuals at the top, a mass of people at the bottom, with carefully defined hierarchical levels in between. In contrast, the kingdom of God is a very "flat" structure because the King Himself desires and has the ability to speak directly with every member of His kingdom on a daily basis! The most vulnerable part of every military force is its "command and control" system. Think of a vast army in which the Commander in Chief, the top strategist, speaks directly to every soldier on the ground in real time. With billions of members in every tribe and nation of the world, the kingdom of God is already unstoppable and ultimately undefeatable. We slow down if we fail to equip our frontline people and when we try to imitate or compete with earthly kingdoms and organizations.

Discussion Questions:

1. Does God have a worldwide and eternal plan for His kingdom?
2. Can I expect the world to become a better and better place before the return of the Lord?
3. Why is there conflict between the systems of the world and the advancement of God's kingdom?

Prayer Point:

Lord, You loved the whole world enough to send Jesus to die for it. Please give me Your worldview and show me your perfect love for every nation.

Chapter 42

What Is a Nation?

The nation is the most important social and political entity in the modern age. However, there is no universally accepted definition of what forms or causes people to become identified as a single nation. As a result, national identity is the source of debate and struggle all over the world today. Can any nation be truly multicultural or multiracial or must there always be at least one dominant culture, language, or race? Is it the obligation of a dominant core group to provide complete equality to minority groups living alongside? What happens when the traditionally dominant group is no longer dominant? How to define a nation in today's world poses a dilemma that is at the root of conflicts that powerfully influence all of modern politics and impact the lives of billions.

What is the difference between a nation and a political state? A nation may refer to a large group of people who are somehow connected by shared history, race, language, or culture. The ways people in a nation are connected are diverse. They may be obvious or very subtle, physical or even imaginary. On the other hand, the basic definition of a state is a little clearer than that of a nation, but in no way freer from conflict. A political state tends to have geographic territory and some form of sovereign government capable of making and enforcing law over its citizens.

Can any nation be truly multicultural or multiracial or must there always be at least one dominant culture, language, or race?

Today, there is no major power that is considered a "pure" nation-state where the political state is comprised of a single ethnic group and united by a common language and culture within established and recognized geographic borders. Two nations that exalted the "pure" ethnic group approach to nationhood in the first half of the twentieth century were Germany and Japan. The disastrous results of the Second World War influenced the world to de-emphasize ethnocentric national models. Increasingly efficient international networks of travel and communications, along with the globalization of the world's economy, are slowly but progressively bringing the world together, especially in mega-metropolitan areas, into a

Separating or grouping people into nations is part of God's redemptive plan of salvation for the world.

pluralistic "global village." However, at the same time, powerful forces of religion, racial prejudice, and global economic shifts continue to contribute to a worldwide cultural and political clash of civilizations.

Against this complex mosaic of races, cultures, and states, the question arises, "What is the role of the kingdom of God?" Does the Bible address these important issues of our time? Where does God stand in all of this? The Bible clearly states that God does have a redemptive plan for all nations, that is, for "every tribe and tongue and people and nation" (Revelation 5:9).

Christianity has a two thousand-year history that has lasted through the eras of kings and kingdoms, empires, world wars, democracies, and super-powers. However, today we may not be well equipped to meet new and greater challenges of nation building, globalization and our post-modern age. Evangelicals seem to understand God's plan for individual salvation and we have learned to "focus on the family," but there is no deep or shared understanding of God's plan for a nation as a whole. We know that Jesus is the "Prince of Peace" and we know His kingdom's reign will bring peace on earth but, other than prayer, Christians do not agree practically on how this is going to happen.

Separating or grouping people into nations is part of God's redemptive plan of salvation for the world. We know from the Bible that God created individuals and also families, clans, tribes, and nations for His good purposes on earth. God made humans in His image and said to them, "Be fruitful and multiply, and fill the earth, and subdue it" (Genesis 1:28). After the fall, Adam and Eve had children and families began to migrate across the earth. Sin infected the human heart and spread like a deadly virus through the population. After the flood, the three sons of Noah multiplied into families and tribes. It is here, in Genesis chapter 10, that the word *nations* first appears in our Bibles. "From these the coastlands of the nations were separated into their lands, every one according to his language, according to their families, into their nations" (Genesis 10:5).

The genealogies recorded in the book of Genesis indicate that as humanity developed on earth, families grew into tribes or clans, and as time passed, ethnically related tribes made agreements with each other to the extent they came together into larger people groups known as nations.

At this point, God stepped directly into the human picture again with His plan to bless and redeem humanity. He called Abram (whose name God later changed to Abraham) from his home country and people to be like an immigrant, even a refugee, a pioneer, starting something new at an advanced age and virtually alone. God spoke these now-famous words:

> Go forth from your country,
> And from your relatives
> And from your father's house,
> To the land which I will show you;
> And I will make you a great nation,
> And I will bless you,
> And make your name great;
> And so you shall be a blessing;

> And I will bless those who bless you,
> And the one who curses you I will curse.
> And in you all the families of the earth will be blessed.
> (Genesis 12:1-3)

The rest of the book of Genesis and most of Exodus are about how God created families, tribes, and ultimately a nation from His starting point with Abraham. This divinely created nation was known as Israel after the new name given by God to Abraham's grandson Jacob. The families of Jacob's sons or the "tribes of Israel" are the beginning of the nation promised to Abraham by God. This was not a divine choice based on favoritism, but a purposeful and important part of God's redemptive plan. Israel as a nation was designed and selected to be God's instrument to bless all the nations of the world. Later, in Exodus, God became King of this nation and so Israel became the pattern or template of what thereafter was known as the kingdom of God.

From its beginning with one man, Abraham, the nation of Israel was commanded by God to be ethnically "pure." Membership in the nation was restricted to the genetic children of Abraham, Isaac, and Jacob, although provisions for the just and loving treatment of foreigners were lawfully part of God's reign as King. The divinely commanded separation of Israel from other peoples is why in the New Testament, which came more than one thousand years after the law was given to Moses, the revelation of Jews and Gentiles as equals in God's kingdom is proclaimed by the apostle Paul as the revelation of a "mystery." He wrote, "that the Gentiles are fellow heirs and fellow members of the body, and fellow partakers of the promise in Christ Jesus through the gospel" (Ephesians 3:6).

Humans are designed by God to cling to their families and prioritize people who are related to them by blood or culture. Inspired by the Spirit of God, the apostle Paul described how God was taking His chosen national example of Israel beyond ethnic and cultural "purity" to a pluralism based on shared faith and the sacrificial love of the King Himself. "But now in Christ Jesus you [Gentiles] who formerly were far off have been brought near by the blood of Christ. For He Himself is our peace, who made both groups into one and broke down the barrier of the dividing wall, by abolishing in His flesh the enmity, which is the Law of commandments contained in ordinances, so that in Himself He might make the two into one new man, thus establishing peace" (Ephesians 2:13-15).

Unknowingly, Paul was not only laying the foundation for the growth of Christianity throughout the Gentile world, but also for the rise of many ethnically diverse and democratic societies existing today. In the Declaration of Independence of the United States of America (1776), a new sovereign nation on the American continent, the Founding Fathers wrote, "We hold these truths to be self-evident, that all men are created equal, that they are endowed by their Creator with certain unalienable rights, that among these are life, liberty and the pursuit of happiness." This belief, faith, or sentiment cherished by those men almost three hundred years ago certainly had roots that reached down into the New Testament writing of Paul.

This brings us to the "mystery," or dilemma of modern nation-states. Neither the dream of a racially or culturally "pure" nation nor the vision of a fully pluralistic one is completely achievable outside of God's kingdom. The tension between these two ideals is like a coiled mainspring that drives, and to a large extent forms, modern politics. What we learn from the Bible is that God has a divine plan for every person as well as one for each family, tribe, nation and the whole world!

He created humans to be nurtured and to develop in families. Families of families become tribes; tribes that agree and unite become nations. Families, tribes, tongues (language groups including cultures), and nations are all meant to be important parts of God's redemptive plan for bringing His kingdom to earth. When Jesus gave the Great Commission to His disciples He said, "Go therefore and make disciples of all the nations . . ." (Matthew 28:19). Of course, the example of Jesus' ministry is discipleship in a small tightly knit group of individuals. But the Great Commission reveals God's strategic plan to transform whole nations.

Discipling nations by seeking to gather ever greater numbers of individuals into larger and larger meetings is doomed to failure. This is the fatal flaw in using numbers of people in attendance at weekly meetings as the main measurement of success or failure in ministry. Ultimately, God's strategic plan is that His wise, loving, and redemptive rule will extend over all the earth. God's kingdom fully coming to earth means that all people everywhere will be disciples. However, God has different tactical methods of discipleship at every level—individual, family, tribe, nation, and the world. There are eternal and godly principles that are the same at every level but significant differences too. You cannot lead nations and societies in the same way you lead people you know personally.

Different leaders, chosen, empowered, and developed by God, are gifted to function at different levels and each level is important. When it comes to ruling the world, however, only God is qualified and worthy. In the future, a human ruler known as the Antichrist will attempt to build and control a worldwide system of government, but it will end in disaster. However, God's worldwide sovereignty is already a reality for those who believe and it will be completely realized after Jesus' return to earth.

Discussion Questions:

1. How many different ethnic groups can I identify in the nation where I live?
2. Is there friction between the "tribes" in my nation? Do all agree to be united and governed as one?
3. How can the church be an expression of ethnic diversity under God's justice and mercy in my nation?

Prayer Point:

Lord, give me a passionate love for all the people of my nation. Help me to love them as You do and demonstrate the inclusive nature of Your kingdom.

Chapter 43

Dual Citizens

Every disciple of God's kingdom will always have at least two citizenships, an earthly one and a heavenly one. Although many people hold multiple passports and are citizens of more than one nation, most people have one place that is their home nation and are subject to the laws of that land. These laws may be completely secular or inspired by a non-Christian religion, but the ultimate authority behind law that governs nations originates with God. Read what the apostle Paul wrote to the believers in Rome.

"Every person is to be in subjection to the governing authorities. For there is no authority except from God, and those which exist are established by God. Therefore, whoever resists authority has opposed the ordinance of God; and they who have opposed will receive condemnation upon themselves. For rulers are not a cause of fear for good behavior, but for evil. Do you want to have no fear of authority? Do what is good, and you will have praise from the same" (Romans 13:1-3).

Every disciple of God's kingdom will always have at least two citizenships, an earthly one and a heavenly one.

These Scriptures speak to us today just as they were written almost two thousand years ago. Believers must be submissive to the government authorities that exist in any nation where we live or work because that authority originates with God. God gives all governments some of His authority, power, and responsibility. He raises up rulers and removes them according to His perfect plans and judgment. Our submission to government authority is not dependent on whether we agree with all the policies of the leaders. The legitimacy of government does not depend on our agreement. A government's responsibility is to protect and serve the best interests of the public. God takes responsibility to judge governments when they do wrong. He has also promised to hear the prayers of His people when they cry out against injustice and can remove governmental leaders when they do evil in His sight.

By today's standards, Roman rule of two thousand years ago would be regarded as brutal and unjust. Nevertheless, according to Paul, disciples should pay taxes and make every effort to respectfully submit to imperfect human government, knowing that we have a higher responsibility and allegiance to God. Paul wrote, "For because of this you also pay taxes, for rulers are servants of God, devoting themselves to this very thing. Render to all what is due them: tax to whom tax is due; custom to whom custom; fear to whom fear; honor to whom honor. Owe nothing to anyone except to love one another; for he who loves his neighbor has fulfilled the law" (Romans 13:6-8).

There is no perfect government on earth except the kingdom of God, where Jesus rules as King. But God's word is clear: In God's kingdom, Jesus' law of love is the highest law of all. He commanded us to love God with everything within us, to love our neighbors as we love ourselves (Matthew 22:36-40), to love each other sacrificially (John 15:13-17), and to love our enemies (Matthew 5:44).

The love Jesus commanded is more than emotion. It is practical and it has political implications. The days of Jesus and Paul were times of intense political conflict for Israel. We know from history that less than forty years after Jesus' crucifixion revolt against Roman rule would devastate Israel. Jesus Himself was tempted to become involved in the biggest political issue of His day—the growing Jewish struggle against Roman oppression.

> Then the Pharisees went and plotted together how they might trap Him in what He said. And they sent their disciples to Him, along with the Herodians, saying, "Teacher, we know that You are truthful and teach the way of God in truth, and defer to no one; for You are not partial

> to any. Tell us then, what do You think? Is it lawful to give a poll-tax to Caesar, or not?" But Jesus perceived their malice, and said, "Why are you testing Me, you hypocrites? Show Me the coin used for the poll-tax." And they brought Him a denarius. And He said to them, "Whose likeness and inscription is this?" They said to Him, "Caesar's." Then He said to them, "Then render to Caesar the things that are Caesar's; and to God the things that are God's." (Matthew 22:15-21)

Jesus was tested by His powerful Jewish enemies, the Pharisees and Herodians, who asked whether it was lawful for the people of Israel to pay tax to Caesar. Knowing that most of the people hated Roman rule, they wanted to trap Jesus into taking a side in the national debate and making a foolish choice between His base of loyal Jewish followers and the Roman government.

Hatred of Rome, and especially Roman taxes, was strong in the region of the Galilee. Jesus' mostly Galilean disciples included at least one who was a radical anti-Roman, Simon, the Zealot (as well as a collector of Roman taxes, Matthew). Jesus answered wisely, saying, in effect, we are dual citizens and owe obedience both to earthly and heavenly rulers. He said this knowing the Pharisees, and even the Herodians, as Jews, would have to agree that their duty to obey God is the greater of the two.

Today, disciples of Jesus face situations similar to those in Jesus' day. We know that God is just and merciful to all without favoritism. But there is great pressure to take sides in the political debates around us. We are constantly tempted to support this popular cause, this political party's platform, this government policy, this ethnic agenda versus that one. Sometimes we feel pressure from others to become identified with a particular side in the fiercely fought conflicts of our time.

To begin with it's good for believers to be involved in the issues of our day. We should participate in our society as good citizens. We should vote, debate, discuss, even run for office! However, it is a mistake to be consumed with debate and solely *identified* with an issue, a government policy, or a political party. Here's what Paul the apostle wrote: "But refuse foolish and ignorant controversies, knowing that they produce quarrels. The Lord's bond-servant must not be quarrelsome, but be kind to all, able to teach, patient when wronged" (2 Timothy 2:23-24). "For our citizenship is in heaven, from which also we eagerly wait for a Savior, the Lord Jesus Christ who will transform the body of our humble state into conformity with the body of His glory, by the exertion of the power that He has even to subject all things to Himself" (Philippians 3:20-21).

Whatever we do or say as citizens, we need to do in the name of Jesus. He is our identity, our King, our reason for entering the public square as citizens of our nation. There should be individuals among us who are called by God to serve professionally in politics. They should and must speak out regarding the issues of the day. However, all believers have dual citizenship and our heavenly one must be prioritized because it is important not only for us but for others as well. We want the unbelievers in our society to know the church as disciples of Jesus, not primarily as the people who support this political leader or that one, this party or that one, this side on an issue or that one.

It is vital for the salvation of the world that the public knows us first and foremost as the people of truth who, out of obedience to God, love all other people. Our identity is that we will do what is right before God, reaching out in love to others in need regardless of which side they are on.

Scholars think Paul's letter to Rome was the last major epistle he wrote. It was written from Corinth around AD 58. About six years later in AD 64, after the great fire in Rome, Nero, the Roman emperor, started his violent persecution of the Christians. Most historians think Paul was executed outside of Rome about that same time.

Paul had been born a Roman citizen, so he understood their thinking and political system. When he wrote his letter, he already knew that Roman rule could be a deadly enemy of the gospel and the Jewish people. After all, Roman authority had crucified Jesus. Still, Paul wrote that believers should submit to the Roman government. It cost the Roman disciples much suffering and sacrifice to submit to their government over the years but in the end, Rome fell and their faith changed the world.

Even though Paul, inspired by the Spirit, wrote that believers should obey government authority and respect political leaders, there will be times when we must respectfully disagree and even refuse to obey. Defying the decree of the Babylonian king, Daniel continued his prayers to God. He was punished, but God delivered him from the lions' den. The disciples, Peter and John, defied the Sanhedrin council and refused to stop preaching about Jesus. It is not always easy to decide how to serve both God and man. There is no simple formula. The only answer is Jesus' Spirit in our lives. We must trust in Him for wisdom and be ready to explain to others why we make this commitment to love and serve both God and our society.

Paul saw that it was the dawning of a bright new day when the gospel began to be preached in Rome. He wrote, "The night is almost gone, and the day is near. Therefore, let us lay aside the deeds of darkness and put on the armor of light" (Romans 13:12). He urged the disciples in Rome to awaken to the spiritual battle they were facing and to "put on" the Lord Jesus Christ.

Similarly, today it is time for us to awaken to the fierce spiritual conflict of our day! The question is whether we will clearly represent Jesus and make Him known by our obedience to sacrificially love every person even when we disagree. This decision may cost us something—we will not always be politically correct, but we will be part of bringing His kingdom to earth.

Discussion Questions:

1. Does God's Word say we should obey our national governments?
2. What do I think it means to be a "citizen" of heaven? (Philippians 3:20)
3. How do I understand Paul's words when he wrote to "put on" the Lord Jesus? (Romans 13:14)

Prayer Point:

Lord, please give me the wisdom and courage to be both a good citizen of my nation and a good citizen of Your heavenly kingdom. Help me to be an example to others who know me but do not yet believe in You.

Chapter 44

Jews and Gentiles Are Equals

Paul, the Messianic Jewish apostle, wrote, "The Gentiles are fellow heirs and fellow members of the body, and fellow partakers of the promise in Christ Jesus through the gospel" (Ephesians 3:6). From Paul's day until now, the relationship between Jews and Gentiles in the New Testament believing community has been of great importance to the church. This is especially true now that the Jewish people have been restored to their land and Messianic Jewish communities are emerging again around the world.

The Jewish people were created and chosen by God for a special role as His example for the rest of humanity. God created the people of Israel, starting from one man, and when He called Abram, God's purpose was that through this man's descendants "all the families of the earth will be blessed" (Genesis 12:3). The divine calling for what eventually became the people of Israel, was to be a model of God's kingdom on earth. In Exodus 19:5-6, God said, "Now then, if you will indeed obey My voice and keep My covenant, then you shall be My own possession among all the peoples, for all the earth is Mine; and you shall be to Me a kingdom of priests and a holy nation . . ."

Many centuries after the events recorded in Genesis and Exodus, Paul wrote that even in unbelief and disobedience, God's choice and purpose concerning Israel would never change. "From the standpoint of the gospel they [the people of Israel] are enemies for your sake, but from the standpoint of God's choice they are beloved for the sake of the fathers; for the gifts and the calling of God are irrevocable" (Romans 11:28-29).

Through the New Testament, we learn that God's plan is for His kingdom to be established through the Person and work of Jesus, the Messiah. Jesus' ministry, which was extended through Paul and the apostles, was to make disciples who were called from among both the Jews and the Gentiles. Israel's role as a blessing to all other nations and the model of God's kingdom can only be brought to its fullness when Jesus is honored as "King of the Jews." Israel's unique role as God's biblical example also reveals that there is a distinctive identity and role for every nation in the kingdom since God is the Creator of all.

Paul the apostle explained this relationship using the image of two olive trees in Romans chapter 11. "But if some of the [Jewish] branches were broken off, and you [Gentiles], being a wild olive tree, were grafted in among them, and became a partaker with them of the rich root of the olive tree, do not be arrogant toward the branches; but if you are arrogant, remember that it is not you who supports the root, but the root supports you. You will say then, 'Branches were broken off so that I might be grafted in.' Quite right. They were broken off for their unbelief, but you stand by your faith. Do not be conceited, but fear" (Romans 11:17-20).

Paul wrote that fear of God is the correct Gentile response to the revelation that by faith in Jesus, Gentiles are "grafted in" to the Abrahamic tree. Today, because we are aware of Israel's suffering over the past two thousand years, it is not difficult to understand his prophetic words about God's severe treatment of the broken off branches. Paul further made the point that Gentile Christians might suffer in the same way as the Jews in God's hands if they lapse into unbelief. In the next verses Paul wrote, "For if God did not spare the natural branches, He might not spare you either. Therefore, consider the goodness and severity of God: on those who fell, severity; but toward you, goodness, if you continue in His goodness. Otherwise you also will be cut off" (Romans 11:21-22).

This reveals a side of God that we are reluctant to examine—His judgment. The Jewish people are His example in their obedience as a shining light and also in their disobedience as an example of chastisement. In God's family of all the nations, He has a multitude of children and He loves each of us with eternal, redemptive love. However, there is only one "older brother" in God's family of the nations and that is Israel. This is the nation that He created, called, and chose to be His model or template for all nations. Knowing the Jewish history of wandering and persecutions over the last two thousand years, I think we would agree they have received a more severe mercy than the rest of us!

> Racism is a denial of God's image in people who are made differently from us.

Does the Bible say Jews and Gentiles are like siblings in God's family? Here's what Paul wrote, "For you are all sons of God through faith in Christ Jesus. For as many of you as were baptized into Christ have put on Christ. There is neither Jew nor Greek, there is neither slave nor free, there is neither male nor female; for you are all one in Christ Jesus. And if you are Christ's, then you are Abraham's seed, and heirs according to the promise" (Galatians 3:26-29).

It is clear that in this family of faith, Jews and Gentiles are equal in value before God but different in the roles to which we are called. We are expected by God to lay aside every resentment and jealousy born of our diversity, to function as one in the body of the Lord. "For He Himself is our peace, who made both groups into one and broke down the barrier of the dividing wall, by abolishing in His flesh the enmity, which is the Law of commandments contained in ordinances, so that in Himself He might make the two into one new man, thus establishing peace, and might reconcile them both in one body to God through the cross, by it having put to death the enmity" (Ephesians 2:14-16).

Racism is a denial of God's image in people who are made differently from us. Racial prejudice is an offense against God as Creator. The difficulty in confronting racism is that so much of it is hidden beneath our consciousness. Our ethnic identities are given to us by God and they are reinforced by our upbringing. Experiencing war, prejudice, humiliation, injustice, discrimination, or violence embeds fear and hatred of others in our human hearts. Teaching and indoctrination about racial stereotypes and inherent inferiority or superiority based on race further strengthens our natural preference to be with people who are like ourselves. It takes the death of a certain part of our human nature to love all races equally, like God does. Nevertheless, this is the call of His kingdom.

The division between Jews and Gentiles from a biblical standpoint is the "mother of all ethnic divisions" because it is the one that God established. This is why making the two into "one new man" through the Lordship of Jesus is such a priority for God. It becomes a template for healing ethnic strife throughout the world. Jews and Gentiles are equal in their need for redemption through the shed blood of Jesus, the Lamb of God. Jesus' suffering is designed to absorb the hatred and the fleshly rivalry between Jews and Gentiles. He died for all, rose from the dead, and gave us His Holy Spirit as a promise of complete equality and perfect love in God's kingdom.

Discussion Questions:

1. Why is it important that God made Jews and Gentiles into "one new man" (Ephesians 2:13-16) in His kingdom?
2. Have I ever experienced racial prejudice? What did it feel like?
3. Why is God's kingdom a place of equal acceptance for all races?

Prayer Point:

Lord, help me to stand against racial injustice and prejudice as Your disciple and especially against hatred of Your people, Israel.

Chapter 45

Men and Women Are Equals

Why is a chapter on men and women in God's kingdom relevant and important in a section about the worldwide aspects of the kingdom? Well, roughly one-half of the world is men and the other half is women! If these two massive groups can be effectively joined for God's purposes, joining mere nations becomes an easier task by comparison. The same verse from Galatians chapter three that defines equality between Jews and Gentiles in the kingdom also addresses the calling and value of men and women. "There is neither Jew nor Greek, there is neither slave nor free man, there is neither male nor female; for you are all one in Christ Jesus" (Galatians 3:28).

God considers men and women completely equal in value. God does not consider one gender inherently superior to the other. However, equal in value does not mean interchangeable in terms of nature, roles, and responsibilities. On the sixth day of creation, according to the Bible, "God created man in His own image, in the image of God He created him; male and female He created them" (Genesis 1:27). Humanity is the only part of the universe created in the image of God and this divine image includes both men and women. In God's original act of creation, there was no distinction in value or intrinsic worth between the two genders. The equality of men and women before God and the love between men and women based on that equality was almost destroyed by the fall into sin. However, through God's redemption offered in the new covenant, equality, diversity, and union were restored.

God considers men and women completely equal in value.

The Bible, however, is clear that the roles of men and women in God's kingdom are different. Overall, God's priority is for men to exercise leadership. In marriage, the husband is the head of the wife and the family (Ephesians 5:23). All the writers of the Bible, all the Levitical priests, and all of Jesus' personally chosen apostles were men. Leadership also means being the first to follow God, the first to sacrifice, the first to become humble and confess sin. Effective spiritual leadership requires the grace of God and the character of a disciple.

Leadership is not simply having a recognized position of authority. Leadership in God's kingdom means pressing forward to *follow* God. When we follow God and others follow us, we become leaders in the body of Christ. Without giving some the grace to follow, giving others the grace to lead is meaningless.

It has been said, "If you think you are leading, and no one is following, you're just going for a walk!" Godly leadership produces godly results in others and so, women who follow God become leaders in their own right. Both men and women need God's grace to lead as well as to follow. Jesus, the greatest leader in the world, was the perfect follower of God. He said, "I do nothing on my own initiative, but I speak these things as the Father taught me" (John 8:28) and "The Son can do nothing of Himself, unless it is something He sees the Father doing" (John 5:19).

While having talents across the spectrum of human abilities, women are chosen and gifted by God to give birth and form character by nurturing young lives. Many women are uniquely gifted to establish communities by developing networks of loving and trusted relationships. In general, men lead and women build (Proverbs 14:1). One is not more important than the other and there are also exceptions. While most of the leaders in the Bible are men, Deborah was a prophetess, a judge, and she also served as a general over the armies of Israel. She called herself "a mother in Israel" (Judges 5:7) but she was, without doubt, an important national leader who exercised life and death authority over men and women in an effective way when the need arose.

Esther, who became a queen, is another biblical example of a woman who, by God's grace, was an effective national leader. In the New Testament, the apostle Paul considered Priscilla and her husband, Aquila, his close "fellow workers" and also mentioned that they led a church in their home (Romans 16:3-5).

In God's kingdom there is equality between men and women as well as diversity within the framework and protection of His sovereignty.

It takes reliance on God's Spirit to recognize and honor the divine identity and calling in ourselves as well as in other people. We especially need God's grace to submit, when it is required, to His calling in others and to hear His voice speaking to us through other people. The term *mutual submission* is often used to describe this godly cooperation in marriage as well as in the body of Christ. While biblical leadership is primarily male, all believers are considered to be a part of the "New Jerusalem" (Revelation 21:2, 9-10) which is called "the bride, the wife of the Lamb." That means in the kingdom of God, men and women alike must develop the "feminine" quality of humble yet powerful purity and submission to love and follow our King throughout eternity.

Our distinct callings, identities, and destinies, as determined by God's grace and perfect plan, are sacred. God's sovereignty determines some things that we must be and some things that we must never seek to be. Within the triune Godhead, there are three distinct persons: God the Father, Jesus, the only begotten Son, and the Holy Spirit. Jesus is the exact representation of God's nature (Hebrews 1:3), but He will never, in all eternity, *be* the Father or take God the Father's place. The same is true about the Holy Spirit. This is biblical, basic, and sacred truth.

In God's kingdom there is equality between men and women as well as diversity within the framework and protection of His sovereignty.

Discussion Questions:

1. Are men and women completely equal in value before God?
2. Is there a difference between equality and functionality in God's kingdom?
3. Why is it important for men and women to work together as equals before God for the purposes of His kingdom to be realized?

Prayer Point:

Lord, cleanse my heart of any attitude that values men more highly than women. Heal and release all the people of Your kingdom to walk together in the light of Your justice and love.

Chapter 46

Learning from Israel's Example

As said before, the nation of Israel was created by God beginning with the calling and gifting of one man, Abraham, whose name means "father of many nations" (Genesis 17:5). When God first spoke to Abraham, He told him the basics of the divine plan that would take thousands of years to complete. God said He would make from Abraham's descendants a great nation that would be a blessing to all the families of the earth (Genesis 12:1-3). This was the divine purpose and calling of what became the people of Israel (named after Abraham's grandson Jacob whose name was changed by God). An unbreakable covenant was the greatest gift God gave to Abraham and his people after him. The promises spo-

God intended Israel to understand that "chosen" nation status only has meaning because of the importance God places on all other nations.

ken by God are all recorded in the book of Genesis.

The apostle Paul, writing much later in his inspired letter to Rome, makes the point that regarding Israel, "the gifts and the calling of God are irrevocable" (Romans 11:29).

Craig Keener, professor of New Testament at Asbury Theological Seminary, wrote, "Paul does not regard God's promises to ethnic Israel as canceled – only deferred (Deut. 4:25-31); God still had a covenant with the ancestors (Deut. 7:8). The grafting in of Gentiles (Rom. 11:17) does not mean that they supplant the Jewish people (Rom. 11:18), as if God has no further interest in the latter. The return of ethnic Israel as a whole to the covenant in the end time would join the grafted-in Gentiles and Jewish remnant that already participate in the covenant."

God intended Israel to understand that "chosen" nation status only has meaning because of the importance God places on all other nations. Israel's role is to be a priestly nation serving all humanity as God's example. Twelve hundred years after Abraham we can see this emphasis in Solomon's prayer at the dedication of the first temple in Jerusalem. He prayed,

> Also concerning the foreigner who is not of Your people Israel, when he comes from a far

> country for Your name's sake (for they will hear of Your great name and Your mighty hand, and of Your outstretched arm); when he comes and prays toward this house, hear in heaven Your dwelling place, and do according to all for which the foreigner calls to You, in order that all the peoples of the earth may know Your name, to fear You, as do Your people Israel, and that they may know that this house which I have built is called by Your name. (1 Kings 8:41-43)

Almost two hundred years after Solomon, the great prophet Isaiah spoke, "Also the foreigners who join themselves to the Lord, to minister to Him, and to love the name of the Lord, to be His servants, everyone who keeps from profaning the Sabbath and holds fast My covenant; even those I will bring to My holy mountain and make them joyful in My house of prayer. Their burnt offerings and their sacrifices will be acceptable on My altar; for My house will be called a house of prayer for all the peoples" (Isaiah 56:6-7).

As a result of God's emphasis on receiving the worship of people not from Israel, when the great temple was completed by Herod in Jerusalem, it included a large outer plaza called the "courtyard of the Gentiles." This area was specifically set aside for Gentiles from all over the world to gather and worship God.

But by the days of Jesus, it had been taken over by merchants who were allowed to change money for the temple offering and sell sacrificial animals to the many Jews who traveled there to worship, especially on the three pilgrim-

In God's kingdom there is equality between men and women as well as diversity within the framework and protection of His sovereignty.

age feasts of Passover (*Pesach*), seeks (*Shavuot* or Pentecost) and Tabernacles (*Sukkot*). This encroachment angered the Lord and He drove them out with strong words. John's gospel records that He used a small whip made out of cords to emphasize God's anger (John 2:13-17).

"Then they came to Jerusalem. And He entered the temple and began to drive out those who were buying and selling in the temple and overturned the tables of the money changers and the seats of those who were selling doves; and He would not permit anyone to carry merchandise through the temple. And He began to teach and say to them, 'Is it not written, "My house shall be called a house of prayer for all the nations"? But you have made it a robbers' den'" (Mark 11:15-17).

Jesus' use of Isaiah's words from chapter 56:7 (see above) shows that it was not necessarily the commerce that bothered Him (Jewish pilgrims from far away needed to change money and purchase sacrificial animals) but rather the location the vendors had chosen and the contempt for the foreigners' right to worship it implied. Quite possibly, the merchants were there, in the temple precinct, because of financial arrangements they had made with the chief priests and if that was so, driving out their source of commissions and kickbacks would have been another reason for powerful people in Jerusalem to desire Jesus' removal.

At the very beginning of His ministry, when Jesus came to Nazareth to read and preach in the synagogue where He had grown up, He read from Isaiah's Messianic prophecy in the first verses of chapter 61 and then boldly proclaimed that He was the One promised in those inspired words. Jesus said, "Today, this Scripture has been fulfilled in your hearing" (Luke 4:21).

Israel was nurtured by God to be the people who would bring His light to other nations, but later it became the chosen nation that chose not to be chosen!

Jesus announced that He was the Person anointed by God, that is, the Messiah in Isaiah's prophecy and on that occasion, the people in Nazareth reacted favorably to His surprising proclamation. The gospel writer Luke recorded the following, "And all were speaking well of Him, and wondering at the gracious words which were falling from His lips; and they were saying, 'Is this not Joseph's son?'" (Luke 4:22). After all, they probably reasoned, if He turns out to be the long-awaited Messiah, how bad could this be for Nazareth? Their little town was certainly not high on the list of "places to visit in the Galilee" at that time! But those verses were only the start of Jesus' message that day. He began to speak of two Jewish prophets who ministered to Gentiles, reminding the synagogue crowd of their obligation as the chosen people to bless the Gentile nations. Then the mood changed radically in that meeting place!

> And He said, "Truly I say to you, no prophet is welcome in his hometown. But I say to you in truth, there were many widows in Israel in the days of Elijah, when the sky was shut up for three years and six months, when a great famine came over all the land; and yet Elijah was sent to none of them, but only to Zarephath, in the land of Sidon, to a woman who was a widow. And there were many lepers in Israel in the time of Elisha the prophet; and none of them was cleansed, but only Naaman the Syrian." And all the people in the synagogue were filled with rage as they heard these things and they got up and drove Him out of the city and led Him to the brow of the hill on which their city had been built, in order to throw Him down the cliff. But passing through their midst, He went His way. (Luke 4:24-30)

The Jewish people of Nazareth in Jesus' day were not just indifferent but hostile to being reminded of their place in God's divine plan for the world. Everyone in the synagogue would already have known Isaiah's prophecies about Israel's calling to bring forth Messianic light to the world. "I am the LORD, I have called you in righteousness, I will also hold you by the hand and watch over you, and I will appoint you as a covenant to the people, as a light to the nations" (Isaiah 42:6).

"He says, 'It is too small a thing that You should be My Servant to raise up the tribes of Jacob and to restore the preserved ones of Israel; I will also make You a light of the nations So that My salvation may reach to the end of the earth'" (Isaiah 49:6).

Israel was nurtured by God to be the people who would bring His light to other nations, but later it became the chosen nation that chose not to be chosen! Jesus once asked whether it is better when commanded by the Father to say "No!" but then regret it and go to do His will or to be the one who says "Yes" and then never obeys. Every disciple should be so passionate in obedience and so fearful to disobey God that we will never refuse to do our Father's will.

As a result of disobedience, Israel experienced the severity of God's judgment. Jesus wept over Jerusalem and said, "Jerusalem, Jerusalem, who kills the prophets and stones those who are sent to her! How often I wanted to gather your children together, the way a hen gathers her chicks under her wings, and you were unwilling. Behold, your house is being left to you desolate!" (Matthew 23:37-38)

In those few words, "Behold, your house is being left to you desolate!" Jesus was prophesying the awful destruction that would come upon Jerusalem not forty years after His crucifixion, the wanderings and persecutions that would follow through the centuries, and even the horrifying terrors of the Holocaust. But He followed that by also saying, "For I say to you, from now on you will not see Me until you say, 'Blessed is He Who comes in the name of the Lord!'" (Matthew 23:39).

Toward the end of His earthly ministry, Jesus said to Jerusalem, "You will not see Me until you say . . ." Today,

Israel has returned as a nation from the long centuries of wandering. In modern Israel, Messianic Jews rephrase Jesus' words filling His promise with fresh meaning. The positive side of "You *will not* see Me *until* you say..." is "You *will* see Me *when* you say . . ." The Scripture "Blessed is He who comes in the name of the Lord" taken from Psalm 118 is prayed, proclaimed, and sung in today's Messianic congregations in Jerusalem and across the land.

Now, Messianic Jews are arising in Israel to welcome Jesus back home while embracing Arab Christians and Gentile brothers and sisters from all the nations. A parallel transformation is also happening in many Christian communities throughout the world. A new generation in churches around the world is recognizing and honoring Israel's prophetic calling and significance.

A new era for Israel and the church is dawning that is destined to impact the world. It is connected to the purpose and power of the Holy Spirit, who is being poured out on the holy bride of the Lord, the body of Messianic Jews and Gentile Christians from every tongue and tribe and nation!

The final question that burned in the hearts of Jesus' personal disciples and His answer to them has special meaning for us today. "So when they had come together, they were asking Him, saying, 'Lord, is it at this time You are restoring the kingdom to Israel?' He said to them, 'It is not for you to know times or epochs which the Father has fixed by His own authority but you will receive power when the Holy Spirit has come upon you; and you shall be My witnesses both in Jerusalem, and in all Judea and Samaria, and even to the remotest part of the earth'" (Acts 1:6-8).

The apostles wanted to know when Jesus, risen from the

dead and filled with authority and power, would restore the rule of God to their nation. Jesus did not say no, but He also did not say when. He answered by implying it was going to be a long process because from that time onward it would not be only Israel but all the world that God would rule as King. Before His crucifixion Jesus had already taught his disciples, “And this gospel of the kingdom will be preached in all the world as a witness to all the nations and then the end will come” (Matthew 24:14 NKJV).

Furthermore, the disciples as “witnesses” would play a key role by being filled with power from the Holy Spirit’s outpouring when the feast of Pentecost came a few weeks later. The international aspects of God’s plan were described centuries earlier in this beautiful part of Isaiah’s prophecy. Today as well, it describes a fulfillment for Israel and a fulfillment for the church.

“Arise, shine; for your light has come, and the glory of the Lord has risen upon you. For behold, darkness will cover the earth and deep darkness the peoples, but the Lord will rise upon you and His glory will appear upon you. Nations will come to your light, and kings to the brightness of your rising” (Isaiah 60:1-3).

Discussion Questions:

1. Is Israel God's example in obedience as well as in disobedience?
2. Did Israel in the days of Jesus fail as God's example of His love for all peoples?
3. What can I learn from Israel's example about the role of the church in society today?

Prayer Point:

Lord, cause us to learn from the example of our "older brother" in God's kingdom, Israel. We want to be a light to the world. Please never allow our fellowships to be seen as inwardly focused or spiritual "clubs" by unbelievers.

Chapter 47

Crossing Cultural Borders

The word *culture* comes from the word *cultivate*, that is, to grow, tend, foster, or nurture. We use this word when we talk about "cultured pearls" or "culturing bacteria" in a laboratory. Cultures are the environment where living things grow and mature. Our human cultures have a powerful role in our development as individuals and socially conscious adults. Our cultures are alive. They are born and grow like coral reefs, a little at a time. Some become thriving ecosystems full of variety, color, and creativity, while others can become hardened around behaviors that are dysfunctional or values that are hostile to God's purposes. Like all living things, cultures can also stop growing, wither, and die.

Some say that culture is like an iceberg floating in the sea. Because of its great weight, only a small portion of an iceberg is visible. The bulk of it is beneath the surface where, as in the case of the *Titanic*, it can pose a danger to whatever gets too close without taking precautions. The surface elements of culture are obvious like language, customs, clothing, foods, tastes in music, and other things. The deeper and weightier aspects of culture are its values and beliefs. What makes them less visible and harder to change is that they are often embedded in the unconscious.

The power of culture is obvious at the level of the tribe because it binds people together around shared values, racial identity, language, traditions, education, and religion. Once a culture forms it is very difficult to change because of the underlying influence it has on young people while they are growing up. Since nations are formed by the agreement of tribes to unite, some countries have a national culture imposed by a dictatorship or religious coercion while others have ongoing dialog and tension between subcultures in their national community. Because culture is so powerful in molding our individual and social lives, its effects can be far-reaching in both positive and negative ways.

All human cultures have good points and dysfunctional aspects too. Look at your own and you will recognize love, justice, and acceptance but if you look more closely you may see cruelty, sexual exploitation, and racism. It is God's great desire to heal all nations by implanting in them the lawful culture of His kingdom. Discipleship has cultural impact and Jesus sent His disciples into the world to make disciples of all the nations. While the word *culture* does not appear in the Bible, there are laws, traditions, festivals, songs, and the stories of heroes, lovers, kings, warriors, and miracle workers in it.

All human cultures have good points and dysfunctional aspects too.

The powerful concept of culture is represented in the Bible by at least two words. The "world" refers to godless, pagan culture and the "law" refers to the divinely given culture of Israel. The apostle John wrote to His disciples, "Do not love the world, nor the things in the world" (1 John 2:15a). The New Testament Greek word for world is *kosmos,* from which we derive the English words *cosmetic* and *cosmopolitan.* It means the interlocking system of things and appearances that characterize this present age. In the verse above, John, a Jewish disciple, may be using Hebrew parallelism to equate the world with the material benefits of the world. These "things" must never be the object of our devotion.

However, Jesus told Nicodemus, a religiously observant Israeli leader, that "God so loved the world [*kosmos*] that He gave His only begotten Son that whoever believes in Him will have everlasting life" (John 3:16). Jesus showed that despite the world's rejection of Him, God still cares enough about His fallen creation to sacrifice what He loves most to redeem it.

From the example of Israel in the Bible, it is not difficult to see the connection between culture and law. The written and unwritten laws embedded in every culture serve to define and protect the values and beliefs that people cherish. Even a casual reading of the Torah shows us that God's law for Israel included commands concerning business and real estate transactions, family relationships, sexual morality, education, justice in the courts, fair treatment of workers and foreigners, foods to eat and not eat, clothes to wear and not wear, songs to sing, values to teach children, praiseworthy attitudes, public health care, and many other important topics. According to the Torah, the entire nation of Israel was meant to be "holy," that is, reserved or set aside for God's use. All of society and culture was meant to reflect the sovereign Lord's glory and lawful reign. The core of Israel's culture, and by extension, the culture of God's kingdom, is contained in the laws of the Bible.

Becoming a disciple of the Lord means being born anew into His kingdom (John 3:7, 1 Peter 1:23) where we also receive a spirit of adoption (Romans 8:15) that makes God our loving Father. Our new citizenship is in heaven (Philippians 3:20). We learn to hear God's Word, understand the Scriptures, and interpret God's law in the spirit of life—not as the burdensome commands of an oppressive and out of touch dictator. The culture of God's kingdom is the environment where this process of growth to maturity, called discipleship, takes place. Yes, God's kingdom has a vibrant culture and it can be like spiritual medicine to the struggling cultures of the world.

One of the most important roles for the local church is to create an environment where young Christians can absorb heavenly culture that molds the way we think, behave, and speak. This is especially important when it comes to how we regard people different from us. Mature Christians and disciples of the Lord should be sensitive to racial and cultural prejudice. We are representatives of a kingdom that includes all peoples and should appreciate the values of multiculturalism.

However, for the dream of cultures mingling together and enriching each other peacefully to be a reality, there must be a higher heavenly authority defining justice and mercy and providing a fair and objective cultural standard for all. Without this, multiculturalism becomes a culture of relativism. Who is to say whose values have priority when conflict inevitably arises? With no shared cultural standard, the result is conflict, injustice, and survival of the loudest, strongest, or most influential.

Disciples of Jesus have a calling and an obligation (Romans 1:14-17) to be faithful to our King, the kingdom to which we belong, and the culture of discipleship that nurtures us. This means displaying the highest values of our culture: love, truth, justice, and the limitless grace of God, wherever we go. We treat all the other cultures of the world with respect, but we cannot deny who we are or to whom we belong. We cross borders of all kinds and bring the culture of the kingdom wherever we are sent.

Discussion Questions:

1. How does the word *culture* relate to a place where living things are nurtured and grown?

2. Does loving all people mean accepting the values found in all cultures?

3. Does God's kingdom have a culture with its own values and beliefs? How would I describe it?

Prayer Point:

Lord, train me in the eternal values and foundational beliefs of the culture of Your kingdom. Empower me to be a living testimony of someone nurtured and brought up in God's house.

Chapter 48

Outsiders Bring Change

It seems that whenever God wants to change an existing culture or to begin an entirely new movement, He finds an "outsider" to do the work. An outsider is someone who does not share the values, ethnicity, customs, or sometimes even the language of the dominant group. In Japan, the word for foreigner is *gaijin*. It is formed by two Chinese characters (called *kanji*). The first character means "outside" and the second one means "person." A foreigner in Japanese culture is literally an "outside person."

Before God made His covenant with Abram and changed his name to Abraham, He first called him to become an outsider. God said, "Go forth from your country and from your relatives and from your father's house to the land which I will show you" (Genesis 12:1). Abraham was an outsider in the promised land for the rest of his life. But God kept His promise to Abraham's descendants, which is found in the next verse, "And I will make you a great nation and I will bless you and make your name great and so you shall be a blessing (Genesis 12:1-2).

Moses was another man whom God turned into an outsider. He was someone whose identity kept being reinvented. Throughout his life, he was never allowed to fully become one with the people around him. From his birth, he was a Hebrew slave raised in Pharaoh's court like a prince of Egypt. At the age of forty, Moses, perhaps desperately struggling for his true identity, murdered an Egyptian overseer who was abusing a Hebrew slave.

After that, he became a fugitive and took refuge among the Midianites where he was a foreigner. Forty years later, he might have been almost completely assimilated. He had married a Midianite woman, raised a family, spoke the language, and was being accepted. Then God called out to him at the burning bush and sent him back to Egypt at the age of eighty.

After confronting Pharaoh, parting the Red Sea, and leading the tribes of Israel for the next forty years, Moses became a legendary leader. But he was never culturally the same as the people he led. During those years in the wilderness, he was the only Israelite among them who had never been a slave. All his countrymen spoke and acted like slaves. They had a slave culture and probably even told slave jokes about the Egyptians. Moses shared none of it. He was a cultural outsider even among his own people.

Of course, Jesus is and was the ultimate outsider. Yes, He became a man and lived among His people Israel, but was there ever before Him and will there ever be after Him, another person in the same category? As the only begotten Son of God, His background is eternally unique. He said to His countrymen, "You are from below, I am from above; you are of this world, I am not of this world" (John 8:23).

By the time He walked this earth, Jesus had already spent an eternity with God, His Father, in heaven. When Jesus taught about the kingdom of God, the only difficulty He might have had was making what was crystal clear to Him understandable to simple and sinful people like us. Jesus spent His time here on earth like a foreigner, even among His own family, but He brought change that has the power to save the world.

The apostle Paul was born into a traditional and religious Jewish family. His family kept the Sabbath, observed the feasts of the Lord, memorized God's Word, and tried to keep the commandments of the Torah. However, Paul was not born in the land of Israel but as a Roman citizen in Tarsus, a Greek-speaking city, which is now in southern Turkey. He might have had non-Jewish playmates as a boy, but while still a youth, he was sent off to Jerusalem and groomed to be a rabbi under Gamaliel, one of the leading Jewish religious leaders of his day. Looking at his life, it is easy to see that Paul never had the luxury of being part of the dominant group in his culture. He was always an outsider.

Paul's earliest years were as a Jewish boy in a Gentile city. Then, in Jerusalem, he was not a native Israeli or part of the Jerusalem "insider" Pharisee and Sadducee cliques. Other young rabbinical students must have had connections with the priestly families, with those who served in the great temple and even the Sanhedrin. But Paul was a Jew of the *diaspora* (dispersion or scattering), who had grown up in a foreign land among Gentiles. Perhaps to compensate, he became an overly zealous "Pharisee of the Pharisees" to the point where he was more radical than even his mentor, Gamaliel, in his persecution of the Messianic sect of Jews who followed the radical preacher *Yeshua* (Jesus).

Later, as a believer, Paul was still an outsider even after his encounter on the road to Damascus with the risen Lord who called him to be a disciple and an apostle. All the original apostles of Jesus were Galileans and had personally walked with the Lord. Paul had none of these credentials. Finally, as a Jew, he would have also been an outsider among the Gentiles to whom he was sent apostolically even though he understood their language and values.

Because of his background, Paul was uniquely suited for the cross-cultural understanding that God gave him by revelation and the apostolic ministry that resulted. Finding his true identity and cultural home in God's kingdom came because of Paul's radical identification with Jesus' death and resurrection.

After he believed in Jesus, Paul became an enemy in the eyes of his own religiously observant Jewish countrymen and former friends, who then tried to kill him several times. Paul fled from the Jewish culture that had nurtured him but he later reappeared, empowered by his new faith.

Paul understood and taught others about the freedom he found in God's kingdom. Paul wrote to the congregation in Philippi he had planted, "For our citizenship is in heaven, from which also we eagerly wait for a Savior, the Lord Jesus

Christ who will transform the body of our humble state into conformity with the body of His glory, by the exertion of the power that He has even to subject all things to Himself" (Philippians 3:20-21).

In the lives of all the biblical leaders mentioned above, being an outsider was an essential ingredient in what God used to make them instruments of change. The truth is that most people have some part of their life that sets them apart from others or some experience that makes them feel like an outsider. Being an outsider or being in touch with the part of you that is outside the bounds of your home environment is an important part of leadership.

Leaders stand apart and have the ability to look at their situation objectively. Leaders look beyond the accepted and present reality to ask "what if?" questions. This kind of creative thinking is necessary for discovering new directions and for making contingency plans when following old ways leads to failure. Sometimes, living in the "what if?" can cause you to become an outsider when everyone else is satisfied with the status quo.

Joseph in Egypt was that kind of leader. As a boy, he was given supernatural dreams of leadership that separated him from others and caused him to live constantly with the question, "What if my dreams are real?" Later, because of his dreams and unique identity, he was rejected by the closest members of his own family and sold as a slave to foreigners.

Unwilling to accept an immoral relationship with the wife of his new master in Egypt, Joseph was thrown into prison as an outcast among outcasts. From his cherished position as the favorite son in a chosen family, Joseph became a foreigner, a slave, and a convict. But thirteen years after he was betrayed by his brothers, only Joseph, of all the men in that great empire, could see what was going to happen to Egypt. He alone could answer Pharaoh's question, "What if our nation's prosperity and power should suddenly come to an end?"

Joseph paid an awful price as an outsider but emerged as one of the greatest leaders of the Bible.

Is it necessary for all God's leaders to be outsiders to their own culture? Absolutely not! Insiders develop and guide the culture from within. Insiders build organizations, create networks of influence, lead churches, political parties, and even nations. In general, insiders bring people together and create systems. God uses outsiders to bring change.

Discussion Questions:

1. When was I ever treated like an outsider by others? How did that make me feel?
2. Why were Abraham, Moses, Jesus, and Paul considered "outsiders"?
3. What are some of the advantages and disadvantages of being an outsider?

Prayer Point:

Lord, help me endure whenever I am treated like an outsider and made to feel rejected. Please allow me to see the positive side of not always being accepted by others.

Chapter 49

Small Is Powerful

This book is being finished during the COVID-19 coronavirus pandemic that began sweeping the world in 2019. This is the first time in living memory when the entire world has become ill with the same disease at the same time. The world's economy was brought to a standstill by tiny particles no bigger than one or two hundred billionths of a meter across. Invisible except to electron microscopes, hundreds of these viruses can fit on an area smaller than the diameter of a human hair!

The world learned that small in size does not necessarily mean weak or powerless. In a similar way, the church world is learning that large in size does not necessarily mean spiritually powerful. The Coronavirus lockdown ordered by government authorities closed the doors of many church meetings. Christians everywhere turned to their phones, computers and the internet to worship, pray, and teach. To meet the unique challenges of our day, the church started to focus on networking scattered individuals into virtual meetings and using video streaming over social media to bring small meetings of believers to a much greater number of people.

The kingdom of God is eternal and does not change, but the church as God's instrument of the kingdom must change. The form that the church takes in any era is by necessity an accommodation to the surrounding culture. The Catholic church's hierarchy resembles a giant kingdom similar to the monarchies from the era in which it was birthed and developed. Some present-day Protestant churches mirror the modern corporations so instrumental in building industrialized nation-states. Today's information-driven societies are influencing the church to become ever more "networked." The church of the future will grow by becoming increasingly decentralized, meeting in smaller groups but connected by technology into vast networks of shared vision and trusted, redemptive relationships. The most dramatic growth of Christianity today is not in the West but in developing countries where acquiring church property may be opposed by the government or prohibitively expensive. Because of the worldwide proliferation of smart phones, increasingly Christian gatherings and conferences will be organized online, greatly reducing the expenses of travel and accommodation so that many more people can participate.

During the COVID-19 pandemic, congregations all over

the world were forced to transition to online meetings. Small teams of ministers delivered whole worship services, complete with songs, teaching, and prayer to congregants' homes by video and computer technology. Online prayer meetings with dozens, hundreds and sometimes thousands of participants logging in from locations around the globe became commonplace. This is progress and spiritual "territory" that should not be given up by the church after the crisis subsides.

In his visionary book *Houses that Change the World*, Christian author Wolfgang Simson addresses what he calls a reformation of structure in the church today. Simson writes, "The church has to become small in order to grow large. Most churches of today are simply too big to provide real fellowship. They have too often become 'Fellowships without fellowship.' The New Testament church was made up of small groups typically between 10 and 15 people."

For twenty years I served as a board member of an organization dedicated to encouraging church growth throughout the world. The chairman of this international board was then senior pastor of the world's largest single church congregation with hundreds of thousands in attendance, and on the board were about sixty other well-known ministry leaders and senior pastors of some of the largest churches in the world.

Every year we would have an international board meeting and a conference in another city around the world. The purpose was always to encourage one another, as well as the tens of thousands who attended the conferences and prayer meetings, to bring God's kingdom to earth by expanding weekly congregational attendance numerically.

A number of the leaders I got to know during those years are greatly gifted servants of God as well as genuinely humble and generous people. However, what I learned before resigning from the board in 2016 is that our focus on numerical growth as the primary indicator of success in ministry can be shortsighted.

Our focus on numerical growth as the primary indicator of success in ministry can be shortsighted.

The problem is that it is easy to mistake the form of the church in any given era for its primary function. The function of the church is to interpret and apply the love and lawfulness of God's kingdom to our generation in order to make disciples of Jesus. Producing numerically larger congregations by influencing people to attend huge weekly meetings can build successful ministries, but producing disciples is what ultimately extends God's kingdom in any nation.

The cell-church model, which advocates dividing congregations into small groups sometimes called home groups, to facilitate more intimate fellowship, teaching, and prayer became popular a generation ago and by now has many forms around the world. The smaller size of these groups alone does not make them more effective for the Lord. Vision and leadership are what make the crucial difference. If the cell model is employed to further the goal of growing the "mother" congregation ever larger, then the cells will not succeed in developing new leaders, who hear from God and become fruitful by moving into new areas of ministry. They will primarily produce followers loyal to the goal of numerical growth.

The forms that the church adopts should follow rather than determine its function.

Like the restrictions on Christian meetings caused by the COVID-19 pandemic, persecution from governments that are hostile to Christian faith, although painful, can be beneficial to the church. If persecution takes the form of severely limiting the size of groups that can meet together or even prohibiting all religious meetings, it means that small groups of believers must each have a responsible leader who knows and trusts every other member of the group. Jesus was the greatest developer of leadership in others who ever walked this earth! Although He also had an effective ministry to large crowds, He concentrated on working with relatively small groups of disciples. The Spirit of Jesus still operates among us today in the same way. If the fire of persecution forces the church to produce more small groups and more leaders, the result will be positive in ultimately extending God's kingdom.

The forms that the church adopts should follow rather than determine its function. If the function of the church is to produce disciples, then the church should be designed as a "factory" of redeemed and spiritually mature human lives. Most business managers understand that in manufacturing, the focus has to be kept on the quality and performance of the product and not on the size of the factory. If management increases the workforce and invests in facilities or capital equipment while continuing to produce fewer and lower quality products, soon that business will have to shut its doors.

Is it possible that some churches today are like power-generating stations that burn a lot of fuel and generate electricity but consume all the power they produce in order to increase their size? Every year a bigger power plant is built but few wires are being installed to light up communities in the darkness beyond!

This is why God's basic law in His kingdom is about love that nurtures people into their personal calling and divine destiny. Jesus gave His life for the world because of love for believers and non-believers alike. As the "Good Shepherd" He was the greatest pastor who ever lived. He could have built the largest church organization of His era, but He simply refused to do so. He pushed on daily to form God's image in His few disciples, commanding them to love as He loved and to take up their own crosses and follow Him. That is why we are here, still following Him and still motivated by the same love to make disciples, even two thousand years after He finished His work and handed responsibility for His kingdom on earth to others.

Machines that could "think" like humans were imagined and dreamed about for centuries, but the principle of the modern digital computer only emerged around the time of the Second World War. By the 1950s, the race was on to produce bigger and more powerful computers and an entire industry was born around companies like IBM, Honeywell, NCR, Control Data, and others. The first digital computers were huge single machines, called "mainframes," which required a staff of specialists to run and maintain them. Soon computers were becoming more powerful and downsizing so that they could be found in many offices, research institutes, and factories operated by employees who did not need specialized training.

Then came networking and the personal computer. Groups of smaller computers networked together were found to be more powerful, flexible, and cheaper than larger machines. With the invention of the internet, the network became more important than the computer itself. Tiny computers, called “smartphones”, now literally in the hands of children, instantly process massive amounts of data from the “cloud,” which can be anywhere on the planet. The computer that was once the center of an entire industry is now simply a means to access a worldwide web of information. By becoming smaller the computer does much more than ever before.

This is a modern picture for the church of the future. The rise of the internet made a major impact on the way modern cultures go about their daily business. “Brick and mortar” stores and malls are giving way to online shopping and home delivery. In the same way, “brick and mortar” churches will give way to congregations that meet in small groups for fellowship and equipping disciples but are massively networked to reach and share resources with millions of trusted brothers and sisters worldwide. Large churches can be successful in making disciples if they keep their primary focus on spiritually equipping everyone and continually developing new leaders. This means having a strategy for growth through smaller, more autonomous subgroups. If you belong to a large church and recognize that the corporate worship service is not sufficient by itself to develop you as a disciple, seek opportunities to grow spiritually with a few others in addition to your weekly church attendance.

When we visit places in Europe where Christianity was established over one thousand years ago, it is instructive to look carefully at the impressive cathedrals that were built as places of fellowship, teaching, and worship. Some of those cathedrals took over a century to build and would cost billions of today's dollars. We understand now those days are over and for the purposes of the Lord to be fulfilled in the end times, such projects don't need to be undertaken again.

In the same way, investments in church facilities that stretch today into tens, even hundreds of millions of dollars per project is a growth model that is passing away. The most important resource in the church has always been people who are focused on growing as disciples. Having a large, comfortable building is a great blessing but the church of Jesus has never required "temples made with human hands" to produce prayer, worship, Bible teaching, and spiritual growth.

Discussion Questions:

1. Are smaller groups better than large meetings for training and equipping disciples?
2. Why does the church put such high value on large meetings? Can Christians benefit from both very small and very large meetings?
3. Should I be part of a small group focused on growing in faith and godly character?

Prayer Point:

Lord Jesus, please deliver me from the attitude that bigger groups are more important than small ones. Help me focus on the few people closest to me and serve them spiritually with the best I have.

Chapter 50

Love Your Neighborhood

Mentioned in Revelation chapter 21, the "New Jerusalem" is a picture of heaven. It is a huge city, actually about the size of Australia on the ground and rising over a thousand miles into the atmosphere. Such a city is built for a God-centered society. It is a new world and God will be there, always present, filling the city with His light. Heaven is described in Scripture as a city. This is the vision that Abraham was seeking by faith.

"By faith Abraham, when he was called, obeyed by going out to a place which he was to receive for an inheritance; and he went out, not knowing where he was going. By faith he lived as an alien in the land of promise, as in a

> After love for God, the greatest heavenly command is to love your neighbor.

foreign land, dwelling in tents with Isaac and Jacob, fellow heirs of the same promise for he was looking for the city which has foundations, whose architect and builder is God" (Hebrews 11:8-10).

In the heavenly city, as in any society, there must be houses where families live, as well as places where groups of families gather or neighborhoods. After love for God, the greatest heavenly command is to love your neighbor. Spiritual neighborhoods exist today. They are groups of people drawn together by God through bonds of family, covenantal friendship, or practical need. These groups meet in their homes to eat, share their lives, encourage each other, and grow together. Recognizing who is my neighbor is at the heart of Jesus' teaching in the parable of the Good Samaritan (Luke 10:25-37).

The church is a reflection of heaven coming to earth and should be composed of neighborhoods where mature disciples bring people together for worship, Bible teaching, doing good works and prayer. The present-day challenge for God's kingdom is to begin forming those neighborhood relationships and building them up person by person, family by family and house by house. This work is a partnership with God that also requires our faith and wisdom. The Scriptures say, "Unless the Lord builds the house, they labor in vain who build it" (Psalm 127:1) and "By wisdom a house is built, and by understanding it is established and by knowledge the rooms are filled with all precious and pleasant riches" (Proverbs 24:3-4).

Apostolic leadership is different from pastoring a large church or speaking evangelistically to massive crowds. Apostles are strategists who raise up other leaders who have diverse gifts and callings. As an example, think of apostles as mayors who want healthy neighborhoods of all kinds everywhere in their cities. Networks of spiritual neighborhoods that grow by meeting from house to house are the optimal shape for the church as we move further into the end times. Meeting often in neighborhood groups requires more discipled leaders but this model will also create more leaders who can disciple others. Groups of spiritual neighbors move the church away from its "spectator" culture where many people sit passively and receive ministry from a few gifted individuals. Multiplication through networks of spiritual neighborhoods prioritizes the development of leaders who can take responsibility for a small group of family members, friends, neighbors, and co-workers who meet face-to-face on a regular basis. Decentralized, networks of smaller groups are less expensive to operate than organizing mass meetings and they survive more readily under persecution. Periodic very large meetings do have a significant place in the kingdom of God. However, their purpose in general is to cast vision, evangelize, or mobilize for specific large-scale projects.

In my personal experience as a minister I have found that, on the whole, the amount of truth from God's Word that can be shared at any given time is in inverse relationship to

Spiritual neighborhoods are the optimal environment for making disciples.

the number of people in the room. The more people that gather the fewer truths that can be spoken and absorbed. If you ever have the chance, as I once had, to address a stadium full of believers you will probably have to be very focused on articulating and reinforcing just one main point!

Christianity is entering the "last lap" of the great race that began in Jerusalem two thousand years ago. Now, finally, the end is in sight. Christians can look across the globe and see the remaining nations and cultures where the gospel of the kingdom has not yet become a witness. The number of resistant populations is shrinking. Today, the fastest growth of Christian faith is found among people groups who were until a short time ago the most hostile to its truth.

Now is the time to realign the church to God's final purposes and prepare it to meet the challenges posed by the ending of this age. Hundreds of millions of people are pressing forward to enter the kingdom of God around the world. In order to respond, a new "army" of responsible young disciples who can be leaders is the critical requirement. Fruitful leaders create other leaders through friendship, love, wisdom, solving problems together, and prayer. Big crowds are not the place for this. The most critical aspect of God's kingdom always takes place in informal groups among friends, in homes, and not in public. Spiritual neighborhoods are the optimal environment for making disciples.

Neighborhood fellowships that met in homes had a vital role in the formation of the earliest church. After the outpouring of the Holy Spirit in Jerusalem in Acts chapter 2, the Scripture says, "They were continually devoting themselves to the apostles' teaching and to fellowship, to the breaking of bread and to prayer. . . . Day by day continuing with one mind in the temple, and breaking bread from house to house, they were taking their meals together with gladness and sincerity of heart" (Acts 2:42, 46).

The church of the future must develop forms that are optimized for the accomplishment of its divine calling. Expecting a modern church organization that is focused on numerical growth to consistently produce high quality disciples is counterproductive. My friend, Rev. Edmund Chan of Singapore, is the founder of the Global Alliance of International Disciplemaking Churches. In his insightful book, *A Certain Kind - Intentional Disciplemaking That Redefines Success In Ministry*, he wrote, "Disciplemaking is not one of the many options in the varied ministries one might be inclined towards. Rather, it is the core calling of God! Jesus did not say, 'Go into the world and launch prayer movements (important as prayer is!),' or 'Go into the world and have excellent worship services,' or 'Go into the world and conduct solid Bible studies,' etc. Jesus said, 'Go into the world and *make disciples of all nations*! It is the core mission of God for the church, towards which all the other ministry concerns contribute."

Disciples are produced by other disciples with whom they share a personal relationship. Basically, we can best disciple the people who become our friends. How many is the optimum number? Well, you can ask yourself the question, "How many real friends do I have?" Everyone is different and there are a lot of studies related to this question but the most common numbers I found are between five and twenty good friends per person at any given time. Jesus, of course, chose twelve.

Friendship by definition is personal and some people for various reasons do not like sharing that area of their lives. However, if the friendship part of our lives as disciples is handed over to the Lord and dedicated to His service, then the skills we have for knowing, loving, and helping our friends become His tools to develop disciples for eternal life and the kingdom of God. We will discover that almost everyone who has made the decision to be a disciple can share their gifts and experience with a few others who enjoy meeting together on a regular basis. Moreover, we will find that some of us are really good at this when we intentionally choose the right group of friends.

The Bible says that Jesus prayed all night before choosing His twelve disciples. These men would become His closest friends and stick with Him to the end. He chose people who were not like Him and some who may not have liked Him at first. Jesus, the perfect Man, chose the friends His Father had already chosen for Him. One of them in His own words was a devil and, when the crisis came, would betray Him. This is such a powerfully human story because we all know that our friends have the power to hurt us. We are careful about who we allow to become our friends. Yet without Judas' betrayal, Jesus could never have accomplished His purpose on earth. God knew all about every one of the twelve disciples He gave to Jesus and worked His eternal plan through their lives and their friendship.

This is the vision of the neighborhood church. It is the

form of the church that captures the power of friendship and brings it to the level of covenant with God. This is one of the most powerful gifts God has given to humans. Soldiers in combat know that when the battle begins, you will risk or even sacrifice your life for the close friends who are there with you. A soldier may join an army out of patriotism, family pride, obligation, coercion, or any other reason. But when it comes to life and death, you lay down your life for your friends. This is what Jesus said is the ultimate demonstration of love. He said, "Greater love has no one than this, that one lay down his life for his friends" (John 15:13).

Small groups of friends that become teams through dedication to a shared goal are very effective in changing our big and complicated world. Steve Jobs, the founder of Apple Inc., was arguably the greatest innovator and business leader of the digital computer era. In a 2003 "60 Minutes" television interview he said, "My model of business is the Beatles. They were four very talented guys who kept each other's negative tendencies in check. They balanced each other and the total was greater than the sum of the parts. And that's how I see business. Great things in business are never done by an individual. They are done by a team of people."

Jesus said to His disciples, "No longer do I call you slaves, for the slave does not know what his master is doing; but I have called you friends, for all things that I have heard from My Father I have made known to you. You did not choose Me, but I chose you, and appointed you that you would go and bear fruit, and that your fruit would remain, so that whatever you ask of the Father in My name He may give to you. This I command you, that you love one another" (John 15:15-17).

Discussion Questions:

1. Have I ever had a spiritual friend who helped me mature as a Christian?
2. What do I expect from someone who is my friend? Can God use friendship to make disciples?
3. Why are homes better places for making disciples than public meetings?

Prayer Point:

Lord, I long to be known as a "friend of God." Would You teach me how to be Your friend and help others to become friends with us?

Chapter 51

Jesus' Signs of the End

The Bible is clear that human history has an ending point, a goal toward which it travels under God's direction. Every day brings us closer to the return of the Lord and the end of this age. The world has been moving toward its final culmination since the creation of humans in Genesis and the days of the patriarchs. History changes but God remains the same. Kingdoms and empires come and go. Israel and the church have also changed with the times, but the sovereignty of God that is expressed through His kingdom in heaven and on earth remains constant and eternal.

Now we are in the end times. In Matthew chapter 23, Jesus predicted that Jerusalem and the people of Israel would not see Him again until they said, "Blessed is He who comes in the name of the Lord!" (Matthew 23:39). Now, Israel is alive again as a modern nation, and Israeli Messianic Jews are beginning to sing and proclaim these same inspired words (Psalm 118:26) to Jesus in congregations all over their land. Two thousand years ago, toward the end of His ministry on earth, the first Messianic Jewish disciples asked Jesus privately, "Tell us, when will these things happen, and what will be the sign of Your coming, and of the end of the age?" (Matthew 24:3). The following is His answer.

> And Jesus answered and said to them, "See to it that no one misleads you. For many will come in My name, saying, 'I am the Christ,' and will mislead many. You will be hearing of wars and rumors of wars. See that you are not frightened, for those things must take place, but that is not yet the end. For nation will rise against nation and kingdom against kingdom and in various places there will be famines and earthquakes. But all these things are merely the beginning of birth pangs. Then they will deliver you to tribulation, and will kill you, and you will be hated by all nations because of My name. At that time many will fall away and will betray one another and hate one another. Many false prophets will arise and will mislead many. Because lawlessness is increased, most people's love will grow cold. But the one who endures to the end, he will be saved. This gospel of the kingdom shall be preached in the whole world

> as a testimony to all the nations and then the end will come. (Matthew 24:4-14)

The five signs Jesus gave in the verses above are becoming increasingly evident in our generation.

1. Deception, false teaching, false Messiahs, misinformation, and "fake news" are characterizing our times. We live in a globalized information age when nations are beginning to focus their rivalries on attacks via the internet using false information meant to disrupt the politics and economics of their enemies and rivals. Post-modern, information-driven culture is fertile ground for bizarre conspiracy theories, racial supremacist ideology, cults, sects, and false religions.
2. Wars and rumors of wars are the new normal. Globalization has not produced a new era of peaceful cooperation and coexistence but rather the empowering of disruptive or dysfunctional societies to influence or threaten the rest of the planet. Hiroshima, Nagasaki, and the Cold War era that followed gave the world a deep fear of nuclear armaments and reluctance in nations possessing them to use such horrific weapons of mass destruction. Today, however, dictatorships like North Korea and Iran are developing nuclear weapons and at the same time the world has entered an era of "limited wars" where powerful nations use foreign proxies in attempts to "cover their tracks" and achieve regional aims. Intelligence agencies and news media are challenged by the sheer number of conflicts taking place in different parts of

the world concurrently. Almost anywhere could suddenly become a new "hotspot."

3. Persecution of believers has risen to new heights in our "enlightened" and "tolerant" age with the list of genocides, mass abductions, beheadings, enforced disappearances, prison terms for Christian workers, and forced closure of churches growing longer each week.
4. Lawlessness is the spirit of our era. Post-modern, post-truth relativism is preached like religious doctrine at universities in the West that were once the greatest centers of open-minded, fact-based learning. Many of those same universities, especially in the United States, were established centuries ago as Bible colleges in the belief, "The truth shall make you free" (John 8:32). Neither liberal democracies nor oppressive dictatorships can stop popular culture from casting off moral and sexual restraints, allowing the abuse of women and children, sexual slavery, human trafficking, and perversion to go mainstream.
5. The good news of God's kingdom is being preached and demonstrated as a "witness" in every nation of the world before the return of the Lord. To preach the gospel of the kingdom, the church must turn away from its many unbiblical beliefs and doctrines and return to its foundations in the inspired Scriptures. As a sign of end time restoration, Israel, the nation that was first chosen by God to demonstrate His kingdom on earth, is back again as if from the dead, after nearly two thousand years of absence. The

> foundation of biblical unity in God's kingdom is being restored as Christians and Messianic Jews join together in faith under one King. This is the Lord's body that is defined not by traditions or church doctrines but in the words of Scripture from Genesis to Revelation.

While we are able to discern a number of important signs of our times that set the stage for the Lord's return, Jesus called this period of history "merely the beginning of birth pangs" (Matthew 24:8, Mark 13:8). Birth pangs, as mothers know, begin with mild contractions and long periods of time between them, but the pains increase in frequency and intensity as the awaited birth approaches.

This is how it will be in these end times: one crisis, like a war, a natural disaster, an epidemic, a market crash followed by a period of quiet, then followed again by another crisis. How do expectant mothers endure the pains of childbirth? Well, I don't know personally! But I do know that in childbirth classes they teach expectant mothers, "Don't focus on the next painful contraction, focus on the baby that is coming!" The pains have a purpose. The tiny child is being positioned and prepared because new life is coming into the world.

Globalization is not just an economic and cultural trend that is interesting or fashionable to discuss. The entire world is being compressed and interconnected in previously unimaginable ways. The Bible predicts that before the return of the Lord, the world will be formed into a single political and economic system that is opposed to the kingdom of God. The ruling power of this system is the spirit of the Antichrist.

"And he causes all, the small and the great, and the rich and the poor, and the free men and the slaves, to be given a mark on their right hand or on their forehead, and he provides that no one will be able to buy or to sell, except the one who has the mark, either the name of the beast or the number of his name" (Revelation 13:16-17).

While we are not yet at this time of the end, we can feel the birth pangs taking place around us and see the outline of things to come predicted in the Scriptures.

The twentieth century experienced two great wars that began in Europe and are sometimes thought of as the first and second part of the same massive conflict. The result was the first truly global war that involved every continent and virtually every nation on the planet. Tens of millions of people died during the years of fighting and the world was forever changed. In this century, we have experienced a truly global pandemic with the outbreak of the Coronavirus (COVID-19) that began in China but then quickly infected almost every nation on earth. The entire world economy was nearly brought to a halt by the rapid spread of this insidious and deadly contagion that respected no political, geographic, racial, or religious borders.

The gospel of the kingdom also defines a global movement. This message of new life and transformation has made its way around the world since breaking out of Jerusalem two thousand years ago. Missiologists tell us the remaining number of people groups and nations that lack a national witness of God's kingdom is steadily falling. The pace of end time events is increasing and the necessity for all church leaders to have a worldwide, prophetic vision is clear.

The return of the Lord is going to be a truly final global

event. It is the end of life as we know it now for every nation on the earth. It will be a day of fearsome judgment and the beginning of an entirely new era led by the presence of God Himself. Should we wish to be alive for this great event? Realistically, the evil of this present time is already enough of a challenge for me! By the time the world reaches its final stages, the intensity of the "birth pangs" will be ferocious and people's hearts will be failing them for fear. Now is the time to prepare and equip younger disciples to face increasingly difficult future challenges while standing firm in faith.

Now is the time to prepare and equip others to face increasingly difficult challenges while standing firm in faith.

The role of the believing body throughout the world is to be focused on becoming "bride-like" in purity, character, and calling. It is our privilege to prepare the way for the King of Kings to appear, claim His betrothed and enter the wedding supper. Whatever the differences there may be in our understanding of eschatology, believers and students of the Bible around the world, in general, agree on three things:

1. Jesus is returning to bring judgment and an end to this age.
2. He is the Bridegroom who is coming to claim His bride, the unified body of all true disciples.
3. He is coming as King to rule the kingdom of God.

The King of Kings is coming to judge the world, vindicate those who by their faith are declared righteous, and punish the selfishly wicked. Among His disciples, Jesus does not want to find lazy complacency, fearful paralysis, prideful triumphalism, or stressed-out perfectionism. The Lord wants to find faith on earth when He returns (Luke 18:8). He is expecting progress not perfection! Jesus said, "Who then is the faithful and sensible slave whom his master put in charge of his household to give them their food at the proper time? Blessed is that slave whom his master finds so doing when he comes. Truly I say to you that he will put him in charge of all his possessions" (Matthew 24:45-47).

Discussion Questions:

1. How do I know that these are the end times? Does this impact my daily life?
2. What are the three things almost all believers agree about concerning the return of Jesus?
3. Why does the Lord stress progress and not perfection in the lives of His disciples?

Prayer Point:

Lord, we know that Your return is coming closer. Please help me and those around me to prepare ourselves and to be a part of Your bride.

Chapter 52

The Days of Elijah

This book began by emphasizing the need for change. God has a word of encouragement for those who are ready to let Him realign their lives. God's word for those who are moving from what they know to what they have never experienced is the same word given by God to Joshua, the disciple of Moses, when he prepared to cross the Jordan into the land of his inheritance: "Be strong and courageous" (Joshua 1:6). When we look for leaders in the Bible who were both strong and courageous, several examples come to mind, but one man, who is on almost everyone's shortlist, is Elijah the prophet.

Elijah's day was a time of steep spiritual decline in Israel.

An apostate king by the name of Ahab had risen to power and together with his queen, Jezebel, they had made idolatry, worship of Baal, the official religion of the northern kingdom. Baal was a fertility god who promised to bring thundershowers with pouring rain throughout the winter, thereby ensuring prosperity for the agricultural economy of the day. Ordinary farmers sacrificed their crops, livestock, and even their children at the altars presided over by ranks of "priests and prophets" to the false god.

Because this religion was abhorrent to the God of Israel, He had commanded His people to cleanse the land of idolatry and never accept the evil of Baal worship. King Ahab, in defiance of God's will, had led his kingdom in the opposite direction. As a result, God spoke through the prophet Elijah that there would be no rain on the land until the Lord spoke again. The complete story is found in the book of 1 Kings chapters 17 and 18.

Even today, despite having massive desalinization plants and advanced water conservation projects, modern Israel still needs sufficient rain each year to supply its needs. Now we are an industrialized, technology-oriented economy, but in the days of Elijah, virtually everyone was a farmer. No rain meant eventual economic collapse. After the first year of drought, the crops died. After the second year of drought, the farm animals died, and after the third year of drought, the people were beginning to die of starvation. Then God spoke again to Elijah and told him to return to Ahab, the king of his nation.

When Elijah returned to Ahab, he was greeted with the accusation that he, Elijah, had caused a national disaster by prophesying drought three years earlier. Elijah responded with "chutzpah" (a Yiddish word originally from Hebrew or Aramaic that means to have audacity or nerve) and said that not he but the king himself was responsible because he had failed to lead the nation toward the righteousness of God's kingdom. Needless to say, it was not a friendly meeting that day, but it was decided that there would be a confrontation on Mount Carmel between Elijah and the false prophets of Baal. The winners would live and the losers would die.

When the day of the contest dawned, Elijah faced three different groups of his countrymen on Carmel. The first group was king Ahab and the ruling government. These people held the levers of political power and had the authority to put Elijah to death. The second group was the false prophets, who controlled the religious establishment of the country. They received income from the people's sacrifices and were supported by the power of the state. The third group was very likely made up of civic leaders from throughout the territory, cultural influencers, and landowners, along with the heads of leading families and clans.

The Bible says that Elijah turned first to the people and said, "How long will you hesitate between two opinions? If the Lord is God, follow Him; but if Baal, follow him" (1 Kings 18:21). Elijah initially turned to the people because God has placed the real power in any nation in the hands of its people. Political and religious leaders may wield great and even life-or-death authority but ultimately, the people decide upon the character of a nation. In short, we usually get the governments and religions we deserve. The people, out of apathy or fear, refused to answer Elijah so two separate altars and two very different sacrifices were prepared on the mountain. The false prophets and Elijah were each to pray before their altar and the God who answered with fire would be the winner. Elijah's altar was a place of pure and wholehearted sacrifice to the living God. Elijah was not a seemingly invulnerable, unapproachable leader. By accepting this challenge he was offering his own body as a "living sacrifice" for the sake of God's purposes in His people to be fulfilled. The altar of the false prophets was a stage for a performance dedicated to religious manipulation and the power to control other people's lives.

Elijah's courage came from the fact that he was not struggling to keep his balance at the very top of the social pyramid.

It is not hard to draw parallels between Elijah's time and our own, no matter where we live. Many corrupt governments are using the power of the state to suppress freedom to worship God and persecute truth tellers or "whistle blowers." There is also a great deal of false religion on the market today, even in the Christian world. What gave Elijah the courage to stand alone against just about everyone who mattered in his society? He faced people at the highest levels, important public figures in positions of recognized authority and prestige. These included the politically powerful, accepted religious leaders, and the non-believing cultural elite who held his faith in contempt.

Elijah's courage came from the fact that he was not struggling to keep his balance at the very top of the social pyramid, but he was standing at the bottom, outside of that whole structure. When referring to the Lord, Elijah was fond of saying, "The Lord before whom I stand." He was, first and foremost, a simple servant of God who used his prophetic gift to speak the truth and turn his nation from destruction.

At the beginning of the day, Elijah turned to the people to challenge them. At the end of the day, when the false prophets had failed, Elijah turned again to the same people, who had refused to respond in the morning, gathered them together, and prayed for them. That is when the fire fell from heaven and changed everything.

This is the spirit and the power needed to turn a new generation of leaders in the nations toward the restoration of God's kingdom. As in the days of Elijah, it still takes faith, courage, and sacrifice to change the way the church teaches and practices Christianity. Nevertheless, change is required now. Christians, who are the spiritual sons and daughters of Abraham, must be turned back to the patriarchs of Israel and their biblical Hebraic roots. God spoke through the prophet Malachi and promised He would rejoin these long-separated generations with the spirit of Elijah in the end times. "Behold, I am going to send you Elijah the prophet before the coming of the great and terrible day of the Lord. He will restore the hearts of the fathers to their children and the hearts of the children to their fathers, so that I will not come and smite the land with a curse" (Malachi 4:5-6).

The Bible says Elijah was an ordinary man like you or me (James 5:17), yet he is considered one of the greatest of Israel's prophets. We know the fire that fell originated in heaven, but Elijah's personal strength and courage came from the fact that he stood apart from the striving and social climbing that characterize human society then as now. Elijah said, "I alone am left, a prophet of the Lord . . ." but he wasn't ever really alone because he stood with the Lord on solid ground at the bottom of the human pyramid. May the spirit and power that was in Elijah restore faith and courage to the Lord's disciples in the end-time church.

Today, the world order is changing politically, economically, as well as culturally, and a fierce new era of disruption and struggle is beginning. Some nations and regions will rise and others will falter. In the days ahead, we must simultaneously deal with increasing chaos as well as authoritarian oppression in various parts of the world. The "birth pangs" of the end times predicted by Jesus in Matthew 24 are upon us. He said that lawlessness will attack love at every human level and cause many hearts to become cold; ethnic groups will clash with bloodshed and religious persecution will rage. God's kingdom and His purposes, however, will continue to move powerfully ahead. Jesus said, "But many who are first will be last, and the last, first" (Matthew 19:30).

The global disruptions of our day point to the emergence of a new body of disciples who are like the sons of Issachar in the Bible, who understood their times and had knowledge of what Israel should do (1 Chronicles 12:32). These sons of Issachar arose to stand wholeheartedly with David in a time of disruption and crisis as he was ascending to the throne in Jerusalem. Today the urgent prophetic call is to bring forth disciples whose allegiance to Jesus and God's kingdom is absolute. Dedicated discipleship is the highest qualification for ambassadors of the King who bring His good news to the nations.

Jesus said, "This gospel of the kingdom shall be preached in the whole world as a testimony to all the nations, and then the end will come" (Matthew 24:14). Now is the time for all disciples of the Lord to arise, put on our spiritual equipment, pray and work together to bring His magnificent kingdom!

Discussion Questions:

1. Do I understand why Elijah was such an important prophet in the Bible?
2. Does the will of the people for good or evil eventually change a nation? Do we need leaders like Elijah now?
3. What was it like in Israel during the days of Elijah? Am I facing challenges like that today?

Prayer Point:

Lord, You said through Malachi that You would send Elijah before the end of this age. In my heart I want to be anointed like he was! Would You pour Your Spirit of strength, courage, and wisdom upon me?

References

Chapter 1 – Organic Growth

Ross, Reuven and Yanit, *Go and Make Disciples! A Vision for Strategic Disciple Making,* (Self-published, www.making-disciples.net, 2000). Kindle edition page 1.

Ross, Reuven and Yanit, *The Call to Radical Discipleship: A Study of Matthew 5-7,* (Self-published, www.making-disciples.net, 2015). Kindle edition.

Coleman, Robert E., *The Master Plan of Evangelism,* (Grand Rapids: Revell, a division of Baker Publishing Company, Ebook edition created in 2010). Kindle edition page 21.

Collins, Jim, *Good to Great – Why Some Companies Make the Leap and Others Don't,* (New York: HarperCollins Publishers Inc., 2001), page 13.

Chapter 5 – Identity of a Disciple

Bruce, A. B., The Training of the Twelve – How Jesus Christ Found and Taught the 12 Apostles; A Book of New Testament Biography, (Pantianos Classics first published in 1871). Kindle edition location 357.

Chapter 6 – Socks and Shoes of Discipleship

Westminster Shorter Catechism is a catechism written in 1646 and 1647 by the Westminster Assembly, a synod of English and Scottish theologians and laymen intended to bring the Church of England into greater conformity with the Church of Scotland. From Wikipedia.

Ladd, George Eldon, *The Gospel of the Kingdom – Scriptural Studies in the Kingdom of God,* (Grand Rapids: William B. Eerdmans Publishing Company, 1959) page 117.

Tan, Kim, Chapter on "Holistic Mission" in *Forming Christian Habits in Post-Christendom,* Editors: James Krabill and Stuart Murray (Harrisonburg: Herald Press, 2011).

Dr. Kim Tan is also author of *The Jubilee Gospel – The Jubilee, Spirit and the Church,* (Milton Keynes: Authentic Media, 2008).

Chapter 7 – Giving Up to Gain More

Murray, Andrew, *With Christ in the School of Prayer,* (Andrew Murray Books, 1895). Chapter 6, Kindle edition location 583.

Foster, Richard, *Celebration of Discipline – The Path to Spiritual Growth,* (London: Hodder & Stoughton Ltd., 1989). Section on The Purpose of Fasting. Kindle edition page 68.

Chapter 8 – Hearts of Gold

Arterburn, Stephen and Stoeker, Fred, *Every Man's Battle – Winning the War on Sexual Temptation One Victory at a Time,* (Colorado Springs: WaterBrook Press, 2002). Chapter 8, page 92.

Chapter 11 – De-Greecing God's House

Pawson, David, *De-Greecing the Church – The Impact of Greek Thinking on Christian Beliefs,* (Pamphlet in the "Explaining" series). (Woodley: Anchor Recordings Ltd., 2017), pages 7 and 10.

This pamphlet is available for download as well as two audio lectures with the same title and material through the official website: www.DavidPawson.org.

Sacks, Jonathan, *The Great Partnership – Science, Religion and the Search for Meaning,* (New York: Schocken Books, a division of Random House LLC, 2011), page 61.

Rabbi Lord Jonathan Sacks wrote, "Science takes things apart to see how they work, [biblical] religion puts things together to see what they mean." (*The Great Partnership,* page 39).

Bivin, David and Blizzard, Roy Jr., *Understanding the Difficult Words of Jesus – New Insights from a Hebraic Perspective,* (Shippensburg: Destiny Image Publishers,

Revised Edition, 1994). Last paragraph of chapter one. Kindle edition location 89.

Chapter 13 – Restoring the Unity of the Bible

Kaiser, Walter C. Jr., *Recovering the Unity of the Bible: One Continuous Story, Plan, and Purpose,* (Grand Rapids: Zondervan, 2009). Chapter 1. Kindle edition location 308.

Walter C. Kaiser Jr. is an American evangelical Old Testament scholar, writer, public speaker, and educator. Kaiser is the Colman M. Mockler distinguished Professor of Old Testament and former President of Gordon-Conwell Theological Seminary in South Hamilton, Massachusetts, retired June 30, 2006. - *Wikipedia*

Chapter 14 – Interpreting the Bible

Bible study resources for digital devices:

Olive Tree Bible Software (www.olivetree.com) I like Olive Tree for its simplicity and ease of use. It's not very expensive and works very well on my iPad. The New American Standard Bible with Strong's Numbers – (NASB Strong's add-on for the mobile app) is particularly helpful.

Logos Bible Software (www.logos.com) Logos is the "Big Daddy" of Bible study resource programs. It is loaded with features and can be technically challenging. Logos has everything you need in one package. Designed for ministers, it can be customized to various levels of study needs.

Accordance Bible Software (www.accordancebible.com)

Less expensive and considered easier to use than Logos, this set of Bible translations and study tools is very popular with serious students of the Bible.

Chapter 17 – The Disciples' Last Question

Calvin, John, *Commentary Upon the Acts of the Apostles - Volume First.* Edited from the original English translation of Christopher Fetherstone by Henry Beveridge, Esq. (Grand Rapids: Christian Classics Ethereal Library Lord.ccel.org, first translation from original Latin in 1585). Chapter one. Kindle edition location 432.

Chapter 18 – Faith + Works = Salvation

Pawson, David, *Once Saved Always Saved? A study in Perseverance and Inheritance,* (London: Hodder & Stoughton, 1996), page 124.

Chapter 19 – Gospel to the Jews

Kolatch, Alfred J., *The Jewish Book of Why,* (Middle Village: Jonathan David Publishers, Inc., 1981), page 58.

Chapter 27 – Freedom from Striving

Bruce, F. F., *Paul: Apostle of the Heart Set Free,* (Grand Rapids: William B. Eerdmans Publishing Company, reprinted 1996), page 21.

Chapter 28 – Other People Hold the Keys

Quotes from Mahatma Gandhi found on internet and article "Gandhi, Christ and Christianity" by Pascal Alan Nazareth. He cites:

Deshpande, M. S. (ed.) *Light of India or Message of Mahatmaji,* 3rd ed. (Ahmedabad: Navajivan Publishing House, 1978).

Gandhi, M. K. (1948): *Non-Violence in Peace and War,* Volume I, page 181.

King, Martin Luther, "I Have a Dream" speech given on August 28, 1963, during the March on Washington for Jobs and Freedom. (https://www.americanrhetoric.com/speeches/mlkihaveadream.htm)

Chapter 29 – The Value of Law

Bragg, Melvyn, *12 Books That Changed the World,* (London: Hodder & Stoughton, 2006).

Chapter 32 – Grace Is Amazing

Yancey, Philip, *What's So Amazing About Grace?,* (Grand Rapids: Zondervan, 1997), page 13.

Chapter 33 – Law and Freedom

Bonhoeffer, Dietrich, *The Cost of Discipleship.* Translated from German in 1937. (New York: Collier Books, Macmillan Publishing Company, 1963).

Chapter 40 – Paul's Freedom

Smith, Martin, "I Could Sing of Your Love Forever," Band: Delirious? Album: Cutting Edge 2, 1995.

Lewis, C. S., *Surprised by Joy: The Shape of My Early Life.* Date of first publication 1955. Ebook produced by: Marcia

Brooks, Mark Akrigg, Stephen Hutcheson, and the online Distributed Proofreaders Canada team at http://www.pgdp-canada.net. Kindle edition location 211.

Chapter 46 – Learning from Israel's Example

Keener, Craig S., *IVP Bible Background Commentary – New Testament,* (Downers Grove: Intervarsity Press, 1993), page 447.

Chapter 49 – Small Is Powerful

Simson, Wolfgang, *Houses that Change the World – The Return of the House Churches,* (Carlisle: OM Publishing – an imprint of Paternoster Publishing, 1998), page xvii.

Chapter 50 – Love Your Neighborhood

Chan, Edmund, *A Certain Kind - Intentional Disciplemaking that Redefines Success in Ministry,* (Singapore: Evangelical Free Church, 2013), pages 223-224.

Jobs, Steve, Quote on "60 Minutes" television interview, 2003. https://youtu.be/pGvnJJxBAlc

Quotations on the Back Cover

Bonhoeffer, Dietrich, *The Cost of Discipleship.* Translated from German in 1937. (New York: Collier Books, Macmillan Publishing Company, 1963) page 47.

Lewis, C. S., *A Mind Awake - An Anthology of C. S. Lewis.* Edited by Clide S. Kilby. (San Diego: A Harvest Book, Harcourt Inc., 1968) page 30.

Graham, Billy, "What's the Cost of Following Jesus Christ?" Audio clip from the Billy Graham Minute, https://billygraham.org/audio/billy-graham-whats-the-cost-of-following-jesus-christ/